HAMLYN ALL-COLOUR
▶▶WORLD▶▶
ENCYCLOPEDIA

HAMLYN ALL-COLOUR

▶▶WORLD▶ ▶ ENCYCLOPEDIA

CONTRIBUTORS:
Robin Kerrod, Roy Woodcock, Mark Lambert,
Peter Lafferty, Andrew Langley, Neil Grant,
Brian Williams and Brenda Clarke

HAMLYN

Jacket Illustrations by: Selwyn Hutchinson

Illustrations by: Peter Bull; Martin Salisbury, Gerry Wood, Tony Morris, (*Linda Rogers Associates*); Brian Watson, Mick Loates, Maurice Pledger, Pat Harby, David Moore, Alan Male, David Webb, David Cook, Craig Warwick, Jack Pelling, Tony Gibbons, Keith Duran, John Lupton, Chris Prothero, Richard Hook, Jon Davis (*Linden Artists*).

Published in 1988 by
The Hamlyn Publishing Group Limited,
a division of Paul Hamlyn Publishing
Michelin House, 81 Fulham Road, London SW3 6RB

ISBN 0 600 55527 5

Printed in Italy

Contents

Photographic acknowledgements

Aldus Archive, London 84 left; All-Sport, London 228, 232–3 top and bottom: Chris Cole 227 bottom, Tony Duffy 225 bottom, Adrian Murrell 227 top, Vandystadt/Jean Marc Barey 227 centre; Ardea, London 13; Australian Overseas Information Service, London 55 left and right, 106; Barr & Stroud Ltd, London 180–1 top; Bridgeman Art Library, London 222–3 bottom (copyright DACS): Fabbri 75, 211 bottom right (copyright DACS), Giraudon 210 top; British Aerospace, Bristol 163, 166–7; British Airways, London 139; BBC Enterprises, London 28 top; British Leyland, Oxford 143; British Museum, London 64; British Steel Corporation, London 138; Cadbury Schweppes Ltd, Bournville 152 bottom; California Institute of Technology and the Carnegie Institution of Washington, reproduced by permission from the Hale Observatories, Pasadena 8, 11 top and bottom, 18–19 bottom; Camera Press, London 205 bottom, 208–9 top and bottom; Camerapix 200 bottom left, K. N. Ramanathan 199 top right; Canadian High Commission, London 47; The Church of Jesus Christ of Latter-Day Saints, London 199 left; Bruce Coleman, Uxbridge 120 bottom: Jen and Des Bartlett 56–7 bottom, Jane Burton 90, Francisco Erize 119; Avions Marcel Dassault-Breguet Aviation, Paris Jacket bottom right; EEC Information Service, London 206; Mary Evans Picture Library, London 76; Ford Prison, Littlehampton 205 top; Geoscience Features Picture Library, Ashford 24–5; Studio Hachette, Paris 68 left; Handford Photography, Croydon 145 left; Michael Holford, Loughton 72; Hutchison Library, London 200 top; The Illustrated London News Picture Library 200 bottom right; ICI Petrochemicals and Plastics Division, Welwyn Garden City 141 bottom; Trustees of the Imperial War Museum, London 82 (copyright DACS), 83; India Office Library, London 80; Japan Information Service, London 136–7 bottom; Kobal Collection, London 215 bottom, 221 (all three); Frank Lane Agency, Stowmarket: G. Moon 123; The Lewis Textile Museum, Blackburn 79; Library of Congress, Washington 78; Mansell Collection, London 69, 162; Metropolitan Museum of Art, New York 210 centre; National Aeronautics and Space Administration, Washington 14 top and bottom, 15 top and bottom, 18–19 top, 20–1, 28 bottom, 132, 150 bottom, 166, 167, 168, 169 left and right, 170, 170–1 top and bottom; National Coal Board, London 147 bottom; National Dairy Council, London 155 top and bottom; National Trust Photographic Library, London 126 bottom; NHPA, Ardingly 97; Nature Photographers, Basingstoke: S. C. Bisserot 100, 153 top, N. A. Callow 216 bottom, Andrew Cleave 92, Martyn Colbeck 25, 26 top, Michael Leach 113, E. C. G. Lemon 56–7 top, Hugh Miles 42, Paul Sterry 115 bottom, 120 top, 127, J. Sutherland 36 bottom, Derek Washington 27 bottom, 115 top; North West Thames Regional Health Authority, London 185; Novosti Press Agency, London 37; Octopus Publishing Group, London Jacket top left, 60, 68 right (photographed at the Galleria dell'Accademia, Venice), 141 top, 144, 145 right, 157, 160, 194, 216 top, 222–3 top, 229 left, 230 right: W. F. Davidson 111, Peter Green 89, Peter Loughran 94, 120 centre right, 153 bottom, Erwin Meyer 211 left (photographed at the Kunsthistorisches Museum, Vienna), Bruno del Priore 210 bottom, Constantino Reyes Valerio 196 bottom, 212, John Webb 211 top right (photographed at the National Gallery, London); The Photo Source, London 26 bottom, 27 top, 44, 48 top, 154 top, 199 bottom right, 203: Peter Beney 33, Central Press 197, Clive Friend 40 bottom, 45 bottom, G. C. Garner 61, Nick Meers 177, E. Nagele 49 bottom; Photostage, London 217; League of the Red Cross and Red Crescent Societies, Geneva: L. de Toledo 207 left; David Redfern, London 85 bottom; Ann Ronan Picture Library, Taunton 178 top; Royal National Institute for the Blind, London 173; Science Photo Library, London 136–7 top; Shell International Petroleum, London 146; Crown copyright, Slough Laboratory 120 centre left; South Dakota Division of Tourism, Pierre 152 top; Spectrum Colour Library, London 32, 35 left, 40 bottom, 42–3, 112, 158 top, 200 centre, 201: D. and J. Heaton 218, Jean Kugler 198 left; Suzuki 142 bottom; TASS, London 207 right; The Telegraph Colour Library, London 50 left, 134, 175, 179; Judy Todd, London 24 top, 41 bottom, 63, 126 top, 130, 196 top and centre right; Weir Westgarth Ltd, Wokingham 180–1 bottom; The Government of Western Australia, London 159; Zal Holdings Ltd, London 45 top; Zefa Picture Library, London jacket top right, 50 right, 85 top, 142 top, 154 bottom, 192–3 top, 213 top, 214, 215 top, 226, 230 left: P. Bading 22, Dr Baer 198 right, D. Baglin 192–3 bottom, E. and P. Bauer 122, T. Braise 150 top, E. G. Carle 49 top, Bob Croxford 39 bottom, Damm 41 centre, R. Halin 52, Günter Heil 52–3, Hiebeler 229 right, Hoffmann-Burchardi 58–9 bottom, Honkanen 36 top, Hubrich 225 top, Jonas 231, P. Kapa 46, Kotoh 213 centre, Foto Leidmann 118, Robert Lorenz 165, McCutcheon 147 top, Maroon 215 centre, Photri 84 right, M. Pitner 48 bottom, Neville Presho 39 top, G. Rettinghaus 187, K. Röhrich 34, Robin Smith 54–5, 213 bottom, V. Stapelberg 16, Starfoto 41 top, W. Stoy 23, H. Sunak 51, Theojac 17, Vontin 58–9 top, Ung. Werbestudio 40 top, W. Westermann 35 right.

Works by Miró (page 82), Picasso (Tate Gallery, Penrose Collection, pages 222-3) and Andy Warhol (Harry N. Abrams Family Collection, page 211) are © ADAGP, Paris and DACS, London 1988.

The Mysterious Universe

THE UNIVERSE AND SPACE

What is the biggest thing you can think of? An elephant? An aircraft carrier? A suspension bridge? The Earth? The Sun? It is none of these. The biggest thing of all is the universe. Everything there is belongs to the universe.

Mostly the universe is made up of nothing – just empty space! Dotted here and there in this space are planets, stars and clouds of gas and dust. The Earth we live on is a planet. A planet is a body that travels

Right **The famous Horsehead nebula is a great mass of dark gas in the constellation Orion.**

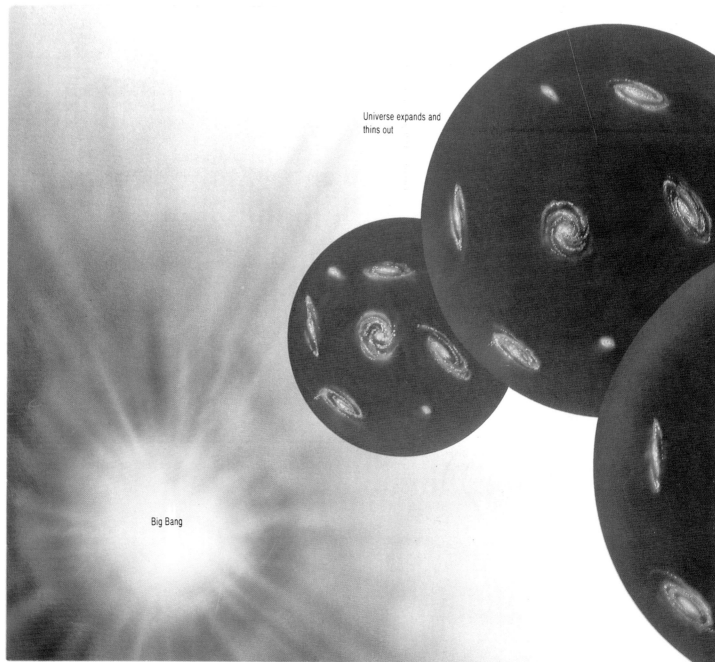

Big Bang

Universe expands and thins out

through space in a circle around the Sun. The Sun is a star (see page 11).

We can live on Earth because of the layer of air around it. We must breathe air to live. Once we go above the layer of air, we are in space. For humans, space is a deadly place. There is no air to breathe; it is scorching hot in the Sun, and freezing cold in the shade. And there are invisible rays that can harm you.

A galaxy of stars

The Sun gives light and warmth to the Earth. It is like the other stars you see in the night sky. But it looks very much bigger and brighter because it is very much closer to us.

The Sun and all the other stars we can see travel through space together. They form a kind of star island floating in a great ocean of space. There are many other star islands, or galaxies, dotted throughout space, with nothing in between.

Most of the galaxies are shaped like a disc, with a bulge in the middle. And like a record disc, they spin round in space. Many galaxies have beautiful curving arms of stars that emerge from the centre bulge of stars.

Astronomical numbers

How many stars can you see in the night sky? If you were very patient and had enough time, you might be able to count about 2,000. And if you looked through a telescope, you could see thousands upon thousands more. All these stars belong to our galaxy.

Astronomers, the people who study stars, think that there are about one hundred thousand million stars in our galaxy. In figures this is 100,000,000,000! The stars we see are also a very long way away, millions of millions of kilometres. Other galaxies are millions of times farther away still!

No one really knows how many stars there are in the whole universe, or how big the universe is. All we can say is that there are more stars in the universe than we can imagine, and the universe is bigger than we can imagine. Maybe it just goes on for ever and ever.

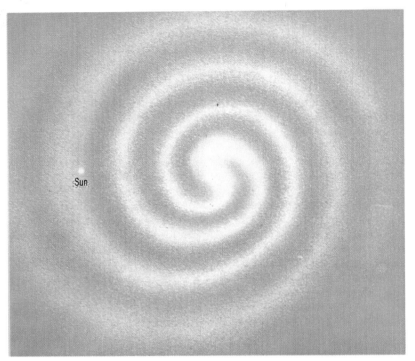
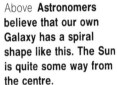

Above **Astronomers believe that our own Galaxy has a spiral shape like this. The Sun is quite some way from the centre.**

Left **Our universe came into being as a great explosion astronomers call the Big Bang. It has been expanding ever since.**

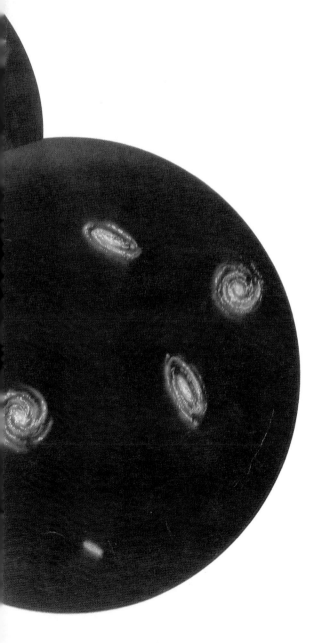

Light and dark

The space between the stars in the galaxies is not always empty. In some places it is filled with clouds of gas or dust. Each cloud is known as a nebula. Some nebulas shine brilliantly against the blackness of space. Other nebulas are dark. They blot out the light from any stars behind.

But the darkest things in the universe are black holes. They are what is left when big stars explode and die. They have an enormous gravity, or pull, and swallow everything near them, even light.

The brightest things in the universe are quasars. They are too big and too far away to be stars. And they are too small to be galaxies. Yet they are as bright as hundreds of galaxies put together!

THE STARRY SKIES

The sky at night is a beautiful sight. The twinkling stars look like jewels sparkling on black velvet. When you look carefully, you notice that some stars are brighter than others. And many of the bright stars make patterns in the sky. If you look at the same part of the sky night after night, you will notice that the patterns stay the same. We call these patterns, the constellations. They stay the same, year after year, century after century.

In ancient times stargazers imagined that the star patterns looked like animals or people. And they gave them suitable names, such as the Great Bear, Orion the Mighty Hunter, and the Swan. We still use these names for the constellations.

The whirling heavens

One night, look up at the stars at different times. What do you notice? The constellations seem to have moved around the sky. They haven't really moved. It is you, or rather the Earth you are standing on, that has moved. The Earth spins round in space, once every 24 hours. This makes the Sun seem to move across the sky during the day, and the stars move across the sky during the night.

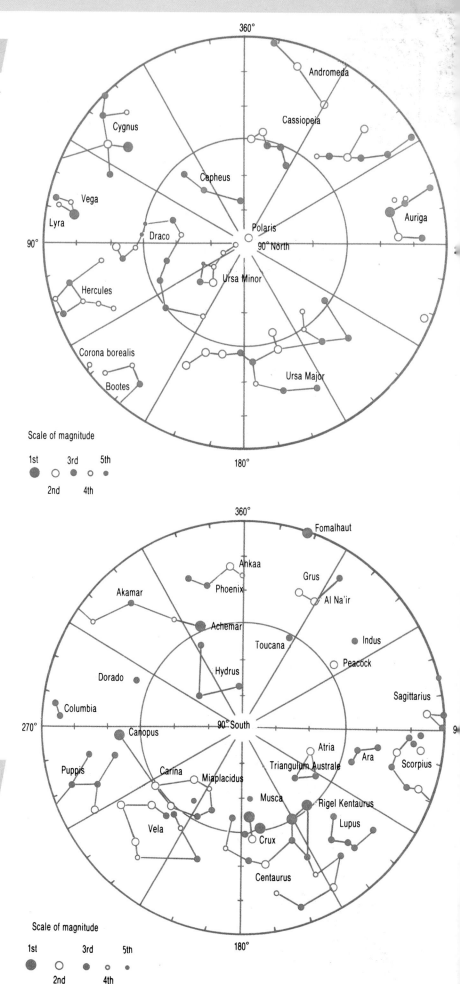

Scale of magnitude

1st   3rd   5th

2nd   4th

Scale of magnitude

1st   3rd   5th

2nd   4th

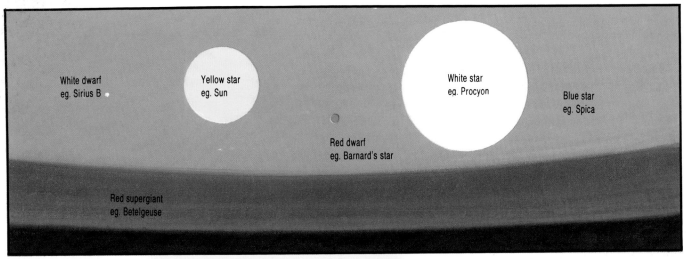

White dwarf
eg. Sirius B

Yellow star
eg. Sun

White star
eg. Procyon

Blue star
eg. Spica

Red dwarf
eg. Barnard's star

Red supergiant
eg. Betelgeuse

Above **The Sun is a medium-sized star. It is much bigger than red and white dwarfs, but tiny compared with supergiants.**

Right **The Crab nebula is what remains of a supernova that took place in AD 1054.**

Clusters of stars

The stars in the constellations look close together in the sky, but usually they are not. They only look close because they happen to lie in the same direction in space. Usually they are very far apart.

But some stars are close together. We call them star clusters. There is a well-known cluster in the constellation of the Bull called the Seven Sisters. Just with your eyes you can usually see its seven bright stars. If you look at it through a telescope, you can see very many more. In other star clusters the stars are packed tightly together in the shape of a globe (ball). We call them globular clusters. They are made up of thousands of stars.

Dwarfs and giants

To our eyes all of the stars look much the same. But they are not. Some stars are small, some are big and others are truly gigantic. We call them dwarf, giant and supergiant stars. Stars also have different colours: bluish-white, yellow, orange and red.

The star we know best is our Sun. Astronomers call it a yellow dwarf star. They know of red supergiant stars that are hundreds of times bigger and brighter than the Sun.

But all the stars – dwarfs or giants, red or yellow – are big balls of hot gas. They give out fantastic amounts of energy as light and heat. The gas doesn't produce energy by burning, like the gas in a gas fire. The energy comes from inside its atoms. This is similar to what happens in a nuclear power station on Earth (see page 151).

THE SUN'S FAMILY

The most important thing that happens every day is that the Sun rises. It brings us light and warmth. Without the Sun, the Earth would be a cold, dark place. It would also be dead. No plants would grow because

Below **We can easily see the Pleiades star cluster with the naked eye.**

they need light and warmth. There would be no animals because they need to eat plants to live.

The Sun seems to travel across the sky every day. It rises in the east and sets in the west. But really it is the Earth, not the Sun, that moves. The Earth spins round in space once every 24 hours. We call this time, our day. The Earth also travels through space in a great circle around the Sun every 365 days. We call this time, our year.

Eight other bodies circle around the Sun. They are the planets. The name "planet" means "wandering star". Some of the planets do indeed look like stars and move around the constellations. The planets are the most important members of the Sun's family, or solar system.

Two planets circle nearer to the Sun than the Earth does. The others circle much farther out. Going out from the Sun, the planets are Mercury, Venus, (Earth), Mars, Jupiter, Saturn, Uranus, Neptune and Pluto. Pluto is the smallest planet, Jupiter is the largest – it is 11 times bigger in diameter than the Earth is and weighs $2\frac{1}{2}$ times as much as all the other planets in the solar system put together.

Many moons

Many of the planets have smaller bodies circling around them. We call these bodies satellites, or moons. The Earth has one – the Moon. Mars has two moons. Jupiter and Saturn together have at least 40!

We know more about our Moon than about any other heavenly body. It is our nearest neighbour in space – and astronauts have travelled there and walked on the surface (see page 168). The Moon is a ball of rock, only about a quarter the width of the Earth. It is a dead world because there is no air around it. It is covered with great flat plains known as seas, or maria. But

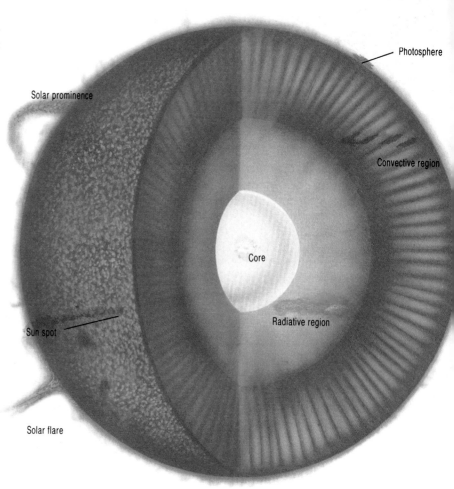

Photosphere

Solar prominence

Convective region

Core

Radiative region

Sun spot

Solar flare

Above **The energy of the Sun comes from nuclear reactions in the core. It travels outwards by radiation and convection currents. The surface is very disturbed, as boiling gas erupts in fountains.**

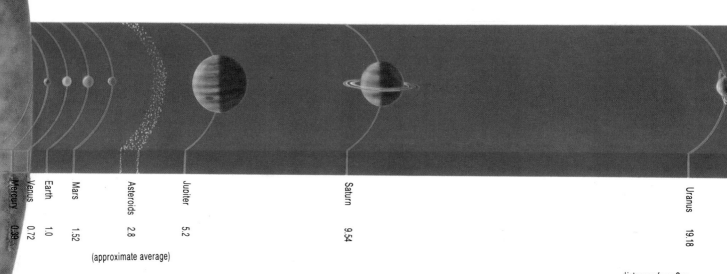

| Mercury 0.39 | Venus 0.72 | Earth 1.0 | Mars 1.52 | Asteroids 2.8 (approximate average) | Jupiter 5.2 | Saturn 9.54 | Uranus 19.18 |

distances from Sun relative to Earth)

there is no water on them. They are the dark areas we can see on the Moon. The bright areas we see are highlands and mountain ranges. All over the surface in the highlands and the plains there are pits, or craters. They were formed when rocks from outer space crashed into the Moon.

Shooting stars and comets

There are bits of rocks whizzing around the solar system. Sometimes they run into the Earth. When they hit the air, they heat up and start to glow red-hot. At night you often see them as bright streaks in the sky, and we call them shooting stars. The proper name for them is meteors.

Usually the rocks are tiny, and they burn away to dust. But sometimes the rock is large and crashes down to the ground. We then call it a meteorite.

From time to time other bright things appear in the night sky. Sometimes they grow a kind of tail, which can stream half-way across the sky. They are comets. Comets are lumps of ice and dust, rather like dirty snowballs.

We see comets only when they come close to the Sun, for that is when they start to glow. Some comets come and go regularly. The most famous is Halley's comet, which returns to our skies every 76 years. Its latest visit was in 1986.

Above **The Arizona meteor crater was created when a huge meteorite hit the Earth about 50,000 years ago. Over 1200 m across, it has been well preserved by the desert climate.**

Below **The diagram shows the relative distances of the planets from the Sun. It gives an idea of the vast scale of the solar system.**

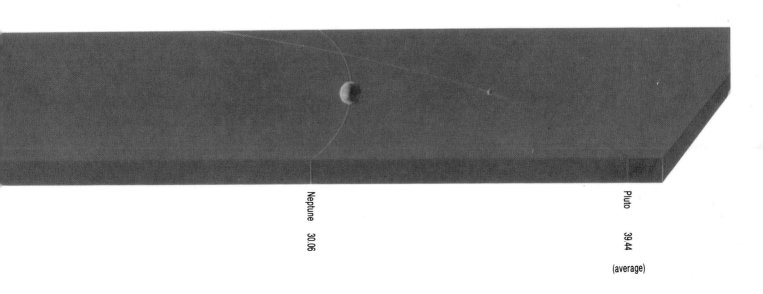

Neptune 30.06

Pluto 39.44

(average)

LOOKING AT THE PLANETS

The illustrations on pages 12 and 13 give you some details about the eight planets that appear in our skies. They show the different sizes of the planets, and how they are arranged in space.

Mercury, Venus and Mars are quite near to the Earth. And like the Earth, they are balls of rock. Jupiter and the other planets are many times farther away. Jupiter is also quite different from the Earth. It is not made of rock, but mainly of gas. It is a giant of a planet, which could swallow over 1,000 Earths! Saturn, Uranus and Neptune are great gas balls too. Pluto is probably made up of ice and rock.

Planet spotting

You can easily see three of the planets – Venus, Jupiter and Mars – just with your eyes if you look at the night sky at the right time. And if you have a pair of binoculars or a telescope, you should be able to make out the others, too. Venus is easiest to spot. You can see it as a bright star in the east at

Below **Space probe Mariner 10 spied clouds in the thick atmosphere of Venus.**

sunrise or in the west at sunset. Then we call it the morning or the evening star.

Jupiter is nearly as bright. You can see it shining in different parts of the sky on many nights of the year. Mars is not quite so bright, but it is easy to spot because it is orange-red in colour. We often call it the Red Planet. It is much more difficult to see Mercury and Saturn. And it is impossible to see the other planets because they are so far away.

Too hot, too cold

We haven't been able to visit the planets yet, but we have sent spacecraft to spy on them. These space probes have made some startling discoveries. They have found that Mercury and Venus are hot enough (450°C/842°F) to melt some metals! Venus has a thick atmosphere of heavy gas that would crush humans to death. Nothing could live on Mercury or Venus anyway because of the heat.

Mars is much cooler than the Earth, but it could just be warm enough to let some kind of life grow. People once thought that there were intelligent beings called Martians on the planet. But we now know this isn't possible. Space probes have landed on Mars

Left **One of the most memorable pictures of the Space Age, showing the Apollo 11 lunar module returning to orbit after the historic first Moon landing in July 1969. Below is the bleak lunar landscape, studded with craters. In the distance is planet Earth, adding a splash of colour to the scene.**

and have not found any signs of life at all. There certainly couldn't be life on Jupiter and the other distant planets because they are far too cold.

The space probes have made many other exciting finds. On Mars they have found a "Grand Canyon" 5,000 km (3,000 miles) long and a volcano 30 km (20 miles) high. On Saturn they have found that the winds blow at over 1,600 km/hr (1,000 mph). On one of Jupiter's moons they have spotted volcanoes erupting. They also solved the mystery of Jupiter's Giant Red Spot. Close-up photographs now show that it is actually a vast, whirling storm.

ETs welcome

So among the planets of the solar system there appears to be life only on Earth. But most astronomers think that there are other living things elsewhere in the universe. Some of them are probably intelligent beings like us. We call them extraterrestrials, or ETs.

Some people say they have already seen and even talked to ETs! The ETs, they say, came to Earth in alien spaceships, or UFOs (unidentified flying objects), but most people don't really believe this.

Left **A Viking lander on the plains of Mars in July 1976. The soil is strewn with small rocks and is rusty red. The sky is pinkish because of the dust it holds.**

Below **This Viking picture shows near the centre the Martian "Grand Canyon".**

THE STARGAZERS

People have stargazed at night for thousands of years. Astronomers are the scientists who study the heavens – the planets, the stars, the Moon, meteors and comets.

It is fun just stargazing with your eyes alone. But it is even better to look at the night sky through binoculars or a telescope. Through these instruments the heavens look really beautiful. You will see many more stars, flaming clouds of gas, and the mountains and craters of the Moon. You might one day be lucky enough to discover a new comet and have it named after you!

Observatories and telescopes

Astronomers usually work in places called observatories, where they observe, or look

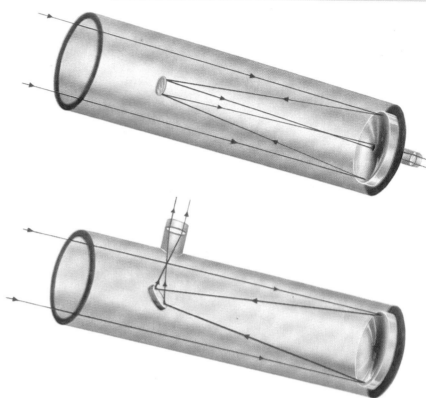

Left **Two common types of reflecting telescopes, which both collect light with curved mirrors. In the Cassegrain type, the light is reflected back down through the mirror for viewing. In the Newtonian type the light is reflected out the side for viewing.**

Below left **The world's biggest steerable radio telescope, at Effelsberg, near Bonn, West Germany.**

Below right **Telescope domes at Pic du Midi observatory in the French Pyrenees.**

at the heavens. Observatories are usually found in the mountains, thousands of metres high. Up there the air is clear, clean and still. And there are no bright city lights to spoil the view of the night sky.

Astronomers have been studying the stars with telescopes for nearly 400 years. And telescopes are still their most important instruments. The early telescopes used glass lenses to gather the light from the stars. The lenses worked in much the same way as a magnifying glass, making distant things appear closer and bigger.

But most astronomers now use telescopes that use curved mirrors to gather the light from the stars. We call them reflecting telescopes. The biggest reflecting telescope is in Russia. It has a mirror 6 m (20 ft) across. It can see unbelievable distances into space, and spot galaxies millions of millions of millions of kilometres away!

Astronomers don't usually look through these big telescopes. Instead, they use them as cameras and take photographs of the heavens. They can see much fainter stars this way. They also look at starlight with other instruments. These can tell them a lot about a star, such as how hot and how far away it is.

Radio Telescopes

Astronomers also use another kind of telescope to look at the heavens in a different way. It is called a radio telescope because it picks up the radio waves that stars and galaxies give out. Most radio telescopes are metal dishes which can be moved to point to any part of the sky. They can work all the time because radio waves reach the Earth day and night.

Astronomy Factfinder

Albedo A measure of how well a planet or moon reflects light.

Aphelion The farthest point from the Sun that a planet or comet reaches in its orbit.

Apogee The farthest point from the Earth that the Moon or an artificial satellite reaches in its orbit.

Apollo Project The American space programme to place men on the Moon. As well as for Moon missions, Apollo spacecraft were used to take astronauts to the Skylab space station.

Asteroid A minor planet orbiting the Sun. Most orbit in a belt between Mars and Jupiter. Over 2,000 asteroids are known.

Astronomical Unit The average distance of the Earth from the Sun, about 150,000,000 km (93,000,000 miles).

Astronomy The scientific study of the heavens.

Atmosphere The envelope of gases surrounding a planet, moon or star. The Earth's atmosphere is about 700 km thick and consists mostly of nitrogen and oxygen.

Aurora A display of lights seen in polar skies. It is caused by electrified particles from the Sun entering the atmosphere.

Big Bang The explosion which is believed to have marked the origin of the Universe.

Binary Star A pair of stars orbiting around their common centre of gravity. Through powerful telescopes, some binary stars can be seen to be two stars.

Black Hole A region of space where the force of gravity is so strong that nothing can escape, not even light. A black hole is believed to form when a massive star collapses at the end of its life.

Brahe, Tycho (1546–1601) Danish astronomer. He made instruments to plot the accurate positions of the planets and stars.

Celestial Sphere An imaginary sphere surrounding the Earth in space.

Comet A body, probably made of ice, rock and gas, which orbits the sun. When it nears the Sun, the solid nucleus gives off gas and dust to form a coma and often a long tail stretching for many millions of kilometres.

Conjunction The close approach in the sky between two planets.

Constellation A pattern of stars, often named after heroes or animals from Greek mythology. There are 88 constellations.

Copernicus, Nicolaus (1473–1543) Polish astronomer. In the face of much opposition, he believed that the Earth and the other planets circled the Sun.

Corona The layer of gas surrounding the Sun. It appears as a pearly-white halo during an eclipse, the only time when it is visible.

Cosmology A branch of astronomy concerned with the study of evolution and structure of the universe.

Eclipse The shadowing of one body by another. A solar eclipse occurs when the Moon passes across the face of the Sun. A lunar eclipse is when the Moon enters the Earth's shadow.

Ecliptic The path of the Sun around the sky each year against the background stars.

Equinox The time when the Sun is directly above the equator, making equal day and night. This occurs around 21 March and 23 September.

Escape Velocity The minimum speed at which a rocket must travel to break free from the grip of a planet's gravity.

Galaxy A mass of stars bound together by gravity. Thousands of millions of galaxies exist, each consisting of thousands of millions of stars.

Galileo (1564–1642) Italian scientist. He was the first observer of the heavens to use a telescope. What he saw confirmed his belief that Copernicus was correct: the Sun was the centre of the solar system.

Geostationary Orbit An orbit at an altitude of 35,900 km (22,300 miles) in which a satellite revolves around Earth every 24 hours, the same rate at which the Earth spins.

Globular Cluster A ball-shaped cluster of many thousands of stars. 125 globular clusters are known in our own galaxy.

Gravity The pull of a planet, moon or star on objects on or near its surface.

Halley, Edmond (1656–1742) British astronomer. He showed that a comet, now named after him, had appeared in the skies at regular intervals before, and predicted it would do so in the future.

Herschel, William (1738–1822) British astronomer, born in Germany. With his specially constructed telescope, he discovered the planet Uranus and many other nebulae, clusters and satellites.

Hubble, Edwin (1899–1953) US astronomer. He founded the study of galaxies beyond our own galaxy.

Interstellar space Space beyond the solar system, in between the stars. There is a great deal of gas and dust floating around in interstellar space.

Kepler, Johannes (1571–1630) German astronomer. He devised laws of planetary motion, which describe the paths taken by the planets in their orbits around the Sun.

Light year The distance that a beam of light travels in one year. It is about 9.5 million million km (5.9 million million miles).

Luminosity A measure of a star's brightness. It is also known as magnitude.

Magnetosphere The magnetic region surrounding the earth, really the Earth's magnetic field extending out into space.

Meridian An imaginary line in the heavens passing through the poles in the celestial sphere and directly over the observer.

Meteor A tiny particle from space, no more than the size of a grain of sand, which enters the Earth's atmosphere and burns up. The streak of light we see when this happens is called a shooting star.

Top **The planet Jupiter, photographed by Voyager I.**

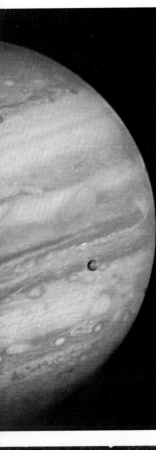

Above **A great spiral galaxy, very similar to our own.**

Meteorite A lump of rock or metal from space which plunges through the atmosphere to hit the Earth's surface.

Milky Way The faint band of light which is seen crossing the sky on clear nights. Seen through a telescope, it becomes thousands of stars: it is actually a cross-section through the plane of our own Galaxy.

Moon Earth's natural satellite, about 384,000 km (238,000 miles) away. Natural satellites of other planets are also called moons.

NASA The National Aeronautics and Space Administration. It is the US government body concerned with the peaceful exploration of space.

Nebula A cloud of dust and gas in space. Nebulae are believed to be the early stages in the birth of a new star.

Neutron Star A tiny, compressed star left behind after a massive star has been destroyed in a supernova explosion.

Newton, Isaac (1642–1727) British scientist. By his laws of gravity, he showed that the same force which governed the fall of apples also governed the orbit of the Moon and all the planets.

Observatory A building designed and equipped for observing the skies. It usually houses a powerful telescope.

Occultation The passing of a moon or planet between the observer and another celestial body, causing that body to disappear temporarily.

Opposition The position of a planet when it lies opposite the Sun with the Earth in between.

Orbit The path in space of one body around another. Orbits are usually elliptical (oval) in shape.

Perigee The nearest point to the Earth reached by the Moon or an artificial satellite in their orbits.

Perihelion The nearest point to the Sun reached by the planets or comets in their orbits.

Planet A non-luminous body orbiting around the Sun. There are nine planets in our solar system, but other stars almost certainly have planets.

Pulsar Believed to be a rapidly spinning neutron star, which gives out a flash of radiation like a lighthouse beam every time it turns.

Quasar A very highly luminous object far off in space. Although it appears to be many thousands of times smaller than a galaxy, it gives out the light of hundreds of galaxies.

Radio astronomy A branch of astronomy concerned with the study of radio energy given off by stars or regions of space.

Radio telescope A device for collecting radio waves from space. Most are shaped like huge dishes.

Red dwarf A star much smaller and cooler than the Sun. They are only faintly visible.

Red giant A star much larger and brighter than the Sun. Stars swell up into red giants at the ends of their lives.

Satellite A natural or man-made object that orbits

a planet. The first man-made satellite was Sputnik I, launched in 1957.

Shooting Star A popular name for a meteor.

Solar System The collection of nine planets, their moons and various asteroids and comets that all orbit the Sun.

Solstice The time when the Sun is farthest north or south of the equator, making longest or shortest day. This occurs around 21 June and 22 December.

Space probe A vehicle launched into space equipped to obtain information about other bodies in the solar system.

Space Station An enclosed structure in which astronauts can live and work for long periods. Early space stations were Salyut and Skylab.

Spectrum The rainbow-coloured band of light formed when visible, or white, light is separated. Study of a star's spectrum can tell us a great deal about what it is made of.

Sputnik A series of Soviet satellites. Sputnik 1, launched in October 1957, was the world's first artificial satellite. The series ended in 1961.

Star A heavenly body which produces its own heat and light. They are glowing balls of various sizes consisting mostly of hydrogen gas.

Sun Our parent star, situated at the centre of the solar system. It is a star of average size and brightness (a ''yellow'' star), but appears so much more prominent to us than other stars because it is much closer.

Sunspot A dark patch on the Sun's surface caused by a cooler region of gas. The number of sunspots waxes and wanes about every 11 years, a period known as the solar cycle.

Supergiant A star of enormous size and luminosity compared with the Sun.

Supernova The explosion of a star, several times larger than the Sun, at the end of its life. The core of the erupted star is left behind as a neutron star or a black hole.

Telescope An instrument for making distant objects visible to the human eye. Light is collected using lenses, mirrors or photographic equipment and magnified.

Transit The passage of a body, such as a planet, across the face of the Sun, as seen from the Earth.

Universe Everything that exists. It contains all the millions of star galaxies. Many astronomers believe it has been expanding since its origin in the Big Bang.

Voyager Two US space probes that travelled to the outer planets of the solar system. They have sent back a wealth of new information and photographs of Jupiter, Saturn and Uranus.

White dwarf A small, extremely hot star about the size of the Earth. A white dwarf is believed to be the likely fate of the Sun thousands of millions of years into the future.

Zenith A point on the celestial sphere directly above the observer.

Zodiac The band of 12 constellations through which the Sun appears to pass during the year.

Our Planet Earth

Long, long ago people used to think that the Earth was the centre of the universe. They thought that all the heavenly bodies circled around the Earth. But now we know differently. The Earth is only a tiny speck in the universe! It is one of the planets that circle around the Sun.

But Earth is special among the planets, for three main reasons. One, it is surrounded by a layer of air, or atmosphere, which we and other living things can breathe. Two, most of its surface is covered with water. Three, the water and the land are full of living things – plants and animals of all shapes, sizes and colours. No other planet has any of these things.

People long ago also thought that the Earth was flat. If you went too far, they said, you would fall over the edge! In time they realized that the Earth must be round. You could sail right around it and arrive where you started. Pictures of the Earth taken by astronauts show this to be true. The Earth is a ball of rock spinning in space.

Below **The Earth has a layered structure of core, mantle and crust.**

Right **An astronaut's view of the Earth floating in space.**

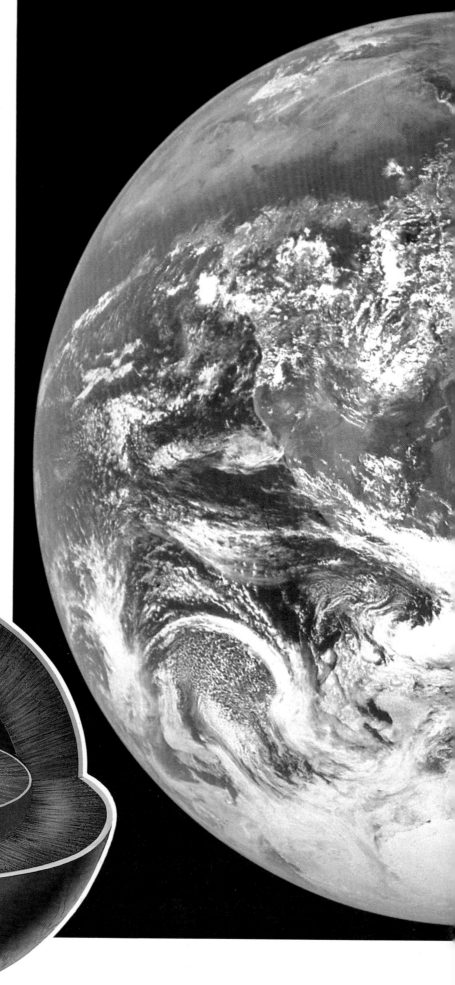

Crust

Mantle

Core (liquid)

Core (solid)

Inside out

When you look at the Earth from space, it looks mainly blue, with brown patches and flecks of white. The blue areas are the waters of the oceans. Oceans cover more than seven parts out of ten of the Earth's surface. The brown patches are the land areas, or continents. They make up less than three parts in ten of the surface. The white flecks on the Earth are the clouds, which move through the atmosphere.

The Earth measures 12,756 km (7,926 miles) around the middle, or the Equator. The continents form part of the Earth's outer layer, or crust. The crust is up to about 60 km (40 miles) thick on the continents, but only about 6 km (4 miles) thick under the oceans. The crust is made up of solid rock. Some of it is flat; some is raised up into hills and mountains.

Underneath the crust is a very much thicker layer of rock. It is called the mantle. The rock is hot and under great pressure. It can move slowly, and this brings about violent changes in the crust (see page 23).

In the centre of the Earth there is a thick core. The outer part of it seems to be liquid. The core is made up of metals, probably iron and nickel. Scientists think that these metals are the reason why the Earth acts like a giant magnet (see page 133).

In the beginning

The Earth was born about 4,600 million years ago, at the same time as the other planets. At first it was a ball of boiling red-hot rock. Gradually the surface cooled down and became hard, forming the crust. Gases came out of the rocks to form the atmosphere. Steam formed clouds and it began to rain. After a very long time, the rains provided the water for the seas.

About 3,000 million years ago, the first signs of life began to appear in the seas. Nobody really knows how this happened. But it took ages and ages before lots of living things appeared. We find the remains, or fossils of early creatures in ancient rocks. The first human beings did not appear on Earth until about four million years ago. (See also page 60.)

DRIFTING CONTINENTS

Below **Where two plates meet each other, volcanoes may erupt, and mountain ranges build up.**

Bottom left **When two plates stick, then suddenly slide past each other, violent earthquakes occur. They wreak havoc when they strike built-up areas, as here in a town in Alaska.**

Bottom right **A map of the plates that form the Earth's crust.**

There are six main land areas, or continents on the Earth. You can see what they look like on the maps between pages 32 and 57. The biggest one is Eurasia. This covers all of Europe and Asia. Next in size comes Africa, which is joined to Eurasia.

Across the Atlantic Ocean are the continents of North and South America, which are also joined together. The continent of Antarctica is in the far south of the world, around the South Pole. The smallest continent is Australia, also in the southern hemisphere (half) of the world.

Continental jigsaws

If you look at the shapes of the coasts on each side of the Atlantic Ocean, what do you notice? They look as though they would fit together like the pieces in a jigsaw. North America would fit against Europe and northern Africa, and South America would fit against southern Africa.

Scientists now believe that long ago these continents were joined in this way. Then they started to drift apart, and water got in between to form the Atlantic Ocean. This idea is now called continental drift. It explains how the land areas of the world came to be like they are today.

About 200 million years ago all the land on Earth was in one great mass, called Pangaea. Then the land masses that became the continents began drifting apart. This is because the parts of the crust they were on began moving. We call these parts, plates.

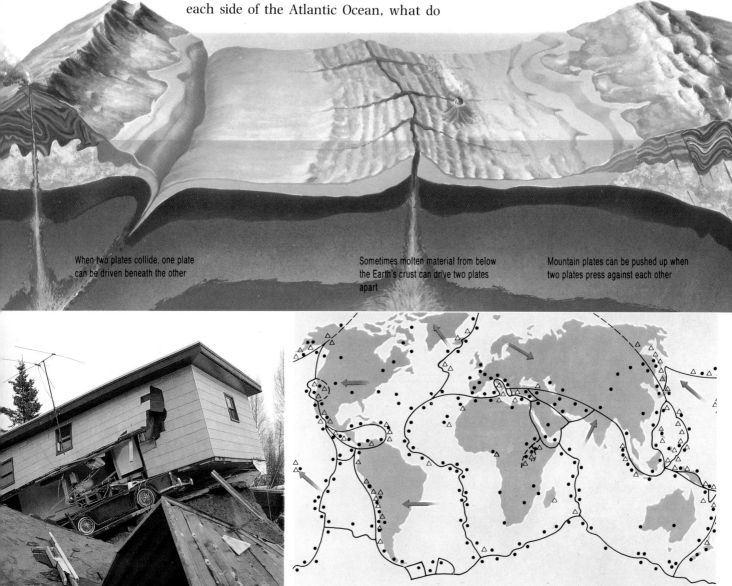

When two plates collide, one plate can be driven beneath the other

Sometimes molten material from below the Earth's crust can drive two plates apart

Mountain plates can be pushed up when two plates press against each other

→ Plate movements   △ Volcanoes   ● Earthquake areas

Moving plates

The whole of the Earth's surface is made up of plates, which are all slowly moving. Movement of the plates brings about many changes on Earth. It makes the oceans get wider, builds mountains, and causes volcanoes to erupt and earthquakes to happen.

In some places, the plates are moving apart. Where this happens, hot molten rock rises from below to form new crust. In other places the plates push against each other. This may cause the land in between to rise and wrinkle, forming mountains. The highest mountains in the world, the Himalayas, were formed in this way. Sometimes when plates push together one plate dips below the other. This causes underground rocks to melt. Sometimes the molten rock forces its way up to the surface resulting in a volcano.

We call the molten rock that pours from a volcano, lava. It is red-hot and can travel a long way before it cools and becomes solid. Many volcanoes erupt (pour out lava) time and time again in magnificent fireworks displays. The ash and lava they throw out makes them grow into the shape of a cone.

When a volcano erupts, the ground nearby shakes. The ground shakes much more violently when there is an earthquake. Earthquakes happen in regions where two plates of the crust are moving past each other. Sometimes the plates get jammed, and then suddenly free themselves. This sends a shock rippling through the ground which can bring down buildings and even destroy whole towns within minutes. As many as 10,000 earthquakes take place all over the world every year. Luckily, only about ten are strong enough to cause damage and loss of life.

Below **An erupting volcano is one of the most terrifying and yet beautiful sights nature has to offer. The great volcanoes on Hawaii, such as Mauna Loa and Kilauea, are in almost constant eruption, sending out rivers of molten lava, as here. Most of the world's volcanoes are extinct, but some are only dormant ("sleeping"): they can erupt without warning. Mount St Helens, in Washington state, USA, erupted in 1980, killing 57 people by burying, burning and suffocation.**

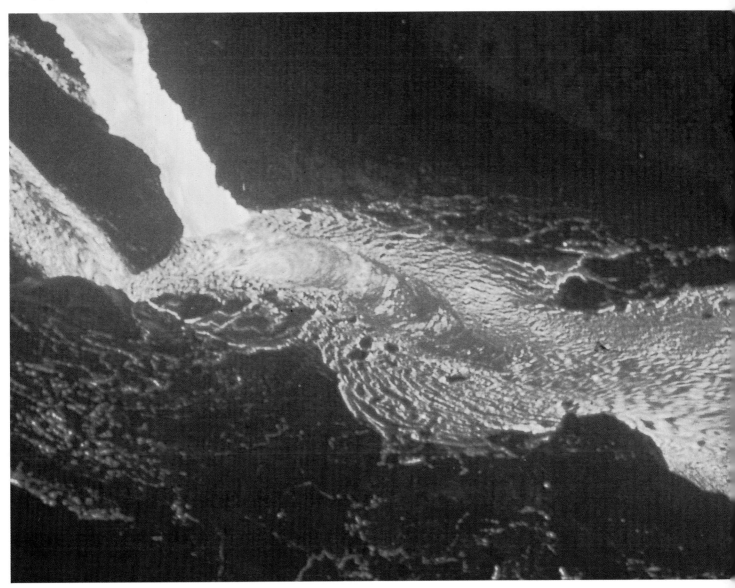

ROCKS AND MINERALS

The Earth's crust is made up of solid rock. You can see this rock in many places, such as in the mountains or along the coast. In other places the rock is buried beneath layers of soil. But you can usually find pieces of rock on the surface in the form of stones and pebbles.

There are many different kinds of rocks. A common one is granite. It is attractive to look at and is very hard. It is often used to make statues and as a building stone. Chalk is another common rock. You can sometimes see brilliant white chalk cliffs at the seaside, for example, along the south coast of England. Chalk is a soft rock. Slate is a rock that can be cut into thin sheets. It is used for the roofs of houses.

Three types of rocks

Granite, chalk and slate are examples of three different types of rocks. Each type was formed in a different way. Granite was

Above left **A slate quarry in Wales. Slate is a layered rock formed by heat and pressure deep inside the Earth's crust. Slate is a metamorphic, or changed rock.**

Above **This great mass of rock in Yosemite National Park, USA, is granite. It formed when molten rock cooled slowly beneath the surface. Granite is an igneous rock.**

Far left **The white cliffs along the southern coast of England are composed of chalk rock. It is made up of the remains of tiny sea creatures that lived many millions of years ago. Chalk is a sedimentary rock.**

Left **When you examine a thin slice of rock under a microscope, you can see the different minerals it contains. In this slice of basalt rock, the large crystals are augite. In between are tiny crystals of mica and feldspar.**

formed from molten rock. The rock pushed its way nearly to the Earth's surface and cooled there, quite slowly. We call it an igneous, or fire-formed rock. The lava that comes from volcanoes is another igneous rock.

Chalk is a rock that was never hot or molten. It is actually made up of the skeletons of tiny creatures that lived in ancient seas. When the creatures died, their skeletons fell to the bottom. Over millions of years layer upon layer of skeletons piled up. They gradually were squeezed together into a hard mass, and became rock.

Many rocks were formed in this way, from layers of sediments, or material that fell to the bottom of the sea. We call them sedimentary rocks. Sandstone is a sedimentary rock formed from sand. Shale is a sedimentary rock formed from mud.

Slate is an example of what is called a metamorphic, or changed rock. Once it was shale, which is quite soft. Then deep underground the shale became heated and squeezed. It turned into hard, flaky slate. Marble is another changed rock. It was once a soft chalky rock called limestone.

Minerals and crystals

If you look closely at pieces of rock, you see that they are made up of many small shiny specks. These are tiny crystals of different substances, which we call minerals. In many granite rocks you can see three kinds of crystals – pink, white and black. The white ones are a mineral called quartz. It is one of the commonest minerals.

Sometimes the crystals in the rocks grow large and into the most beautiful shapes. They can be cut in special ways to make gems for jewellery. The finest gems of all are diamonds. They are very hard and sparkle brilliantly in the light. Sapphires, emeralds and rubies are also very precious gems.

Other minerals don't look so impressive, but they are still important. These minerals are used in industry, and some are used to make metals. They are called ores. The most important of these are the iron ores, which are used to make iron and steel. The ores are changed into metals by being heated at extremely high temperatures in furnaces. This process is called smelting (see page 139).

SHAPING THE LANDSCAPE

Have you been at the seaside during a storm? If you have, you will have seen the waves crashing down on the shore with great force. They can do a lot of damage to sea walls and seaside roads and buildings. In other places, the waves pound the rocks along the shore. In time, they would shatter the rocks into pieces, and then wear away the pieces into pebbles and tiny specks of sand. The breaking down and wearing away of the rocks is called erosion.

The sea is just one of the many things that cause erosion of the Earth's crust. The weather is another. For example, rain water gets into cracks in the rocks, and on cold nights it freezes into ice. The ice takes up more space than the water, and this forces the cracks apart. Little by little, the surface of the rocks breaks up.

Running water

Rivers also cause erosion of the land. They wear out a channel as they flow over the ground. Over many years they can cut through the rocks to form deep valleys and gorges. In the United States, the River Colorado has cut a gorge in places over 1.6 km (1 mile) deep. It is called the Grand Canyon, and is one of the natural wonders of the world.

Sometimes river water contains traces of acid. When it flows over the rocks, it may start to dissolve them, rather like water dissolves sugar. Gradually the acid river water widens the cracks in the rocks. In time the cracks grow into underground

Below **In desert regions sand whipped up by the wind sand-blasts the rocks into weird shapes.**

Bottom **Great glaciers carve their way through the mountains.**

Above **Water dripping in underground caves creates giant stalactites and stalagmites.**

Below **Over millions of years the River Colorado has cut 1600 m deep into the rocks to form the Grand Canyon. In the layers of rocks in the Canyon walls, we can read much about the history of the Earth.**

tunnels and caves. In these caves you often see great "icicles" of stone hanging from the roof. We call them stalactites. Stone pillars called stalagmites often rise from the floor.

Rivers of ice

In very cold climates of the world snow can stay on the ground all year long. As more snow falls, it builds up into a thick layer that becomes squeezed into ice. We call this layer an ice sheet or glacier. Huge glaciers cover much of the island of Greenland in the far

north of the world, and the continent of Antarctica in the far south. Many smaller glaciers are found in high mountain ranges all over the world.

In the past, during the Ice Ages, glaciers covered much of North America and northern Europe. They covered all of the British Isles except the far south. We can still see the marks they made on the landscape, even today.

In the mountains, glaciers often form in valleys. As the weight of ice builds up, the glaciers start to move downhill. The ice carries rocks along with it, and these wear away the valley floor, like a rough file. Many glaciers melt as they go downhill, and rivers form at their feet. Some glaciers reach the sea. Then they break up into great chunks, as icebergs, which float away.

Sandblasting

In the great hot sandy deserts of the world, it is the wind that causes most erosion. The wind picks up the grains of sand and carries them along. The sand scrapes away at everything it touches and makes the rocks into weird shapes. Most of the erosion takes place near the ground and some of the rocks end up looking like mushrooms.

WEATHER AND CLIMATE

By "weather" we mean the state of the atmosphere where we happen to be: how hot it is, whether it's raining or snowing, if the wind is blowing, and so on. The scientists who study the weather are called meteorologists. They try to forecast the weather, to tell us what it is going to be like. They now use weather satellites to help them. These satellites take pictures of the cloud cover over the Earth, enabling them to watch the development and movement of weather fronts in far more detail than is possible from traditional weather reports. They also measure the temperature all over the world. They can follow how the weather is changing hour by hour. This helps the meteorologists make better forecasts. Unfortunately, they are not always right!

Air movements

The weather changes all the time as great masses of air travel through the atmosphere. The heat from the Sun is what drives the air about. The Sun heats up the land, and the land heats the air above it. The hot air rises, starting off a wind that moves over the surface.

When the wind passes over seas and

Below **To help them predict weather, forecasters now use computers, which process data from weather stations, ships and satellites.**

Bottom **This is what a hurricane looks like from space. The clouds spiral round a calm centre, or eye.**

lakes, it picks up moisture (water) in the form of vapour (gas). When the moist air rises high into the sky, it cools. The vapour turns into little drops of water or specks of ice. We see them in the sky as clouds.

Hail and gale

When the water drops in a cloud grow bigger, they become heavier and heavier.

Eventually they fall from the sky as rain. If the air is very cold, ice crystals form and fall to the ground as snow. In a thundercloud, the water drops freeze into hailstones. Some hailstones grow as big as cricket balls before they fall! They can do a great deal of damage when they hit the ground.

The wind can also do great damage when it blows hard. In a gale, winds can blow at speeds of up to 100 km/hr (60 mph). They can uproot trees and blow the tiles off roofs. But the wind can blow even harder. This happens during the great storms we call hurricanes and cyclones. Then the winds can reach speeds of over 160 km/hr (100 mph). They can blow down houses and toss cars about like toys.

Climates

The weather changes from day to day and from season to season. But the pattern of weather for a particular region is much the same year after year. We call the usual weather pattern of a region, its climate. Every part of the Earth has its own climate.

We usually describe a climate by its temperature and by the amount of rainfall it has every year. The hottest climates are found near the Equator. This is the part of the Earth that gets most sunshine. It also rains a lot there. We call this climate tropical. There are other places away from the Equator that are also very hot, but have little if any rain. They have a desert climate.

Going farther away still from the equator, the climate gets cooler. Summers are warm, but winters are cool and wet. This is a temperate climate. The regions around the North and South Poles are the coldest. These frozen deserts have a polar climate.

Below **Generally, winds blow from high pressure to low pressure areas. This is complicated by the Earth's rotation: winds are deflected to the right in the northern hemisphere and to the left in the southern.**

North Pole

Cold   Cold

Cool   Cool

Warm   Equator   Warm

Cool   Cool

Cold   Cold

South Pole

North Pole

High   60°N
Low
High   30°N
(Horse latitudes)
Low
Doldrums   Equator
High
(Horse latitudes)   30°S
Low
60°S

South Pole

Prevailing winds

Trades

Westerlies

Polar Easterlies

Right **The amount of water in the air has a great effect on the weather. Water passes into and falls out of the atmosphere in a never-ending cycle. Water evaporates from the sea and rivers. Plants also give off vapour. When moist air rises into the sky, it forms clouds as it cools and condenses back into water droplets. When they become large enough, they fall to the ground as rain, or in freezing conditions, as snow.**

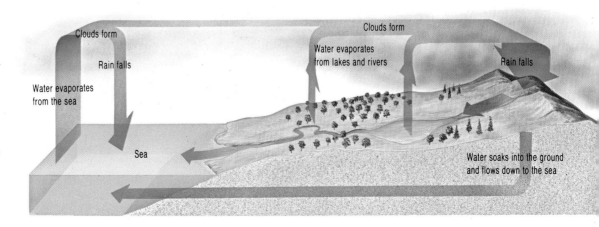

Clouds form   Clouds form

Rain falls   Water evaporates from lakes and rivers   Rain falls

Water evaporates from the sea

Sea   Water soaks into the ground and flows down to the sea

Earth Factfinder

Alluvium Mud, silt and sand deposited by running water. An alluvial fan will form when a fast-flowing mountain stream reaches flatter land.

Anticyclone A region of high pressure in the atmosphere. It usually brings bright, sunny weather.

Atoll A circular or horseshoe-shaped coral reef surrounding a lagoon.

Basalt A fine-grained igneous rock, dark in colour. It is formed from solidified volcanic lava.

Continents

	sq km	sq miles
Asia	42,700,000	16,500,000
Africa	29,860,000	11,530,000
N. America	24,307,000	9,385,000
S. America	18,221,000	7,035,000
Europe	9,800,000	3,800,000
Australia	7,635,000	2,948,000
Antarctica	15,500,000	6,000,000

Continent A large land mass, consisting of part of the Earth's crust which rises above the ocean floors. The seven major unbroken land masses of the Earth, together with their continental shelves occupy about 30 per cent of the Earth's surface.

Continental Shelf The sea bed surrounding the continents, usually not more than about 180 m (600 ft) deep. Beyond the continental shelf, the continental slope drops steeply to the ocean floor.

Core The central mass of the Earth. It probably consists mostly of iron and has a diameter of about 6,900 km (4,300 miles).

Crust The outer layer of the Earth. It is 10–40 km (6–25 miles) thick.

Cyclone A region of low pressure in the atmosphere. It is also called a depression, and usually brings wet weather.

Delta The area of sediments, often fan-shaped, built up from alluvium deposited at the mouth of some rivers. The river may be split up into a number of channels as it enters the sea.

Desert A large area of land with very little rainfall – less than 250 mm (10 in) a year. Deserts may be hot (e.g. Sahara) or cold (e.g. Gobi).

Largest islands

		sq km	sq miles
1	Greenland	2,130,265	822,500
2	New Guinea	794,090	306,600
3	Borneo	751,078	289,993
4	Madagascar	589,683	227,678
5	Baffin I.	476,066	183,810
6	Sumatra	431,982	166,789
7	Great Britain	229,522	88,619
8	Honshu	226,087	87,293
9	Ellesmere	198,393	76,600
10	Victoria	192,695	74,400

Earthquake Shock waves produced by sudden movements in the Earth's crust. The vibrations can have a great effect on the Earth's surface, causing great cracks to appear and triggering landslides.

Equator The imaginary line encircling the globe midway between north and south poles.

Erosion The wearing away of the Earth's surface by the action of water, ice or wind. Rivers, glaciers and the sea are all responsible for a great deal of erosion.

Fault A crack in the Earth's crust, either side of which layers of rock have moved out of line with one another.

Fjord A long, deep and steep-sided sea inlet in a mountainous area. It was originally a valley eroded by a glacier, before being filled in by the sea.

Oceans and seas

		sq km	sq miles
1	Pacific Ocean	165,000,000	64,000,000
2	Atlantic Ocean	81,500,000	31,500,000
3	Indian Ocean	73,500,000	28,350,000
4	Arctic Ocean	14,250,000	5,500,000
5	Mediterranean Sea	2,850,000	1,100,000
6	South China Sea	2,486,000	960,000
7	Bering Sea	2,274,000	878,000
8	Caribbean Sea	1,942,000	750,000
9	Gulf of Mexico	1,855,000	716,050
10	Sea of Okhotsk	1,525,000	589,000

Fold mountains Mountains formed from the bending of layers of rock in the Earth's crust. The Rockies are an example of fold mountains.

Highest mountains

		metres	feet
Asia			
1	Everest (Himalaya)	8,848	29,028
2	Godwin Austen (Karakoram)	8,611	28,250
3	Kanchenjunga (Himalaya)	8,579	28,146
4	Makalu (Himalaya)	8,470	27,790
5	Dhaulagiri (Himalaya)	8,172	26,810
South America			
	Aconcagua (Andes)	6,960	22,835
North America			
	McKinley	6,194	20,320
Africa			
	Kilimanjaro	5,888	19,317
Europe			
	Elborus (Caucasus)	5,633	18,481
	Mont Blanc (Alps)	4,810	15,781
Antarctica			
	Vinson Massif	5,139	16,860
Oceania			
	Caestensz (Nassau Range)	5,000	16,404

Front The dividing line between air masses of different temperature and humidity (the amount of moisture in the air).

Geography The study of the Earth's surface, including its climate, landscape, and human activity.

Geology The study of the origin, structure and composition of the Earth.

Geyser A fountain of hot water occasionally shooting out from the ground in volcanic regions. There are spectacular examples in New Zealand and Iceland, where the name comes from.

Glacier A mass of ice that creeps slowly down a mountainside. In the past, vast glaciers have deepened and straightened river valleys.

Hurricane A severe storm in which high winds blow in a spiral pattern towards the centre, the eye.

Ice age A period when temperatures are much lower than normal and large parts of the Earth's surface are covered with ice. The last great Ice Age ended around 18,000 years ago.

Largest lakes

		sq km	sq miles
1	Caspian Sea (Asia)	440,300	170,000
2	Superior (N. America)	82,400	31,820
3	Victoria (Africa)	69,480	26,820
4	Aral (USSR)	67,340	26,000
5	Huron (N. America)	59,575	23,010
6	Michigan (N. America)	58,000	22,400
7	Tanganyika (Africa)	32,890	12,700
8	Great Bear (Canada)	31,600	12,200
9	Baikal (USSR)	31,470	12,150
10	Great Slave (Canada)	28,930	11,170

Igneous rock Rocks which have been formed from volcanic lava that has solidified on or beneath the Earth's surface.

Lava Molten rock thrown out from beneath the Earth's surface (where it is known as magma) during a volcanic eruption.

Lightning A flash of light in the sky caused by a discharge of electricity between clouds or between clouds and the Earth. Thunder is the sound of lightning.

Magnetic Poles The ends of the line of magnetic force that run north and south through the Earth. They vary in location, but are never far from the true north and south poles.

Mantle The layer of rock lying between the crust and core of the Earth. It is about 2,900 km (1,800 miles) thick and makes up the bulk of the Earth's volume.

Metamorphic rocks Rocks whose structure or composition has been changed by great heat or pressure in the Earth.

Meteorology The study of the Earth's atmosphere and weather.

Highest active volcanoes

		metres	feet
1	Cotopaxi (Ecuador)	5,978	19,613
2	Popocatapetl (Mexico)	5,452	17,887
3	Sangay (Ecuador)	5,410	17,749
4	Tungurahua (Ecuador)	5,033	16,512
5	Cotacachi (Ecuador)	4,937	16,197
6	Klyuchevskaya (USSR)	4,850	15,912
7	Purace (Colombia)	4,756	15,604
8	Wrangell (Alaska, USA)	4,269	14,005
9	Tajmulco (Guatemala)	4,210	13,812
10	Mauna Loa (Hawaii, USA)	4,168	13,675

Mineral The substance of which rocks are composed. Minerals are tiny crystals of a natural, solid and inorganic (not living) material.

Longest rivers

		km	miles
1	Nile (Africa)	6,695	4,160
2	Amazon (S. America)	6,520	4,050
3	Mississippi-Missouri-Red Rock (N. America)	5,970	3,710
4	Yangtze (Asia)	5,470	3,400
5	Yenisei (USSR)	5,310	3,300
6	Mekong (Asia)	4,500	2,800
7	Zaire (Africa)	4,375	2,710
8	Amur (USSR)	4,345	2,700
9	Ob (USSR)	4,345	2,700
10	Lena (USSR)	4,310	2,680

Peninsula A piece of land that is almost an island, although not completely separated from the mainland. Italy is a peninsula.

Plate tectonics The movement of plates – large areas of the Earth's crust separated by faults – over the surface of the globe.

Rift Valley A long valley formed where a block of land has sunk between two parallel faults. A fine example is the Great Rift Valley which runs from Syria to East Africa.

Sedimentary rocks Rocks which have been formed from mineral or organic (living) fragments that have been deposited by water, ice or wind. Clay, sandstone and limestone are sedimentary rocks.

Soil The loose, upper layer of the land surface made up of rock particles, and decaying plant and animal material.

Tides The regular rise and fall of the sea level caused by the gravitational pull of the Moon and the Sun.

Highest waterfalls

		metres	feet
1	Angel (Venezuela)	807	2,648
2	Cuquenan (Venezuela)	610	2,000
3	Ribbon (USA)	490	1,612
4	W. Mardalsfoss (Norway)	467	1,535
5	Upper Yosemite (USA)	436	1,430
6	Gavarnie (France)	421	1,385
7	Tugela (South Africa)	421	1,385
8	Glass (Brazil)	403	1,325
9	Krimml (Austria)	381	1,250
10	Takkakaw (Canada)	366	1,200

Valley A stretch of lower land running between hills. A valley may be formed by the action of rivers, glaciers or faulting, or by a combination of any of these. A river valley is usually V-shaped; a glaciated valley is a U shape.

Volcano Openings in the Earth's crust, usually mountains shaped like cones. During a volcanic eruption, lava spouts up from the central vent.

Wadi A dry valley in a desert. Wadis are carved out by torrential streams which flow during rare periods of rain. These powerful erosive forces combined with wind erosion and weathering produce the very steep sides of a wadi.

Greatest depths

		metres	feet
1	Mariana Trench (Challenger Deep)	11,520	37,800
2	Tonga Trench	10,630	34,885
3	Philippine Trench (Galathea Deep)	10,540	34,580
4	Kuril Trench (Vityaz Deep)	10,375	34,045
5	Japanese Trench (Ramapo Deep)	10,372	34,035
6	Kermadec Trench	9,995	32,788
7	Guam Trench	9,632	31,614
8	Puerto Rico Trench (Milwaukee Deep)	9,200	30,246
9	New Britain Trench (Planet Deep)	9,140	29,987
10	Bonin Trench	9,088	29,816

Water cycle The continual movement of water between the Earth and the atmosphere. Water evaporates from the sea, rivers and vegetation, then condenses into clouds. It falls to the ground as rain or snow.

Water table The level of water in the ground. Rainwater that has seeped through the soil and through cracks or tiny holes (pores) in the rocks beneath collects where it cannot penetrate further.

Weathering The wearing away of the Earth's surface by exposure to the atmosphere. Changes in temperature or the chemical reaction between oxygen and rock material are examples of the weathering process.

Wind The movement of air masses across the surface of the Earth.

Countries of the World

EUROPE

Europe is the smallest continent, only 4,929,000 sq km (1,903,000 sq miles) in area, but most of the countries contain a lot of people. It is a wealthy continent and there are many areas with very good agriculture such as near Paris (France), in East Anglia (Britain) and in the Po Valley (Italy). Europe can produce more food than is needed. There are also big towns and regions with steel works, chemicals factories and many other industries.

The climate of Europe changes from west to east, because the damp and mild air from the Atlantic cannot spread over the whole continent. There are also changes from north to south because it is much colder in Norway and Sweden than it is near the Mediterranean. In northern Europe the winters are often snowy and the temperature falls below freezing point, but in the south the winter temperatures will be 5–10°C (41–50°F). Northern summers are only about 15°C (59°F) but in the south the temperatures are 25–30°C (77–86°F). Western Europe (Britain and France) is quite mild in winter (about 5°C or 41°F) but Poland and Germany have temperatures about five degrees below zero. The rainfall is always much heavier in the west than in the east because most of the moisture comes from the Atlantic. In Britain average rainfall totals are about 750–1,000 mm (30–40 in), but in eastern Europe the totals are only about 500 mm (20 in).

There are many small countries in Europe and there are many different languages. In Switzerland most of the people need to speak French and German, and some also speak Italian and Romansch. There are two languages in Belgium. In Iceland, most of the people learn three or four languages.

Northern Europe includes Scandinavia and Finland. Scandinavia consists of the three countries; Norway, Sweden and Denmark. Norway is very mountainous with the highest peak of Galdhopiggen 2,661 m (8,091 ft) high. There are icecaps and glaciers in the mountains and along the coast are fjords. These are steep valleys cut

Above **Every year, thousands of tourists crowd to see Buckingham Palace, Queen Elizabeth II's London home.**

Far right **An olive grove in Spain. Olive trees thrive in a Mediterranean climate: they give oil and wood as well as olives.**

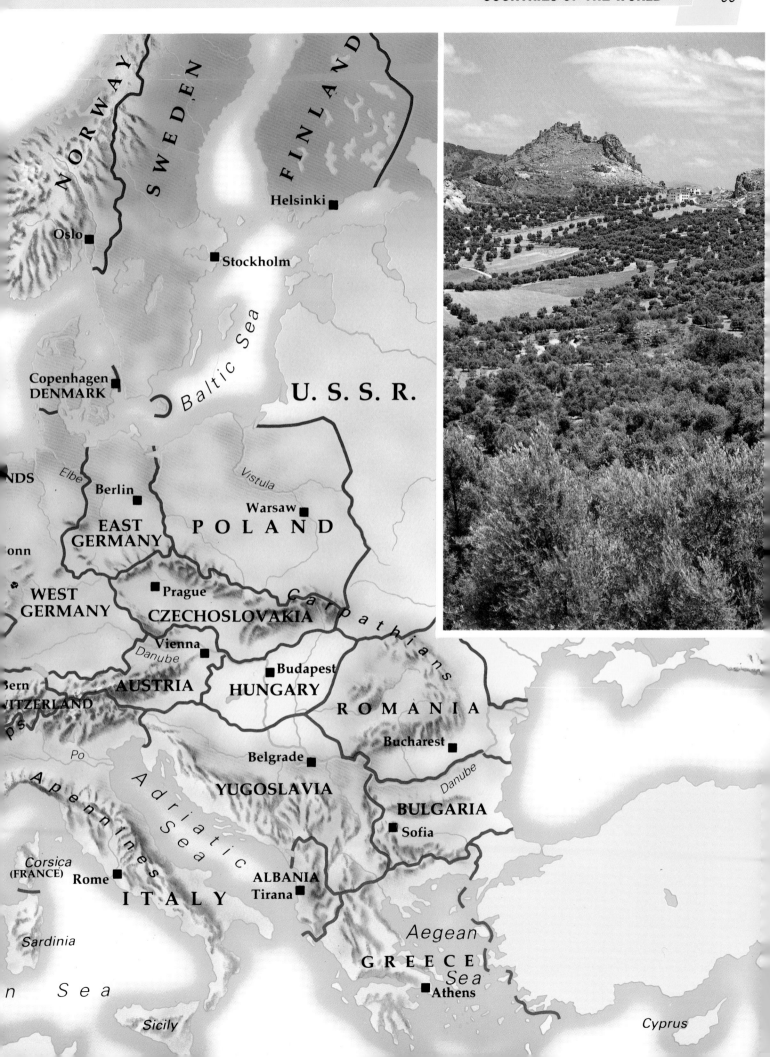

NORWAY

SWEDEN

FINLAND

Helsinki

Oslo

Stockholm

Baltic Sea

Copenhagen
DENMARK

U. S. S. R.

NDS

Elbe

Berlin

Vistula

Warsaw

**EAST
GERMANY**

P O L A N D

onn

**WEST
GERMANY**

Prague

C a r p a t h i a n s

CZECHOSLOVAKIA

Vienna

Danube

Budapest

Bern

AUSTRIA

HUNGARY

R O M A N I A

WITZERLAND

ps

Po

Bucharest

Belgrade

Danube

Apennines

Adriatic Sea

YUGOSLAVIA

BULGARIA

Sofia

Corsica
(FRANCE) Rome

ALBANIA
Tirana

I T A L Y

Aegean

Sardinia

G R E E C E
Sea

Athens

n *S e a*

Sicily

Cyprus

by glaciers a few thousand years ago which were then drowned as the sea flooded in. The main lowland area of Norway is in the east near Oslo where the best farming land is found. Many of the farmers in Norway take their cattle up the mountain to patches of good grass in summer, but have to go back down to the valleys in winter when the snow begins to fall.

Much of Norway is covered by coniferous trees and millions of these are cut down each year to provide pulp for making newspapers. Sweden and Finland both have large areas of forests as well, with spruce, larch and fir trees. All these countries use their fast-flowing streams and rivers to make hydro-electricity and so they do not have dirty industrial towns like those in Germany, Belgium and Britain where coal has been the main source of energy. Finland and Sweden both have a large number of lakes which are good for boating and fishing. The attractive scenery encourages people to go out into the countryside and many tourists come from foreign countries. In the far north of Sweden and Finland there are still a few groups of Lapps who herd reindeer which they use for milk and meat as well as clothing.

Denmark is different because it is low lying and mostly used for farming. There is a big area of fertile soils, many of which are formed of deposits left by the ice during the last ice age. Denmark consists of a peninsula called Jutland and several islands. The main islands are Funen where Odense is the main town, and Zeeland where Copenhagen, the capital, is situated. The eastern side of

Zeeland is very close to Sweden. The farmers in Denmark grow crops as feed for animals. They earn most of their money from milk, butter, cheese and ham, from the millions of dairy cows and pigs.

Western Europe is made up of Britain, Ireland, France, Belgium, Netherlands, Luxembourg, West Germany, Switzerland and Austria. These are all wealthy industrial countries where factories make steel, machines, motor cars, computers and hundreds of other products. These are mostly

Below **Most of upland Scandinavia is covered by coniferous trees. Rivers are used as natural transport to float the logs down to a sawmill. Wood and paper are important exports of both Norway and Sweden.**

used in Europe but some goods are exported all over the world.

The Mediterranean countries have a much sunnier and warmer climate than the rest of Europe which is why millions of tourists go there for holidays from Britain, Germany and Scandinavia. Olives and grapes grow well in the warm climate, but there are many other crops too.

East European countries have communist governments and there are many big farms called collectives where all the peasants share the work. Much of the countryside is hilly and covered with woodland, but there are some big towns and industries as well. Some of the biggest towns such as Budapest, Belgrade and Bucharest are in the Danube valley.

There are a few very famous islands in Europe, notably Iceland in the north, and Sicily and others in the south. Iceland is never very hot but does have hot springs and pools where people can bathe out of doors all through the year. Many tourists go to Iceland to see these hot springs, as well as the geysers and volcanoes. There are many spring flowers and many interesting wild birds. It is not a land of ice, in spite of its name, but it does contain the Vatnajokull, the biggest ice cap in Europe.

Sicily is very much warmer and grows oranges and lemons. It is also famous for its volcano, Etna, which is active every few months.

There are many other islands in the Mediterranean, such as Cyprus, Crete, Corsica and the Balearics all of which attract many visitors from further north.

Many of the countries in the west and south of Europe are now part of the European Economic Community (the EEC). There were originally six members of this community, France, West Germany, Italy, Belgium, Netherlands and Luxembourg and they all joined together in 1958. In 1973, the United Kingdom, Denmark and Ireland joined to bring the total up to nine. Since then, Greece, Spain and Portugal have also become EEC members.

Below **The Alps are one of Europe's most popular holiday resorts. Many skiers are attracted to the snowy mountain slopes (the "piste") and excellent facilities provided.**

Bottom **The Ruhr is the industrial heartland of West Germany.**

USSR

The Soviet Union or USSR (Union of Soviet Socialist Republics) is partly in Europe and partly in Asia. It is made up of a number of republics, of which Russia is the largest. The European section reaches as far east as the Ural Mountains and south to the Caucasus Mountains. It is a very large country of 22.4 million sq km (8.65 million sq miles) and has a population of over 280 million.

In the south of the country near the Black Sea, the climate is Mediterranean with mild winters and hot sunny summers. Nowhere else in the country remains mild in winter; Siberia in the north is very cold indeed. In north-east Siberia the town of Verkhoyansk has average temperatures of minus 40°C (−40°F) in January. In the spring, the ice in the soil and rocks melts to make everywhere wet and marshy.

Farming is difficult in many parts of the USSR because of the cold, but in European Russia there are some rich farming areas. Best of all is in the Steppes of the Ukraine, where the natural grassland has been ploughed up to grow wheat, barley, sun-flowers and maize. Near Moscow too, the farming is good: cereals and vegetables are grown and sheep and cattle are reared.

The most southerly part of the USSR near Samarkand and Tashkent is almost desert and the towns are in oases. Rivers flow from

Above **The Russians use ice breakers to keep open the sea route through the Arctic Ocean.**

Below **The Kremlin, Moscow, viewed from across the river.**

the high mountains such as the Pamirs (where Mount Communism reaches a height of 7,495 m (24,590 ft) and provide water for irrigation. Fruits and cotton are the most important crops.

The USSR is very rich in minerals, oil, natural gas, coal, iron, manganese, gold and many other metals. Some of these are mined in southern Russia and near the southern end of the Ural Mountains and a few are mined in Siberia. Roads and railways have been built into these cold and isolated areas to encourage people to live there. The most famous of all the Russian communication lines is the Trans-Siberian railway which runs from Moscow to Vladivostok, a distance of 9,300 km (nearly 6,000 miles).

There are several large rivers and lakes in the USSR. The rivers Lena, Yenisey and Ob all flow across Siberia into the Arctic Ocean. When not frozen, they are used for floating logs down to the coast.

Bottom **Georgia is a republic in the Caucasus, in the south of the USSR. It has a warm climate and is a rich agricultural region.**

ASIA

Asia is the largest continent and contains nearly 3,000 million inhabitants. Southern parts of Asia are hot and wet equatorial regions where temperatures are about 25°C (77°F) every month and there is heavy rain in most months to give a total of 1,500–2,500 mm (60–100 in) in the year.

In India, China and neighbouring countries the monsoon climate is found: winds blow in from the sea during the summer part of the year bringing heavy rain. The winds then change direction in winter and blow out from land to the sea, bringing dry weather. So, in summer, these monsoon areas can have up to 2,000 mm (80 in) of rainfall, though certain areas only receive 500 mm (20 in) or less. In winter, most of the monsoon areas are very dry – grass shrivels up, the trees have to be able to survive without water, and it is difficult to grow any crops. The summer monsoon is vital because if there is not enough rain the people cannot grow enough food to last them through the dry months.

In the north of China and Korea, the winters can be very cold with temperatures below freezing point, although summer temperatures can be over 20°C (68°F).

The islands off the east coast, Japan and the Philippines, are generally wetter than the mainland because they get some rain in the winter months. This makes it easier to grow more food.

At the western edge of Asia the climate is very different because there is little rainfall. Saudi Arabia is a huge desert country where it is hot all through the year, with temperatures of 20–30°C (68–86°F). The other Middle East countries are also covered by a great deal of desert or poor scrub vegetation.

There are massive mountain ranges in Asia, notably the Himalayas, but there are also high mountains in China, Afghanistan, Iran and Burma. Indonesia, Japan and the Philippines contain a large number of volcanoes too, as one of the most active parts of the earth's crust is where the western edge of the Pacific Ocean meets the eastern edge of Asia.

Most of the USSR is in Asia and in addition to that country, there are five major regions which make up the conti-nent: the Middle East, Southern Asia, South East Asia, the islands of Indonesia, Philippines and Japan, and China.

The Middle East is where Asia meets Africa and Europe. It is mostly very dry with a lot of desert land, although irrigation schemes along the Tigris and Euphrates rivers have been in use for more than 6,000 years in the area called Mesopotamia. There are newer irrigation schemes in Israel,

Right **A town in Nepal near the Chinese border.**

Far right **A Buddhist monk in a temple in Thailand. The religion of Buddhism was founded in India but there are now over 220 million Buddhists spread throughout the world.**

where agriculture has become very important in places.

The Middle East is best known for its enormously rich deposits of oil, especially in Saudi Arabia which has been the world's greatest oil producer for several years. Saudi Arabia and Kuwait and other smaller countries export a lot of oil, particularly to Japan and the USA. Iran has deposits of oil and some other minerals too; cotton, wheat and rice are major crops. Iraq also has large deposits of oil, and produces 80 per cent of the world's dates. Several small countries are wealthy because of their oil, for example, Bahrain, and the United Arab Emirates, a country which consists of seven

Amur

Ulan Bator

MONGOLIA

Gobi Desert

Tien shan

R.

K2

Himalayas

TIBET

NEPAL
Katmandu
Everest
BHUTAN

Ganges

BANGLADESH
Dacca

NDIA

BURMA

Irrawaddy

Bay of
Bengal

SRI
LANKA

olombo

DIAN OCEAN

CHINA

Hwang Ho

Yangtze Kiang

Si Kiang

Peking

Pyongyang

NORTH
KOREA

SOUTH
KOREA

Seoul

JAPAN

Tokyo

Taipei

TAIWAN

HONG
KONG

Hanoi

LAOS

VIETNAM

Vientiane

Mekong

THAILAND
Bangkok

KAMPUCHEA

Phnom
Penh

South
China
Sea

Manila

PHILIPPINES

BRUNEI

MALAYSIA

Kuala
Lumpur

SINGAPORE

INDONESIA

Jakarta

Rangoon

small states which have joined together.

Southern Asia consists of India, Pakistan, Bangladesh, Sri Lanka, Afghanistan, Bhutan and Nepal. These countries are affected by the monsoon climate, but some areas in India and Bangladesh are very wet – 2,000 mm (80 in) or more – whereas Pakistan and north west India are very dry – only 250 mm (10 in) per annum. Pakistan's agriculture depends on irrigation from the river Indus and its tributaries; cotton, rice and wheat are important crops. Sri Lanka, an island, also grows rice, and has plantations of rubber and tea. Bangladesh grows rice for

Below **The Taj Mahal at Agra, India, made of marble and sandstone is one of the most beautiful buildings in the world.**

Right **An oil refinery in Iraq. Many oil installations have been attacked during the Iran–Iraq war.**

Above **Rice terraces in the Philippines.**

Right **A flourishing industry in manufacturing electronic goods has brought wealth to South Korea.**

Below **The Great Wall of China was built in the 3rd century BC as a defence against warring tribes.**

food, and jute for making sacking or the backing for carpets. It is a low-lying and densely populated country which frequently suffers from flooding. India grows vast quantities of rice, wheat, sugar cane and other crops. Afghanistan, Bhutan and Nepal are sparsely populated mountain states.

South East Asia contains several countries: Burma, Thailand, Laos, Kampuchea, Vietnam and Malaysia. Much of the land is mountainous and still covered by forests, though there are lowlands along the coasts and in the river valleys. As the forests are being cut down, serious soil erosion problems are arising: the soil gets washed into the rivers which overflow their banks and cause serious flooding in the lowlands. In the lowland areas such as the Red, Mekong, Chao Phraya and Irrawaddy valleys, rice is very important. Malaysia has some important rubber and pineapple plantations as well as rice growing areas. There are valuable mineral deposits in Burma, Thailand and Malaysia, while the small state of Brunei is quite wealthy because of oil. The even smaller city state of Singapore is wealthy because of trade.

The island nations of Indonesia, Philippines and Japan are spread out over thousands of kilometres in the Pacific. They produce huge quantities of food and Japan is one of the world's greatest industrial nations, famous for its electronic goods. Japan consists of four main islands: Honshu, Hokkaido, Kyushu and Shikoku. There are over 7,000 islands in the Philippines group, though only 11 major islands. The islands of Indonesia are spread out over 12 million sq km (4.5 million sq miles).

China and her neighbours are cooler than the other regions of Asia and grow temperate crops (for example, wheat and millet) as well as rice. There are many large towns now, and industrial development is well under way. Over 20 per cent of the world's people live in China. To the north of China is Mongolia, a sparsely populated country with a large area of desert and poor grassland. Korea and Taiwan have been developing many industries in recent years. Korea was formerly just one country, but the North and South are now divided by a boundary which follows the 38th parallel of latitude.

AFRICA

The Equator runs through the middle of Africa near where the large river Zaire reaches the Atlantic. The other large rivers of Africa are the Niger, which also flows into the Atlantic, the Nile which flows into the Mediterranean, the Zambezi which flows into the Indian Ocean and the Orange which flows across the Kalahari desert before reaching the Atlantic.

The northern edge of Africa has a Mediterranean type of climate with very hot summers (25–30°C or 77–86°F), just like the deserts, but warm wet winters with temperatures of 10°C (50°F). The total rainfall is only 250–500 mm (15–20 in). There are forests on the Atlas Mountains where rainfall is heavier, and thorny scrub in the lowlands.

Further south is the Sahara desert where temperatures are often over 30°C (86°F) and rainfall is rare. Occasional thunderstorms will bring some heavy showers. Beyond the Sahara moving southwards, the rainfall gradually increases. Where it is 500–750 mm (20–30 in), tall tropical grasses grow, forming the savanna areas of northern Nigeria, Ghana, Sudan and other countries.

In the latitudes of southern Nigeria and Zaire the rainfall is up to 2,000 mm (80 in), and this is heavy enough to support dense tropical forests. The east African countries of Kenya, Tanzania and Uganda are on a plateau which is cooler and drier than the Zaire valley, and so the landscape here is grassland instead of forest. In this grassland area are scattered acacia trees and a rich variety of wild animals, including lions, giraffes, zebras and gnus.

South of the Equator there is more tropical grassland, in Angola, Zimbabwe and Zambia, and beyond that is the Kalahari desert. This is a smaller desert than the Sahara, because southern Africa is much narrower than north Africa.

The extreme south of Africa is similar to north Africa as it has a Mediterranean-type climate, particularly around Cape Town. The winters are mild and wet, while summers are sunny and hot, although here in the Southern Hemisphere the summers are from November to March and the winters May to September.

People

Southern Africa contains groups of people called the Bantu, and many of these were originally subsistence farmers growing maize as their main food crop. Further north in the Zaire forests are small numbers of shifting cultivators who grow yams and sweet potatoes in forest clearings. There are also a few Pygmies who are nomadic hunters and gatherers. On the grasslands of east Africa are the cattle herding tribes such as Masai, but some other groups such as the Kikuyu are settled farmers who grow crops. Nigeria also has settled farming groups,

Below **A small oasis in the Sahara Desert. It is overshadowed by the massive accumulation of wind-blown sand.**

Nouakch
Dakar
SEN
S
L

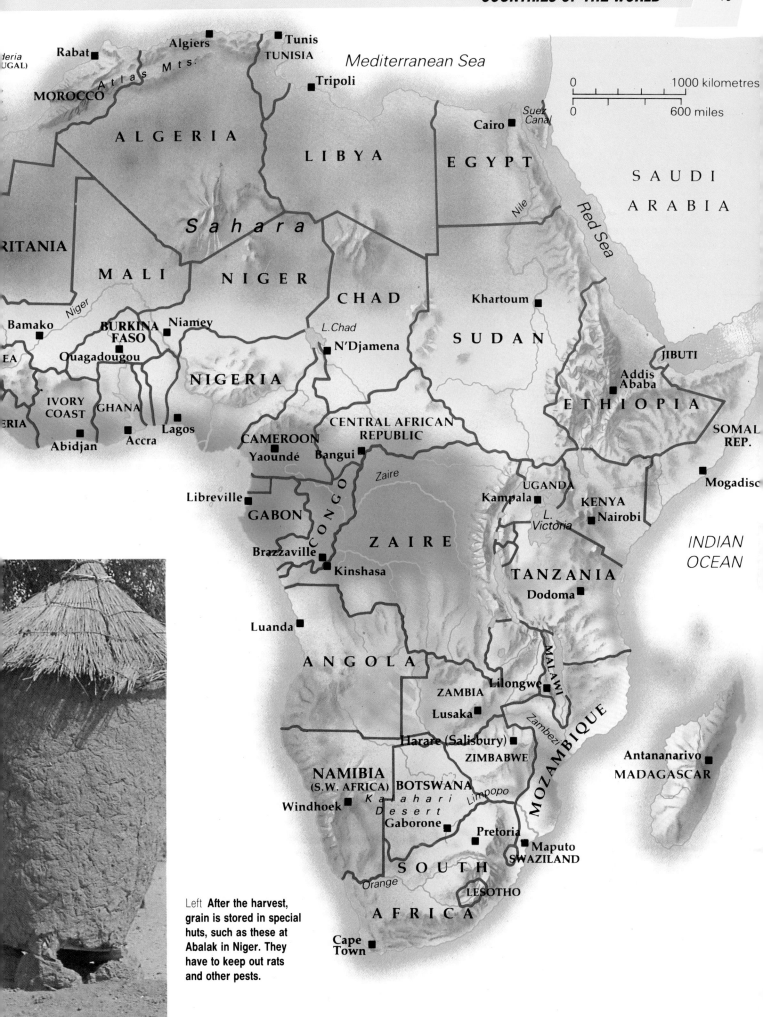

Rabat

Algiers

Tunis
TUNISIA

Tripoli

Mediterranean Sea

Cairo

Suez Canal

MOROCCO

Atlas Mts.

leria (UGAL)

A L G E R I A

L I B Y A

E G Y P T

S A U D I

A R A B I A

Sahara

RITANIA

M A L I

N I G E R

CHAD

Nile

Khartoum

S U D A N

Red Sea

0   1000 kilometres

0   600 miles

Niger

Bamako

BURKINA
FASO

Niamey

L.Chad

N'Djamena

EA

Ouagadougou

JIBUTI

Addis
Ababa

E T H I O P I A

NIGERIA

IVORY
COAST

GHANA

Lagos

CENTRAL AFRICAN
REPUBLIC

SOMAL
REP.

ERIA

Abidjan

Accra

CAMEROON

Yaoundé

Bangui

Zaire

Mogadisc

Libreville

GABON

CONGO

UGANDA

Kampala

KENYA

Nairobi

*L.
Victoria*

INDIAN
OCEAN

Brazzaville

Z A I R E

Kinshasa

T A N Z A N I A

Dodoma

Luanda

A N G O L A

Lilongwe

MALAWI

ZAMBIA

Lusaka

Zambezi

M
O
Z
A
M
B
I
Q
U
E

Harare (Salisbury)

ZIMBABWE

Antananarivo

MADAGASCAR

NAMIBIA
(S.W. AFRICA)

BOTSWANA

*Kalahari
Desert*

Limpopo

Windhoek

Gaborone

Pretoria

Maputo
SWAZILAND

S O U T H

Orange

LESOTHO

A F R I C A

Cape
Town

Left **After the harvest,
grain is stored in special
huts, such as these at
Abalak in Niger. They
have to keep out rats
and other pests.**

44

especially in the wetter forested south, but on the grasslands of the north there are herdsmen and their cattle.

The Sahara contains a few groups of nomadic Bedouin and Tuareg who rear camels, and there are farmers at oases who grow dates, fruit, wheat and vegetables.

Most of Africa is not yet fully developed and the people are still preoccupied with agriculture and attempting to grow enough food for themselves. Large numbers of people have recently been migrating to the towns such as Cairo, Lagos, Nairobi and many others, which have become very congested.

Countries

North Africa contains Egypt, Libya, Tunisia, Algeria and Morocco. Egypt and Libya are mainly in the Sahara desert and so everywhere is dry. The Nile valley is very important for agriculture because of irrigation; cotton, maize and other crops are grown. Cairo, Egypt's capital, is the biggest city in the continent. Libya is a wealthy country because large deposits of oil have

been found. Tunisia, Morocco and Algeria were all influenced by French settlers in the past, and many people still speak French. Near the Mediterranean coast there is some winter rainfall so wheat, grapes, olives and oranges grow well. Further south where it is drier, goats and camels are reared and date palms grown. Morocco and Algeria both contain high mountains of the Atlas Range.

On the southern edge of the Sahara is a region called the Sahel. This includes parts of Burkina Faso, Niger, Chad, Sudan and Ethiopia. There are often shortages of rainfall here and the people cannot grow enough food, and so famines occur. Most of the people are herders but there is sometimes no grass for their animals to eat.

South of the Sahel is a wetter region where good grass grows, in northern Ghana and Nigeria. Here, better cattle are reared and the people have better supplies of food. Maize, millet and groundnuts are grown and there are some irrigation schemes along the rivers Niger and Volta.

The coastal regions of Ghana, Nigeria and neighbouring countries are much wetter. There are plantations of cocoa and palm oil; yams, sweet potatoes and maize are also

Above **The west coast of Africa is extremely fertile, because of great rivers such as the Volta and Niger. Abundant fruits and vegetables are found in the markets, such as this colourful one in Senegal.**

Above right **The economies of Zaire and Zambia depend on mining. Important reserves of copper supply both countries with their principal export earnings.**

Right **The famous flat-topped Table Mountain rises above the South African city of Cape Town. It was here that the Dutch settlers first arrived from Europe in the 17th century.**

cultivated. Similar hot and wet conditions can be found in Zaire where there is still a lot of tropical forest.

East of Zaire are Kenya, Tanzania and Uganda, which are on a plateau and so are not as hot as the Zaire valley. Cattle are reared, maize is grown and there are some commercial farms which grow coffee. The natural vegetation is savanna tropical grassland, which is being preserved in some of the National Parks.

Further south in Zambia, Zimbabwe and Malawi, there is much scrub and grassland. The farmers grow maize and rear cattle, and commercial farms grow tobacco and tea in places. As the climate becomes drier approaching the Kalahari desert, poor quality cattle are reared and few crops can be grown.

In southern Africa, the east coast is much wetter than the west because rainfall is brought in from the Indian Ocean. In the Republic of South Africa there are several good irrigation schemes along the Orange River, and near Cape Town there is enough sun and rain to ripen oranges and grapes. The inland areas are drier and specialize in growing wheat and rearing sheep.

NORTH AMERICA

North America consists of the United States and Canada, and is sometimes called Anglo-America because English is the main language (Central America and South America are referred to as Latin America).

The USA contains 50 states, 48 of which make up the mainland part of the United States; Alaska and Hawaii are the 49th and 50th states. Canada consists of ten provinces (and two territories).

The northern part of the continent is made up of very old hardrocks which are rich in minerals. This area is called the Canadian Shield and stretches from the Rocky Mountains in the west, across past Hudson Bay and Lake Superior, towards Labrador on the east coast. The northern part of the Shield is covered by tundra which is poor grass, mosses and lichen: typical Arctic vegetation. The southern part of the Shield is covered by coniferous forests.

Further south there are differences between the eastern and western sides of the continent. In the east there is a range of mountains called the Appalachians which separate the coastal lowlands from the interior. These mountains were quite a barrier when the early settlers were trying to migrate into the interior of the USA.

The interior is a vast lowland which is drained by the Mississippi and its tributaries, notably the Missouri and the Ohio. The distance from the source of the Missouri downstream to the Mississippi delta is about 6,080 km (3,800 miles), which makes it the third longest river in the world.

West of the Mississippi Basin are the mountains and plateaus of western USA. The highest and biggest range of mountains is the Rockies which reach up to a height of 4,200 m (14,000 ft) and run several hundred kilometres inland. Nearer to the Pacific

Right **Combine harvesters work in groups on the large fields of the Prairies. These vast areas of flat land are used to grow wheat. They stretch for thousands of miles.**

Below **The skyline of New York at night. Limited space on the island of Manhattan forced the city to expand upwards. Skyscraper buildings are the result.**

coast are other mountain ranges including the Sierra Nevada. In the Sierra Nevada is Mount Whitney which at 4,410 m (14,495 ft) is the highest mountain in mainland USA. There are several higher peaks in Alaska, including Mount McKinley which is 6,197 m (20,320 ft) high, the highest of the North American continent.

Central USA and Canada were originally covered by grassland called prairies, over which large herds of buffalo roamed, often pursued by the native Indians. The buffalo and Indians have now gone and much of the grassland has been ploughed up. The northern prairies grow wheat as the main crop, but as the winters are well below freezing point, the seeds cannot be planted until the ground thaws out in spring. It is called spring wheat and is harvested in August. Further south in Iowa, Kansas and Ohio winter wheat is grown. Winter wheat is planted in autumn, grows slowly through the winter and is harvested in July or August. The winter wheat area is part of the Corn Belt where vast quantities of corn (maize) are grown, mostly to be fed to cattle, pigs and poultry, to fatten them up ready for the markets.

East of the Prairies, much of Canada and the USA was covered by forest, because the rainfall is heavier than in the Mississippi Basin. A lot of the forested land has been cleared for towns and farmland, but some still remains in the hillier areas.

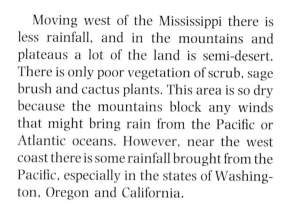

Left **The White House, Washington DC, is the home of the President of the United States.**

Below **California enjoys a warm Mediterranean climate. Fruit produce, such as from these orange groves, contributes to the state's rich economy.**

Moving west of the Mississippi there is less rainfall, and in the mountains and plateaus a lot of the land is semi-desert. There is only poor vegetation of scrub, sage brush and cactus plants. This area is so dry because the mountains block any winds that might bring rain from the Pacific or Atlantic oceans. However, near the west coast there is some rainfall brought from the Pacific, especially in the states of Washington, Oregon and California.

The states of the USA

The 48 states of mainland USA can be grouped into seven main areas. The six most easterly states are collectively known as New England, a region originally settled by the Pilgrim Fathers. The eastern central states include New York and are very industrial, with big coal fields in Virginia and Pennsylvania. In the south east are the states where cotton is one of the main crops (tended in the 17th and 18th century by African slaves). The north central states are important for agriculture, particularly the vast prairies (which extend into Canada) where wheat and other cereals are farmed. Oil and natural gas are mined in large quantities and cotton, tobacco and maize are grown in several of the south central states (which includes the enormous state of Texas).

The mountain states – Arizona, Nevada, New Mexico, Utah, etc. – are sparsely populated but all contain magnificent scenery. The west includes Washington, Oregon and California which are very important for agriculture and forestry, as well as a variety of industries, most famous of which is film-making at Hollywood.

Alaska is a cold, mountainous state which is rich in forests in the south and oil in the frozen north. The 50th state, Hawaii, is a collection of islands in the Pacific for which tourism is one of the most important industries.

The provinces of Canada

Canada consists of ten provinces, each with its own parliament. British Columbia and Alberta in the west are bisected by the

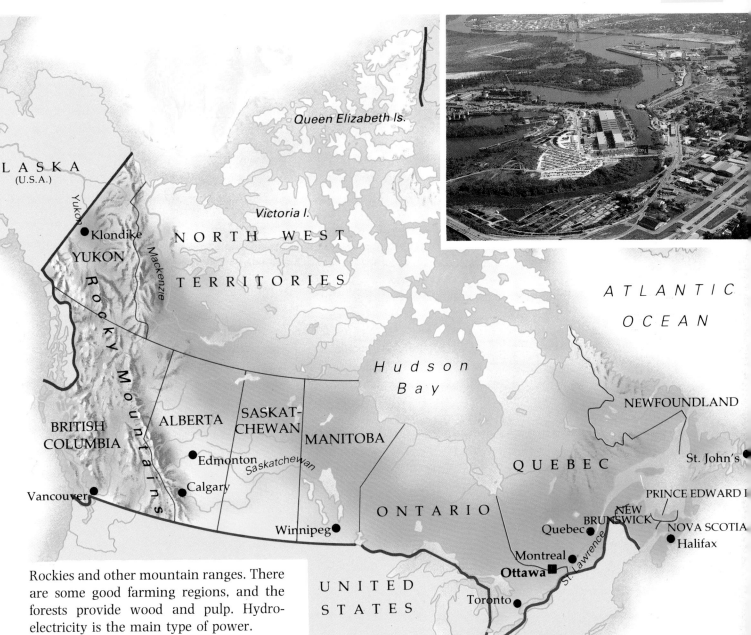

Queen Elizabeth Is.

ALASKA
(U.S.A.)

Yukon

Klondike

YUKON

Mackenzie

Victoria I.

N O R T H   W E S T

T E R R I T O R I E S

R
o
c
k
y
  M
o
u
n
t
a
i
n
s

BRITISH
COLUMBIA

ALBERTA

SASKAT-
CHEWAN

MANITOBA

Edmonton
Saskatchewan

Calgary

Vancouver

Winnipeg

H u d s o n
B a y

A T L A N T I C

O C E A N

NEWFOUNDLAND

Q U E B E C

St. John's

PRINCE EDWARD I

O N T A R I O

NEW
BRUNSWICK

NOVA SCOTIA

Quebec

Halifax

Montreal

St. Lawrence

Ottawa

U N I T E D
S T A T E S

Toronto

Rockies and other mountain ranges. There are some good farming regions, and the forests provide wood and pulp. Hydroelectricity is the main type of power.

Saskatchewan, Manitoba and part of Alberta make up what are sometimes called the Prairie Provinces. Only the southern parts, however, are prairie or grassland. More than 20 million tons of cereal are grown here annually. North of the Prairies is a vast expanse of coniferous forest which stretches from the Rockies to the east coast. The climate is only just warm enough in summer for these trees to grow, and the land is frozen up for four to five months each winter.

Ontario and Quebec are the most populated and industrial areas, particularly around the Great Lakes and St Lawrence seaway. Fishing is the most important industry of the other provinces which are all coastal – Newfoundland, Nova Scotia, Prince Edward Island and New Brunswick.

Top **The docks at Houston, Texas, an important inland port in the southern USA.**

Right **The skyline of Toronto, Canada's largest city, is dominated by the CN tower, 553 m (1814 ft) high.**

CENTRAL AMERICA AND THE WEST INDIES

Central America consists of one large and seven smaller countries. Mexico is really a large plateau with mountain ranges, the Sierra Madre, along the edges. There are small plains along both coastlines. The other smaller countries also have coastlines along the Caribbean and Pacific edges, with high ground inland. This high ground is all volcanic, as the small Central American Republics are really a line of volcanoes which have been joined together by patches of lower land. Izalco in El Salvador is one of the best known as it is frequently flaming.

Southern Mexico and the small republics have forests over most of the lowlands but on the mountains the vegetation is poorer. Bananas are grown in plantations near the coast where the forest has been cleared, and there are coffee plantations higher up in the mountains. Most of the people are poor and grow maize and beans for food. The biggest money earner is the Panama Canal which attracts ships for trade and also a lot of tourists. There are locks in the Panama Canal because the waterway has to cross through a small range of hills.

Mexico is a very large country although much of it is dry and unsuitable for farming. A lot of farmers have migrated into the towns, especially Mexico City which now has over 15 million inhabitants and is one of the world's biggest cities.

Nicaragua is the largest and most sparsely populated of the Central American Republics (excluding Mexico). It has few areas of high land which are suitable for settlement. Guatemala has a wide lowland in the north, and a narrower lowland alongside the Pacific, but the capital city and most of the economic development are in the mountainous interior where the climate is less humid.

There are several large West Indian islands such as Cuba and Jamaica, which have their own governments. Most of the smaller islands are also independent now. They all have sunny climates though often

Below **Mexico City is one of the largest cities in the world. Now the capital city of Mexico, it was built on the ruins of the old Aztec capital of Tenochtitlan.**

Tijuana

Gulf of California

Baja (lower) California

Sierra Madre

Monterr

M E X I

Guadalajara

Aca

Left **Produce from fruit plantations is important to the economies of Central American countries.**

with heavy rainfall too. High temperatures are good for ripening sugar cane, coffee, bananas and other fruits, as well as attracting many tourists from North America and Europe. The islands are generally mountainous and covered in lush forests inland, and several of them are volcanic.

Cuba is the largest of the Caribbean islands and is one of the Great Antilles group. The others in this group are Hispaniola, Puerto Rico and Jamaica. Hispaniola is the second biggest and consists of Haiti and the Dominican Republic.

The Lesser Antilles are all smaller islands and are divided into two groups, the Leeward Islands and the Windward Islands. The largest and most populated are Trinidad and Tobago, with over one million inhabitants.

North of Cuba is the Bahama group of islands, which are made of coral, whereas many of the small islands in the Lesser Antilles are volcanic. Martinique has had one of the biggest eruptions when Mont Pelée blew up in 1902.

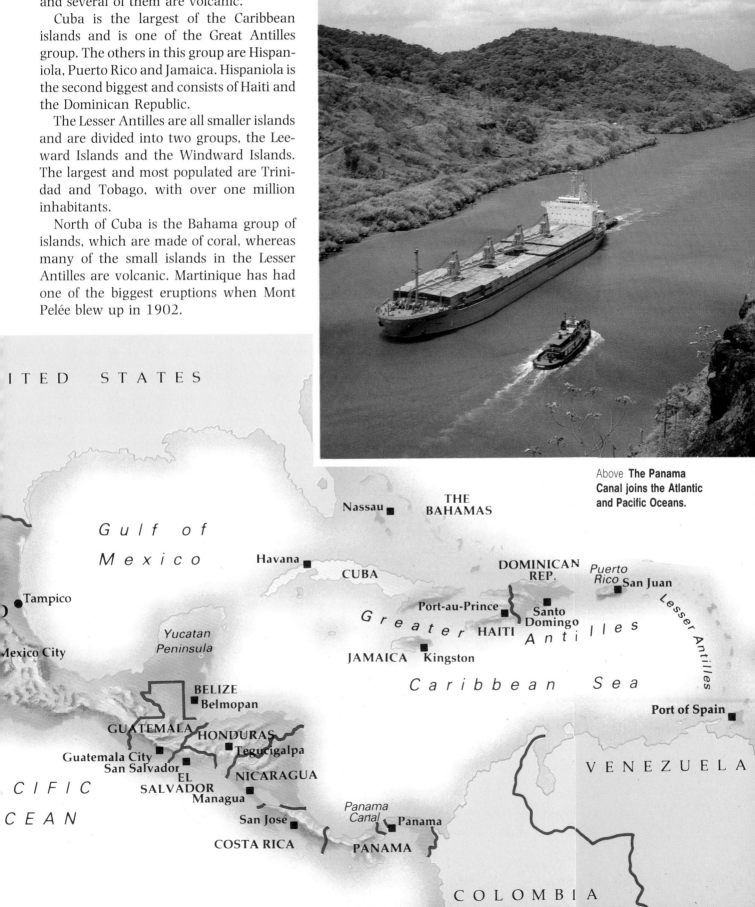

Above **The Panama Canal joins the Atlantic and Pacific Oceans.**

ITED STATES

Gulf of Mexico

Tampico

Mexico City

Yucatan Peninsula

Nassau · THE BAHAMAS

Havana · CUBA

DOMINICAN REP.

Puerto Rico · San Juan

Port-au-Prince · Santo Domingo

Greater Antilles HAITI

Lesser Antilles

JAMAICA Kingston

Caribbean Sea

BELIZE Belmopan

GUATEMALA HONDURAS

Guatemala City San Salvador · Tegucigalpa

EL SALVADOR NICARAGUA

Managua

CIFIC

CEAN

San José

Panama Canal · Panama

COSTA RICA PANAMA

Port of Spain

VENEZUELA

COLOMBIA

SOUTH AMERICA

South America covers an area of nearly 18,000 sq km (7,000 sq miles) and contains 13 countries. The Andes Mountains extend for over 6,500 km (4,000 miles) down the western side of the continent, and there are two large plateaus in the east. These are the Guiana Highlands in Venezuela and Guyana, and the Brazilian Plateau.

The three main lowland areas are crossed by very large rivers: the River Orinoco in Venezuela; the River Amazon, mainly in Brazil; and the River Parana, and its major tributary the Paraguay, in Argentina, Paraguay and Uruguay.

The Orinoco valley contains tropical grassland (called llanos) where cattle are reared. In Argentina there are temperate grasslands (called pampas) where cattle and sheep are reared; large areas have also been ploughed for fields of wheat, maize and flax. Much of the Amazon basin is covered by tropical forest which is increasingly being cleared for road building and farmland. There are other forests in northern Colombia and southern Chile.

South America has a desert along the coasts of Peru and northern Chile. Here, in the Atacama desert rainfall is often less than 25 mm (1 in) each year, but there are rivers which are used for irrigation.

The earliest inhabitants of South America were the Indians. Then the Europeans arrived in the 16th and 17th centuries. One of the earliest explorers was Amerigo Vespucci and the continent was named after him. Christopher Columbus only had a country named after him: Colombia.

The Europeans who settled in Brazil were mainly Portuguese; most of the other countries were settled by Spaniards. There were small numbers of British, Dutch and French in Guyana, Surinam and French Guiana which were formerly called British Guiana, Dutch Guiana and French Guiana.

Brazil occupies nearly half of South America and it is one of the biggest countries in the world. The Amazon lowlands are mostly covered with forest, while the Brazilian plateau has forests and thorny scrub in places. The southern part of the plateau, near São Paulo, is the wealthiest part of the country with some of the best farmland as well as most of the industry.

Argentina is the second biggest country and much of it is pampas grassland, which spreads over into Uruguay. In the west of

Below left **A road cutting through the dense Amazon jungle of Brazil.**

Below **Quito, the capital of Ecuador, is a city with many buildings in the Spanish Colonial style.**

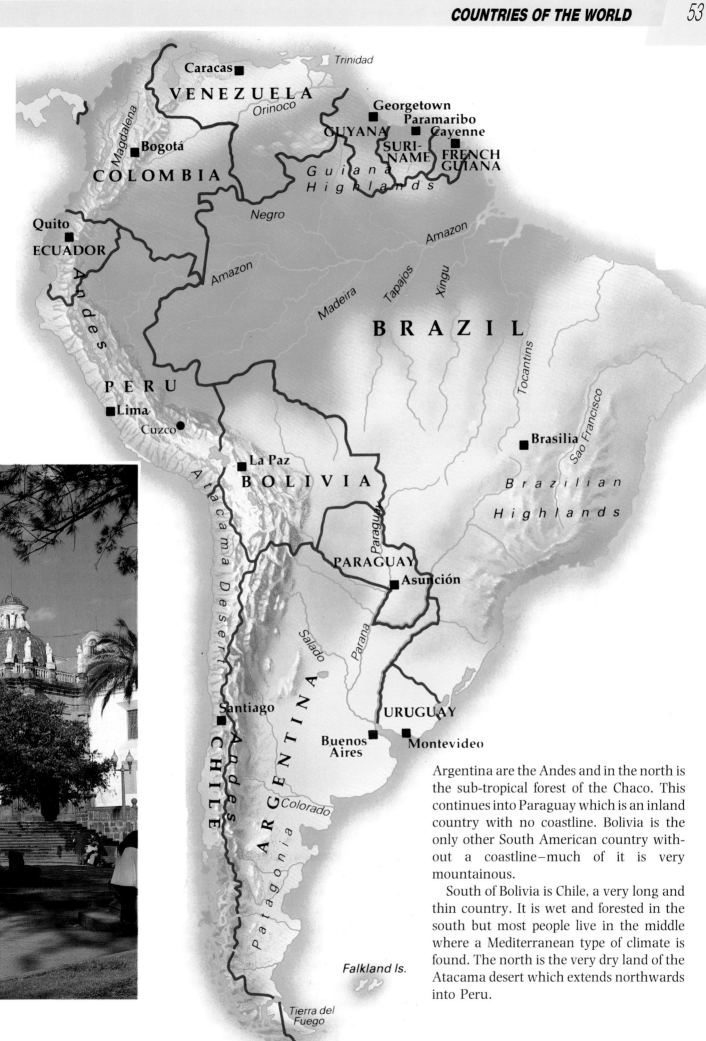

Caracas

VENEZUELA

Trinidad

Orinoco

Georgetown

GUYANA

Paramaribo

Cayenne

SURI-
NAME

FRENCH
GUIANA

Magdalena

Bogotá

COLOMBIA

*Guiana
Highlands*

Negro

Amazon

Quito

ECUADOR

Amazon

Madeira

Tapajos

Xingu

B R A Z I L

Tocantins

A n d e s

P E R U

Lima

Cuzco

Brasilia

Sao Francisco

B r a z i l i a n

La Paz

B O L I V I A

H i g h l a n d s

Paraguay

A t a c a m a   D e s e r t

PARAGUAY

Asunción

Salado

Parana

A R G E N T I N A

URUGUAY

Santiago

Colorado

C H I L E

A n d e s

Buenos
Aires

Montevideo

P a t a g o n i a

Falkland Is.

*Tierra del
Fuego*

Cape Horn

Argentina are the Andes and in the north is the sub-tropical forest of the Chaco. This continues into Paraguay which is an inland country with no coastline. Bolivia is the only other South American country without a coastline–much of it is very mountainous.

South of Bolivia is Chile, a very long and thin country. It is wet and forested in the south but most people live in the middle where a Mediterranean type of climate is found. The north is the very dry land of the Atacama desert which extends northwards into Peru.

OCEANIA

Oceania consists of Australia, New Zealand, New Guinea and numerous small islands in the archipelagoes of Melanesia, Micronesia and Polynesia. These small islands are isolated from each other, as well as being isolated from the rest of the world.

Australia

Most of Australia is desert or semi desert and contains little vegetation and few people. There are still small numbers of the native Aborigines living in the interior. People also live in the interior where irrigation is possible or where there are rich mineral deposits. The largest mining area is in the north west. Iron ore is dug out from mountains and taken by specially built railway lines to the new ports which have been created. Ships then export most of the iron to Japan.

Around the edges of Australia there are wetter areas. In the south west near Perth, temperatures are 20–25°C (68–77°F) in summer (November–February) and 15°C (59°F) in winter. Total rainfall is about 750 mm (30 in), most of which comes in winter (May to September). Fruit and wheat are grown, and millions of sheep are reared inland.

The south east has a wetter, fertile area too, especially around Melbourne and Sydney, where dairy farming is important. Inland, beyond the mountains, the rainfall decreases and very large sheep farms are common.

The rainy area along the coast extends northwards into Queensland and right along the north coast past Darwin. In these wetter parts there are forested areas, ranging from temperate forests in Victoria and

Left **Sheep farming in New Zealand. The country is the world's second largest producer of lamb and mutton.**

are dry enough to produce wheat and other cereals.

Like Australia, New Zealand is a wealthy country and has small deposits of gold and coal, as well as oil reserves.

The thousands of small islands that make up Melanesia, Micronesia and Polynesia are either volcanic or are built up of tiny coral animals. Most of them rely on fishing for food and on tourism.

New South Wales, to tropical monsoon forests in Queensland and Northern Territory. This region is also the most populated and industrialized, especially on the coast.

Above left **Much of the desert landscape of Australia's Northern Territory is semi-desert.**

Above **Sydney Harbour bridge spans the entrance to a fine natural harbour.**

New Zealand

New Zealand is made up of two main islands – North Island and South Island – both of which were well covered with forest. Much of the land has now been cleared for farming, particularly cattle and sheep rearing.

North Island has several volcanoes, is prone to earthquakes and has many hot springs and geysers. Some of the hot water from these underground sources is used to make electricity at geothermal power stations. Electricity is also generated by hydro-electric schemes on both islands.

South Island has a large range of mountains, the Southern Alps, which reach 3,764 m (12,349 ft) at Mount Cook; there are many glaciers here, as well as fjords on the south west coast. The Canterbury Plains

Auckland

Hamilton

Lake Taupo • Rotorua

North Island

Nelson ● ■ **Wellington**

Mount Cook ▲ *Southern Alps*

Christchurch

South Island

Invercargill ● Dunedin

THE ARCTIC AND ANTARCTIC

The Arctic and Antarctic are the two polar regions. The Arctic is in the north and is an ocean surrounded by the land masses of Europe, Asia and North America. Much of the Arctic Ocean is covered by a layer of ice which is always moving.

The most northerly of the land masses which surround the Arctic – Greenland and Ellesmere Island – are covered by snow for most of the year. Svalbard (Spitzbergen) at 80°N is ice free in summer. The island group is owned by Norway though it does have some coal mines worked by Russians.

Many explorers have gone into the Arctic Ocean. Nansen deliberately trapped his boat in the ice, so that he could prove that the ice drifted with the ocean currents. Amundsen, also a Norwegian, was the first man to reach the North Pole and more recently, a nuclear powered submarine actually emerged through a gap in the ice to reach the surface at the North Pole.

Around the edges of the Arctic Ocean, the land is not all permanently covered by snow and ice; some areas of tundra-type vegetation exist, where mosses, lichens, some grass and small stunted trees will grow. Many flowers can be seen in the summer, together with a rich variety of birds and millions of mosquitoes. The animals that live in the Arctic include walruses, polar bears and reindeer. This is also the region where the Eskimoes and Lapps manage to survive.

The Antarctic continent is a large continent surrounded by oceans. It has not always been around the South Pole, as some of the rocks contain coal which was

Left **A scientific research station, on the edge of the Antarctic continent.**

Below left **Penguins in the Antarctic.**

formed in a hot wet climate. Antarctica used to be joined to Africa, South America and Australia but has drifted to its present position during the last 100 million years. All the world's continents are moving about at this slow rate – one or two centimetres each year.

Many explorers have ventured into the Antarctic, and first to reach the South Pole was Amundsen in 1911. He beat the British expedition, led by Scott, by one month.

There are no real settlements but there are always a few groups of scientists at the research stations which are mostly located around the edges of the continent. There is also a permanent American research station at Scott Base at the South Pole which can be reached by air.

Climatic conditions at the Scott Base are some of the worst experienced anywhere in the world. Winter temperatures drop to −60°C (−76°F) and even in summer they may only rise to −20°C (−4°F). In addition, there are frequently strong winds which make conditions even worse, as well as occasional blizzards. The blizzards are partially the result of wind-blown snow which is picked up from the ground rather than fresh snow falling from the sky. Surprisingly, snowfalls are rare and light, but the snow which falls does not melt, and so snow has been accumulating for thousands of years.

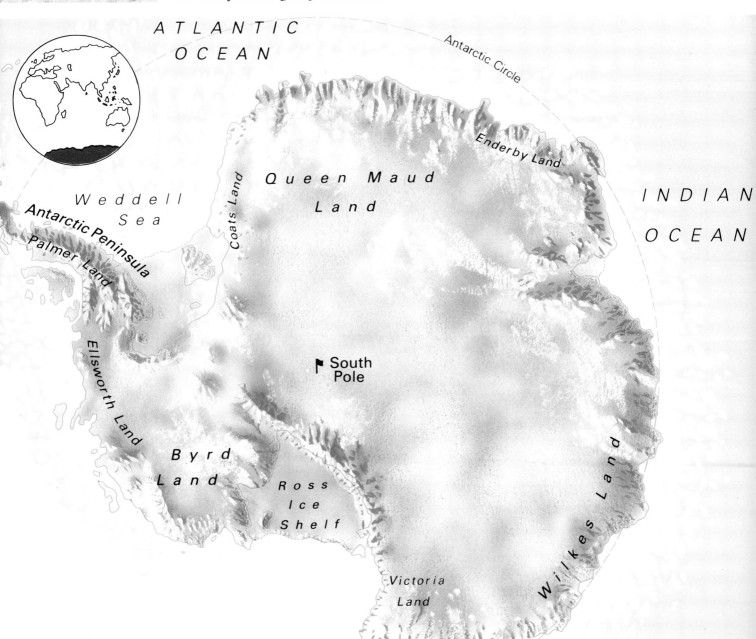

World Nations

AFRICA	area (sq km)	area (sq miles)	population (thousands)	capital
Algeria	2,381,741	919,595	21,718	Algiers
Angola	1,246,700	481,354	8,754	Luanda
Benin	112,622	43,484	3,932	Porto Novo
Botswana	581,730	224,607	1,085	Gaborone
Burkina	274,200	105,869	6,639	Ouagadougou
Burundi	27,834	10,747	4,718	Bujumbura
Cameroon	475,442	183,569	10,106	Yaoundé
Central African Rep.	622,984	240,535	2,608	Bangui
Chad	1,284,000	495,755	5,018	Ndjamena
Congo	342,000	132,047	1,740	Brazzaville
Djibouti	22,000	8,494	430	Djibouti
Egypt	1,001,449	386,662	48,503	Cairo
Equatorial Guinea	28,051	10,830	392	Malabo
Ethiopia	1,221,900	471,778	43,350	Addis Ababa
Gabon	267,667	103,347	1,151	Libreville
Gambia	11,295	4,361	643	Banjul
Ghana	238,537	92,100	13,588	Accra
Guinea	245,857	94,926	6,075	Conakry
Guinea-Bissau	36,125	13,948	890	Bissau
Ivory Coast	322,463	124,503	9,810	Abidjan
Kenya	582,646	224,961	20,333	Nairobi
Lesotho	30,355	11,720	1,528	Maseru
Liberia	111,369	43,000	2,189	Monrovia
Libya	1,759,540	679,362	3,605	Tripoli
Madagascar	587,041	226,669	9,985	Antananarivo
Malawi	118,484	45,747	7,059	Lilongwe
Mali	1,240,000	478,791	8,206	Bamako
Mauritania	1,030,700	397,955	1,888	Nouakchott
Mauritius	2,045	790	1,020	Port Louis
Morocco	446,550	172,414	21,941	Rabat
Mozambique	801,590	309,495	13,961	Maputo
Namibia	824,292	318,261	1,550	Windhoek
Niger	1,267,080	489,191	6,115	Niamey
Nigeria	923,768	356,669	95,198	Lagos
Rwanda	26,338	10,169	6,070	Kigali
Senegal	196,192	75,750	6,444	Dakar
Seychelles	280	108	65	Victoria
Sierra Leone	71,740	27,699	3,602	Freetown
Somalia	637,657	246,201	4,653	Mogadishu
South Africa	1,221,031	471,445	32,392	Pretoria
Sudan	2,505,813	967,500	21,550	Khartoum
Swaziland	17,363	6,704	647	Mbabane
Tanzania	945,087	364,900	21,733	Dar-es-Salaam
Togo	56,785	21,925	2,960	Lomé
Tunisia	163,610	63,170	7,081	Tunis
Uganda	236,036	91,259	15,477	Kampala
Zaire	2,345,409	905,567	30,363	Kinshasa
Zambia	752,614	290,586	6,666	Lusaka
Zimbabwe	390,580	150,804	8,300	Harare

ASIA

	area (sq km)	area (sq miles)	population (thousands)	capital
Afghanistan	647,497	250,000	18,136	Kabul
Bahrain	622	240	417	Manama
Bangladesh	143,998	55,598	98,657	Dhaka
Bhutan	47,000	18,147	1,417	Thimphu
Brunei	5,765	2,226	224	Bandar Seri Begawan
Burma	676,552	261,218	37,153	Rangoon
Cambodia	181,035	69,898	7,284	Phnom Penh
China	9,596,961	3,705,408	1,059,521	Peking
Hong Kong	1,045	403	5,548	Victoria
India	3,287,590	1,269,346	750,900	Delhi
Indonesia	1,904,569	735,358	163,393	Jakarta
Iran	1,648,000	636,296	44,212	Tehran
Iraq	434,924	167,925	15,898	Baghdad
Israel	20,770	8,019	4,233	Jerusalem
Japan	377,708	145,834	120,754	Tokyo
Jordan	97,740	37,738	3,515	Amman
Korea, North	120,538	46,540	20,385	Pyongyang
Korea, South	98,484	38,025	41,209	Seoul
Kuwait	17,818	6,880	1,710	Kuwait
Laos	231,800	91,429	4,117	Vientiane
Lebanon	10,400	4,015	2,668	Beirut
Malaysia	329,749	127,317	15,557	Kuala Lumpur
Maldives	298	115	177	Malé
Mongolia	1,565,000	604,250	1,891	Ulan Bator
Nepal	140,747	54,342	16,625	Kathmandu
Oman	212,457	82,030	1,242	Muscat
Pakistan	746,045	307,374	96,180	Islamabad
Philippines	300,000	115,831	54,378	Manila
Qatar	11,000	4,247	315	Doha
Saudi Arabia	2,149,640	830,000	11,542	Riyadh

Top **Most of Egypt's 48 million population live in the fertile valley of the Nile.**

	area (sq km)	area (sq miles)	population (thousands)	capital
Singapore	581	224	2,558	Singapore
Sri Lanka	65,610	25,332	15,837	Colombo
Syria	185,180	71,498	10,267	Damascus
Taiwan	35,742	13,800	19,135	Taipei
Thailand	514,000	198,457	51,301	Bangkok
Turkey	779,452	300,947	45,218	Ankara
United Arab Emirates	83,600	32,278	1,327	Dubai
Vietnam	329,556	127,242	59,713	Hanoi
Yemen, North	195,000	75,290	6,849	Sana'a
Yemen, South	332,968	128,560	2,294	Aden

EUROPE

Albania	28,748	11,099	2,962	Tirana
Austria	83,849	32,374	7,555	Vienna
Belgium	30,513	11,781	9,903	Brussels
Bulgaria	110,912	42,823	8,957	Sofia
Cyprus	9,251	3,572	665	Nicosia
Czechoslovakia	127,869	49,370	15,500	Prague
Denmark	43,069	16,629	5,114	Copenhagen
Finland	337,032	137,851	4,908	Helsinki
France	547,026	211,208	54,621	Paris
Germany, East	108,178	41,768	16,644	East Berlin
Germany, West	248,577	95,976	61,015	Bonn
Greece	131,944	50,944	9,935	Athens
Hungary	93,030	35,919	10,649	Budapest
Iceland	103,000	39,768	241	Reykjavik
Irish Republic	70,283	27,136	3,552	Dublin
Italy	301,225	116,304	57,128	Rome
Luxembourg	2,586	998	366	Luxembourg
Malta	316	122	383	Valletta
Netherlands	40,844	15,770	14,484	Amsterdam
Norway	324,219	125,181	4,152	Oslo
Poland	312,677	120,725	37,203	Warsaw
Portugal	92,082	35,553	10,229	Lisbon
Romania	237,500	91,699	23,017	Bucharest
Spain	504,782	194,897	38,602	Madrid
Sweden	449,964	173,732	8,350	Stockholm
Switzerland	41,293	15,943	6,374	Berne
United Kingdom	244,046	94,227	56,125	London
USSR	22,402,200	8,650,000	270,376	Moscow
Yugoslavia	255,804	98,766	23,123	Belgrade

NORTH AND CENTRAL AMERICA

Belize	22,965	8,867	166	Belmopan
Canada	9,976,139	3,851,809	25,379	Ottawa
Costa Rica	50,700	19,575	2,600	San José
Cuba	110,861	42,804	10,090	Havana
Dominican Republic	48,734	18,816	6,243	Santo Domingo
El Salvador	21,041	8,124	4,819	San Salvador
Guatemala	108,889	42,042	7,963	Guatemala
Haiti	27,750	10,714	6,585	Port au Prince
Honduras	112,088	43,277	4,372	Tegucigalpa
Jamaica	10,991	4,244	2,337	Kingston
Mexico	1,972,547	761,605	78,524	Mexico City
Nicaragua	130,000	50,193	3,272	Managua
Panama	77,082	29,762	2,180	Panama City
Trinidad and Tobago	5,130	1,981	1,185	Port of Spain
United States	9,372,614	3,618,787	239,283	Washington, DC

OCEANIA

Australia	7,686,848	2,967,909	15,752	Canberra
New Zealand	268,676	103,736	3,254	Wellington

SOUTH AMERICA

Argentina	2,766,889	1,068,302	30,564	Buenos Aires
Bolivia	1,098,581	424,165	6,429	La Paz
Brazil	8,511,965	3,286,488	135,564	Brasilia
Chile	756,945	292,258	12,074	Santiago
Colombia	1,138,914	439,747	28,624	Bogotá
Ecuador	283,561	109,484	9,378	Quito
Guiana, French	90,000	34,749	82	Cayenne
Guyana	214,969	83,000	790	Georgetown
Paraguay	406,752	157,048	3,681	Asunción
Peru	1,285,216	496,225	19,698	Lima
Surinam	163,265	63,037	375	Paramaribo
Uruguay	176,215	68,037	3,012	Montevideo
Venezuela	912,050	352,144	17,317	Caracas

Above **Singapore is a major port, situated at the tip of the Malay peninsula.**

The History of Mankind

PREHISTORIC MAN

The first really man-like animal was *Homo erectus*, "upright man", who walked by swinging his legs from the hip, instead of shuffling like an ape. He had a large brain, made rough shelters from branches, built fires and lived by hunting.

The successor to *Homo erectus* was *Homo sapiens*, "thinking man", the species to which we belong (see page 188). An early example was Neanderthal Man, who lived in the last Ice Age. Although he had a low forehead, his brain was as big as ours. He was a skilful hunter, travelling long distances after game, and he made tools from flints or bones. After the Ice Age ended, about 10,000 years ago, he was replaced by another type, Cro-Magnon Man, who looked more or less like us.

Although they had crude tools, shelter and clothing, our distant ancestors were part of the world of nature like other animals. They were nomads, moving camp when game grew scarce and the forest nearby had been stripped of edible fruits. But a few were able to settle down, for example by lakes where fish provided a regular food supply. The biggest change, perhaps the most important in all human history, came when they learned to be farmers, sowing crops and keeping animals. It was then no longer necessary to keep on the move. A settled life, with plenty of food, allowed civilization to develop.

EARLY CIVILIZATION

Civilization developed in the fertile river valleys of the Middle East about 8,000 years ago. Agriculture began about the same time

Below **We do not know for certain how human beings evolved, but most scientists believe our ancestors looked like these. The earliest, a small ape-like creature called Ramapithecus, lived 12 to 14 million years ago.**

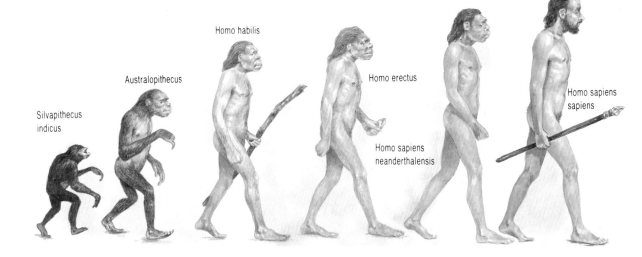

Silvapithecus indicus

Australopithecus

Homo habilis

Homo erectus

Homo sapiens neanderthalensis

Homo sapiens sapiens

Above **Paintings of animals were made on walls of caves in southern France during the Ice Age.** Left **A European village 10,000 years ago.**

in south-east Asia and China, and a little later in Central America. A steady food supply allowed towns to develop, which were dependent on trade and on plentiful wild wheat. By 3000 BC the wheel and a simple plough were in use, and bronze or copper tools were replacing stone ones.

THE SUMERIANS

In Mesopotamia, between the Tigris and Euphrates rivers, Sumerian civilization was well established. The Sumerians lived in city states, with huge brick-built palaces and many temples, for religion dominated people's lives. They used a form of writing known as cuneiform, written in damp clay tablets with a sharpened reed. The Sumerians eventually died out, but their civilization was carried on through successors like the Babylonians, Assyrians and the Persians.

ANCIENT EGYPT

On the banks of the Nile another civilization developed. Unlike the Sumerians, the Ancient Egyptians were a single nation under one ruler. Their civilization was a rich and complicated one with a strict class system and slaves to do the hardest work, as in all early civilizations. It lasted with little change for 3,000 years.

The first Indian civilization appeared in the Indus Valley a little later than in Egypt or Mesopotamia, with which it had trade connections. In China, in the valley of the Hwang Ho (Yellow River), a Bronze Age civilization was established by 1500 BC.

Above **The Sphinx and pyramids (royal tombs) at Giza near Cairo, Egypt, which were built between 4,000 and 5,000 years ago. The largest and most famous of the pyramids was built for Cheops in c.2700 BC. It is 146 m (480 ft) high.**

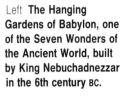

Left **The Hanging Gardens of Babylon, one of the Seven Wonders of the Ancient World, built by King Nebuchadnezzar in the 6th century BC.**

THE GREEKS

The first European civilization was Greek, and even now many of our ideas can be traced back to Classical Greece.

Greek civilization dates from the Minoan age in Crete, which was established before 2000 BC, and also from the Mycenaeans who invaded Crete from Greece. Classical Greek civilization reached a peak in Athens in the 5th century BC, and was later spread over a large region by the conquests of Alexander the Great (a Macedonian, not a Greek) in the late 4th century BC. This later, universal Greek culture is called "Hellenistic" to distinguish it from the culture of Classical Greece.

Although the Greeks learned many things from earlier civilizations, they were unique. Their society was the first to show a capacity for change, and without change there can be no progress. Among the Greeks, much greater value was given to the individual person, and Greek city-states were the first democracies.

We know far more about the Ancient Greeks than we do about any earlier society. Some of their art and much of their writing has survived (see page 216). History, literature, philosophy, politics and science (as we think of them) all began with the Greeks.

Both as a society and as individuals, we seem to know the Greeks as well as we know more recent historical figures. Yet the Greeks were probably less like us than we imagine. Even the great thinker Pythagoras appears strangely superstitious to us today. There is a legend that he celebrated the proof of his famous geometrical theorem by sacrificing an ox to the gods.

Below **A Greek trireme, a wooden warship driven by oars and steered by a paddle. The first triremes were probably built by the Phoenicians in c.500 BC.**

Above **The ideas of the great ancient Greek philosophers are still studied today. The most famous were Plato, Aristotle, Socrates and Pythagoras.**

Top **Greek theatres were built in the open air, usually on a hillside. The centre, or orchestra, is the space in front of the tiered seats where the audience sat.**

THE ROMAN EMPIRE

When the civilization of Athens was at its brilliant height, Rome was a small, struggling republic. Within 200 years it had gained control of Italy. Within 400, under the emperors, it ruled most of the known world. Even at its greatest, the empire was beginning its long decline, yet the Romans ruled Europe for five centuries.

The Roman empire was truly international. A man did not have to be born in Rome to become a Roman citizen, and one of the greatest emperors was a Spaniard. What held the empire together was an excellent system of law and a widely known official language, Latin.

Another vital quality was the talent and thoroughness of the Romans in practical matters like building and engineering. The Romans expected their empire to last for ever, and built accordingly. Some of their roads and buildings can still be seen today. Living standards were more advanced than in any other European society.

By the 1st century AD the Greek and Roman gods did not inspire people with much faith. Other religious groups were growing in strength. By the 4th century Christianity was the official religion of the Roman empire.

Above **The Colosseum was a huge Roman amphitheatre.**

Above right **Julius Caesar, a great Roman statesman.**

Right **The Roman empire at its greatest.**

Below **A Roman siege.**

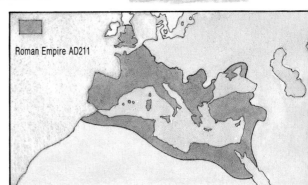

Roman Empire AD211

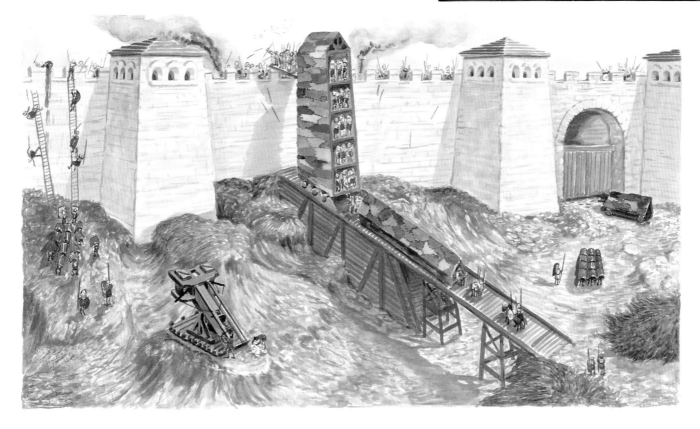

CELTIC CIVILIZATION

In the 4th century the Roman empire split in two. The Eastern or Byzantine empire, with its capital at Constantinople, survived until the 15th century. The Western empire collapsed under attacks from tribal peoples whom the Romans called "barbarians". European civilization took a step backwards.

The Celts were originally a warrior people from central Europe who migrated west and settled in lands that are now France, Belgium, Britain and Ireland. Most of them, called Gauls by the Romans, came under Roman rule by the 1st century AD, but the Romans never conquered Scotland or Ireland, and Celtic civilization lasted in those centuries long after Roman times.

The Celts were ruled by kings and a small class of warriors and priests, known as Druids. They were skilful craftsmen, especially in iron.

After the fall of Rome the Celts came under pressure from Germanic tribes pushed westward by nomadic raiders from the east. Some, known as Anglo-Saxons, settled in lowland Britain so founding the English nation. Another Germanic people, the Franks, established an empire under Charlemagne which stretched from Spain to Scandinavia. It was seen as the successor to the Roman empire, and Charlemagne was crowned as Holy Roman Emperor by the pope in Rome in AD 800. Charlemagne is regarded as one of the founders of both the German and French nations.

Above **Celtic craftsmen made fine metalwork, like this mirror back from Celtic Britain.**

Right **An Anglo-Saxon village. The Anglo-Saxons drove the Celts out of England.**

Below **People who lived a settled life in villages were open to attacks by nomadic tribes seeking new land.**

THE ARABS AND ISLAM

The Middle East, which had been the cradle of civilization, ceased to occupy a central position in human history after the conquests of Alexander the Great. But it was from there that a mighty new power sprang in the 7th century.

Inspired by the new religion preached by Muhammad, the Arabs erupted from the desert into the more fertile lands of the Middle East, Southern Europe and North Africa around them. In less than 100 years they conquered an area larger than the old Roman empire and converted it to Islam.

Although this empire was made up of diverse lands and people, it was united by shared beliefs and, in general, it was a more civilized society than that of Christian Europe. It was, for instance, more tolerant: even the Christians of Egypt and Syria preferred Arab rule to that of Christian Constantinople.

Islam managed to absorb many cultural influences, of which the most important was probably the Classical tradition of Greece. This helps to explain the artistic and scientific achievements of Arab scholars, unrivalled in Christian Europe, in the 8th–10th centuries.

However, within Islam there were frequent disputes and civil wars, especially between orthodox Sunni Muslims and the anti-establishment Shi'a. With changing times and changing dynasties, Arab influence decreased and Islam broke up into a varying number of more or less independent political units, but religion and the Arabic language made Islam a continuing cultural force (see page 198).

Below **Muslim worshippers in the great mosque at Mecca, in Arabia. The square-sided Kaaba was built to contain a holy object called the Black Stone.**

Below left **Inspired by Muhammad, the conquering Arabs spread the religion of Islam over a wide area.**

Bottom **The Crusades began as an attempt by European Christians to reconquer the Holy Land from the Muslims.**

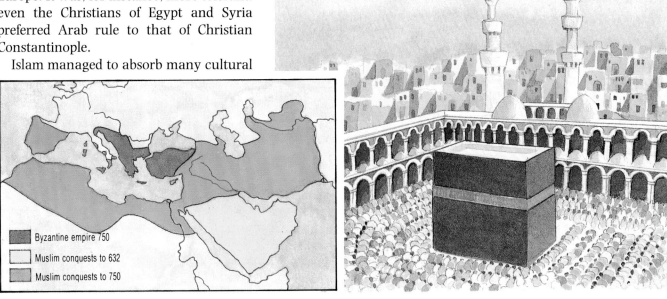

Byzantine empire 750

Muslim conquests to 632

Muslim conquests to 750

MEDIEVAL EUROPE

The last "barbarian" invaders in Europe were the Vikings from Scandinavia, and by the 11th century they, like many earlier raiders, had settled down. Kingdoms had developed, although a king was generally no more than the chief of a powerful, land-owning, warrior class.

Feudalism emerged as the basic social system, common throughout Europe. The basis of feudalism was the holding of land in exchange for military service. The great nobles leased their estates from the Crown, swearing loyalty to the king and promising to fight for him in war.

Landlords and Serfs

A lord's estates were made up of territories which in England were called manors. A manor was, in practice, a self-sufficient village. Practically everything in the way of food, clothing, and tools was made locally. The lord or baron let some of the land out to lesser landholders, who might pay rent in produce or in cash and served as soldiers. But the greater part was worked by serfs. They had to work on the lord's own land part of the time, and also had to pay rent in produce for such things as use of the lord's

Above **Peasants working in the manor fields.**

Right **Medieval people believed that God sent plague as a punishment.**

Below **The power needed to grind grain into flour was often provided by a watermill.**

mill or his bakery. They had free grazing for their animals on common land, but the forests (then much more widespread) were hunting reserves for the nobility.

Although they were not quite slaves, serfs had little freedom. They could not leave the district nor get married without their lord's permission.

The Power of the Church

Religion was the basis of European civilization in the Middle Ages. Bishops and abbots were great landholding lords like the barons. Every village had its church, the clergy had their own courts, and the most advanced form of government in Europe was that of the pope.

The Church had a monopoly of education and of what we would call the media. The priest was probably the only man there who could read and write.

In general the Church co-operated with the State, but as royal governments sought greater power, conflicts arose between pope and ruler. The most famous of these, between the pope and the Holy Roman emperor, the greatest ruler in Europe, concerned the right to appoint bishops (a bishop appointed by the Crown was likely to obey the king; if appointed by the pope, he took his orders from Rome). In England, a quarrel between the king and the archbishop of Canterbury resulted in the murder of the archbishop, Thomas Becket.

In the later Middle Ages, the huge power of the Church was under growing threat. This was partly due to weakness at the top – the failure of successive popes to keep control of the Church – partly to the growing power of kings, and partly to discontent with the way in which the Church was run. Wyclif in England and Hus in Bohemia were the most famous critics.

Miracle plays were performed on a stage in the market place by travelling actors. They taught religious lessons (the monster represents the mouth of Hell).

RENAISSANCE EUROPE

Criticism of the Church came to a head in what we know as the Reformation in the 16th century. An attack on certain Church practices by a German monk, Martin Luther, grew into a deep division which ended the universal authority of the pope and the Roman Church for ever. Protestant churches were founded in many countries, including England and Scotland where Roman Catholicism was banned. Other countries, like France, remained Roman Catholic but contained large Protestant groups. For the next century and more, religious differences added a new element to the conflicts of Europe.

An age of discovery

The Protestant Reformation was linked with the great change in people's ideas which is known as the Renaissance. This word means "rebirth", and it refers to the rediscovery and renewal of the ideas of Classical Greece and Rome. But above all it was an age of curiosity and inquiry. Educated people became intensely interested in mankind and in nature generally. Old beliefs which had been accepted for centuries

were questioned. New facts were discovered and new lands (the Americas) explored.

Change, however, takes time, and the Renaissance did not start or stop suddenly, like a war. It began in Italy, the most advanced country in Europe, round about 1300 and reached its height between 1450 and 1550. But in some parts it had little effect until after 1600. Its influence was not wholly good, either. A famous book on

Left **A street in Renaissance Florence.**

Below left **Columbus's** *Santa Maria*.

Below **A drawing by Leonardo.**

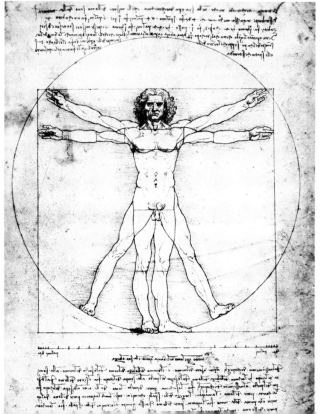

reasons that no one can explain, artists of genius were easily found–extraordinary men like Leonardo da Vinci, who filled his notebooks with drawings of machines that were not to be invented for centuries, or Michelangelo, whose long life spans the height of the Italian Renaissance.

In literature, Rabelais, Cervantes, Sir Thomas More, and greatest of all, Shakespeare (a leading figure of the English Renaissance) are only a few of the famous literary figures of the period.

Developments in science

The new spirit of inquiry led to great advances in science. Copernicus proved that the Earth goes around the Sun, an idea fiercely rejected by the Church, which taught that the Earth is the centre of the universe. Vesalius of Pavia was the first man to make a study of human anatomy. In other sciences too, the knowledge of the ancient Greeks, which had not been improved on in over 1,000 years, was studied more eagerly and, as time went by, often shown to be inaccurate. The Renaissance marked the beginning of an age of more rapid change which has continued, at an ever-growing pace, ever since.

Above **Printing the Bible on an early printing press.**

Left **A knight in armour.**

Below **The massacre of Huguenots (French protestants) on St Bartholomew's Day, 1572.**

politics, Machiavelli's *Prince*, advised rulers to be cunning and ruthless. Murder was common. Wars were frequent.

Great artistic achievements

Partly because we can still see the results, the Renaissance seems to us above all, as a period of great achievement in art. For

70

THE AGE OF KINGS

During the Renaissance Europe took on its modern shape. Strong kingdoms existed in Spain, France, Sweden and England. The Dutch, after a long war of independence against Spain, made their republic the most prosperous state in Europe. Germany and Italy, however, remained divided into a mass of small states.

Eastern Europe was still feudal, but in the West the economy was based on money. The military power of the nobility had declined, and monarchs were therefore more powerful. Historians speak of an "age of absolutism", though the power of the king was never absolute. There were practical limits, chiefly money. The efforts of royal governments to raise more money through taxes resulted in civil conflicts, and in England caused a civil war which, for a short time, put an end to royal government.

The chief example of "absolute" monarchy in Europe was in France under Louis XIV (1643–1715). *L'état, c'est moi* ("I am the State") he is supposed to have said, and he reigned from his magnificent new palace at Versailles. However, Louis' foreign policy caused a succession of wars which steadily weakened France.

Below **Louis XIV's palace of Versailles was designed to make a simple statement: "the man who owns this palace is the greatest king in the world." It was also a sign that the king and his courtiers were losing touch with the ordinary affairs of France, but few people had yet begun to ask if all this extravagance was just.**

Below **The courts and palaces of great Asian rulers, like the Mughal emperors of India, were equally grand in a different style. The Mughals, who gained their empire by conquest, at first showed more tolerance than Christian rulers, but later emperors unwisely tried to crush all opposition by force.**

Bottom **The best-trained soldiers in Europe were the Turkish janissaries.**

EMPIRE BUILDING

The age of strong monarchies in Europe roughly coincided with the reigns of great emperors in Asia. Persia (now Iran), united under the Safavid dynasty in the 16th century, reached a peak of power and prestige under Shah Abbas, "the Great" (1586–1628). His new capital at Isfahan was as brilliant as Versailles, though in a completely different style.

The Safavids belonged to the Shi'a branch of Islam. Other Muslim rulers, notably the Sultan of the Ottoman Turks, were Sunnites. The Ottoman empire was the greatest power in the world in the 16th century. Strong-minded sultans, especially Suleiman "the Magnificent" (1520–66), led their armies, including highly trained professionals known as janissaries, deep into eastern Europe.

They had already captured Constantinople, bringing to an end the Byzantine empire, in 1453. In 1529 Suleiman besieged Vienna, and the Turks long remained a threat to Europe. Vienna was besieged a second time in 1683, but after that Ottoman power declined, though the empire staggered on into the 20th century.

AKBAR'S ENLIGHTENED RULE

In India too a powerful Muslim dynasty was established in the 16th century. The outstanding ruler was Akbar (1556–1605), who extended the Mughal empire over most of the Indian subcontinent. Though won by force, the empire was maintained by good, tolerant government. Akbar married the Hindu daughter of one of the rebellious Rajput princes, and he also welcomed Christian missionaries from Europe. Like European rulers of the time, he was a great patron of the arts.

The Mughals built some of the world's most beautiful buildings, including the Taj Mahal. But later emperors lacked Akbar's wisdom. By the end of the 17th century the Mughal empire was breaking up.

72

Below **A Samurai warrior of medieval Japan. They lived by strict rules of honour and discipline.**

Below right **The Chinese learned how to make silk about 2600 BC and kept the method secret for 2,000 years.**

CHINA AND JAPAN

China was one of the earliest centres of civilization, but it developed in its own way, influenced very little by its neighbours and not at all by Europe. Indeed, in many respects the Chinese were far ahead of Europe, yet they were a conservative people who did not believe in change.

China's long history can be roughly measured by its ruling dynasties. Periods of prosperity usually came near the beginning of a new dynasty, before decline set in and the dynasty ended in civil war.

In the 17th century the Manchu (foreigners, like earlier dynasties) seized power. They extended their rule over east Asia from Burma to Korea. Trade began with Europe (mainly tea and porcelain, or "china"), and under the scholarly emperor K'ang-hsi (1661–1722) China was peaceful and prosperous. Despite later rebellions and money shortages the dynasty survived, and the final breakdown of Manchu China's museum-like culture was postponed until the 20th century.

Unlike the Chinese, the Japanese welcomed the European missionaries. Japanese society was as advanced as western Europe though very different. In particular, it lacked a strong central government; local warlords were constantly fighting each other for land and influence.

Japan was finally unified in the 16th century. Tokugawa Ieyasu (1543–1616) became shogun (the effective ruler, under the emperor), and his family held office for over 250 years. They secured peace and security by a policy of isolation–no foreign visitors, no foreign travel–which was only possible in an island nation with a strong sense of discipline.

NORTHERN EUROPE

Sweden emerged as a nation-state in the 16th century when Gustavus Vasa gained independence from Denmark. During the Thirty Years' War (1618–48), in which all Europe was involved, the victories of Gustavus Adolphus made Sweden a great power. The Baltic Sea became "a Swedish lake".

However, another power was rising in the north – Russia. The Russian tsar was an absolute ruler who governed a nation made up mainly of a small class of landowning aristocrats and a huge mass of serfs. Famine was still a frequent danger and by western standards Russia was primitive.

The dynamic tsar Peter the Great (1682–1725) was determined to modernize the country, and to gain an outlet to the west via the Baltic. Despite the generalship of Sweden's war-loving Charles XII, the resulting conflict ended in Russian victory.

Peter made sweeping educational reforms, created a civil service responsible to the tsar, and stamped out opposition from the quarrelsome nobles. He planned the expansion of Russia to the east, across Siberia to the Pacific and Alaska.

The great mass of the Russian people were not affected by these events. Serfdom was an unsuitable system for a modern state, but neither Peter nor his successors were able to make the great changes required to modernize Russian society.

Right **Peter the Great, who tried to drag his country into the modern age (and, it is said, once worked in an English shipyard).**

Left **Royal palace in Peter's capital, St Petersburg (now Leningrad).**

EIGHTEENTH-CENTURY EUROPE

Russia was just one of the new powers in Europe in the 18th century. Another was Prussia, a Protestant state which challenged Catholic Austria for the future leadership of Germany. All three powers combined to carve up Poland, which disappeared from the map, while Russia expanded farther in the south-east.

European conflicts were spreading further afield. Clashes over trade and colonies had been going on since the Europeans first began to exploit other continents in the 15th century, but they had not greatly affected the affairs of Europe. The Dutch, whose wealth depended on trade and shipping, were the first to realize that trade was

worth fighting for. They fought the English for supremacy at sea in the 17th century, but England's control of the Channel meant that they could not win. Portugal and Spain, the first European nations to expand overseas, had fallen into decline, and France and England were left as the chief rivals in the colonial and naval conflict.

The Seven Years War (1756–63), which was fought in Asia, the Americas and Africa as well as Europe, ended with Britain dominant, having achieved control of India and taken Canada from the French. Although Britain lost its oldest North American colonies later in the century, it gained new lands as a result of the voyages of Captain Cook to Australia and New Zealand.

Top **Cutting cane in the West Indies, a business that made European merchants very rich.**

Above **The wars for trade among European nations were usually won at sea. Armies overseas had to be supplied by ships.**

THE FRENCH REVOLUTION

France still appeared to be a grand and glorious country in the 18th century, but in fact she was on the edge of bankruptcy. The whole system of government was old, unfair and rotten. A growing number of educated people believed that big changes were needed. The changes that actually happened were much bigger than anyone expected.

In 1788 the royal government called a meeting of the Estates General, a representative assembly from all classes which had not met since 1614. It was quickly dominated and finally taken over by the Third Estate–representative of the commoners– which declared itself a National Assembly (1789). Within two years, against a background of revolutionary excitement and violence, it reformed the whole system of law and government in France.

The privileges (and in a few cases the heads) of the nobility and clergy were swept away, along with all relics of the feudal system. Everyone was declared equal under the law, a novel idea at that time. Censorship was abolished and Church estates were nationalized.

The Revolution ended in the dictatorship of Napoleon. He was an able general, sympathetic to the Revolution (despite getting himself crowned emperor), who conquered most of Europe and spread the ideals of the Revolution throughout the continent.

After Napoleon's defeat at Waterloo (1815), the monarchy was restored and the clock was put back to 1788. However, the Revolution loosed forces of liberalism and nationalism which were to dominate European affairs during the next century.

Below left **Napoleon, painted as a conquering hero.**

Below **The guillotine was named after its French inventor in 1789, but the Scots used the same method of execution much earlier.**

AMERICA

The American continents were inhabited by a great variety of peoples whom we call "Indians". In North America the Indian population was rather small. It was greater in Mexico and Central America, where a complicated series of civilizations rose and fell.

The history of the Americas was changed by the arrival of the Europeans, who set up trading posts and colonies. European settlement had dreadful effects for the native American Indians. Disease wiped out whole nations. Many others were enslaved or slaughtered.

The largest colonial empire belonged to Spain. It stretched from southern Chile to northern California, although it was thinly populated with most settlements on the coast. Still, Mexico City in the 18th century was larger than most European cities.

Spanish America, because of its huge silver mines, was rich. North America had no silver and only a few luxury trade goods such as furs, but in the long run it had greater advantages for European settlers. By 1700 about 500,000 Europeans lived along the east coast. They included French, Dutch, Swedes, and Germans, but the largest number came from Britain.

Above **An Algonquin village in the 16th century.**

Right **Civil war in the Inca empire enabled Pizarro to conquer it with 170 men.**

Below **At the "Boston Tea Party" (1773) a mob dressed as Indians threw tea into the harbour rather than pay tax on it.**

guzmã. michvacã.

Many of these colonists had first arrived as religious refugees. New England had first been settled by English Puritans, for whom the Church of England was too Popish, not "pure" enough. Maryland was founded for Roman Catholics, Pennsylvania for Quakers.

There were 13 British colonies strung along the east coast between Florida and Canada (which became British in 1763). London was far away and the colonies enjoyed almost complete self-government. But after 1763 conflicts arose between Britain and its American colonies. The British wanted to impose taxes, such as customs dues, on the colonists. The colonists refused to pay for the reason that, unlike British taxpayers, they had no representatives in the British parliament. Resistance was fiercest in Massachusetts, and it was there that the first shots of the American War of Independence were fired in 1775.

Despite their differences, the Thirteen Colonies united to set up a Continental Congress, declared their independence (in 1776), and formed a combined army under command of George Washington. Although the British forces looked stronger, their commanders made serious mistakes and the two main British armies were forced to surrender. In 1783 the British government recognized the independence of the United States.

An important new power was rising. The United States, although it still allowed slavery, was a democracy, with a written constitution (1787) which laid down the laws of government and recognized that the State exists for the good of the citizen (and not the other way round).

Equally important was the economic potential of the United States. The British government, fearful of Indian resistance, had tried to keep colonial expansion in check. This restriction had been removed, and the way west lay open.

Below **El Alamo was a mission building in Texas besieged by Mexicans in 1836. Its entire garrison was killed.**

Left **American colonists fight the British "redcoats" during the War of Independence. The war followed a long series of quarrels, mostly about paying taxes to the British government.**

Right **Fur trappers and other pioneers led the way in pushing the frontier of settlement farther west, beyond the Appalachian Mountains.**

78

Below **The victory of the North in the Civil War kept the US united.**

EMERGING POWERS

The new American nation rapidly increased its lands, buying territory to the west from France (the Louisiana Purchase, 1803), buying Florida from Spain (1819) and Alaska from Russia (1867). It gained a huge region in the south-west through war with Mexico (1848).

The population and the economy expanded, but serious divisions appeared between the states, especially between North and South. One of the main differences was over slavery, which was legal in the South but not in the North. When the candidate of the anti-slavery Republican party, Abraham Lincoln, was elected president, the Southern states decided to withdraw from the union. This resulted in the Civil War, which raged from 1861 to 1865.

The North had more men, money and machinery, but the South, with fine commanders and great spirit, held on for four years. Lincoln's Emancipation Proclamation in 1863 finally abolished slavery, and the United States came out of the war even stronger.

Below **Railways opened the way for new towns and cities in the West.**

Right **Italian immigrants arriving in New York.**

An expanding nation

Attracted by political freedom and the opportunity to get rich, European emigrants arrived in growing numbers. The frontier moved steadily west, at the expense of the Indians who were cheated out of their lands and forced into reservations. The first railway from the Atlantic to the Pacific coast was completed in 1869. Farming and industry expanded and by the end of the century the United States was the world's leading industrial power.

THE INDUSTRIAL REVOLUTION

A revolution of a different kind also began in late 18th-century Europe. It is called the Industrial Revolution, and it was probably the most important economic change in human society since the beginning of farming. With Britain leading the way, trade, industry and population all expanded at a tremendous rate. The building of railways stimulated even faster growth.

In less than a century, life for many people changed dramatically. Small market towns, unchanged for centuries, turned into smoky, industrial cities (complete with slums) in one human lifetime.

Employers grew rich, or went bankrupt. The new class of industrial workers, working in shocking conditions, began to organize trade unions. The ideas of the French Revolution and the obvious injustices of society provoked a "year of revolutions" in 1848 with outbreaks in nearly every country. In the same year Marx and Engels published their *Communist Manifesto*.

THE GROWTH OF NATIONALISM

Revolutionary outbreaks were often linked with nationalism. This resulted in the creation of newly unified states, for example, Italy and the Prussian-dominated German empire, which became the most powerful state in Europe.

Nationalism was at work in other continents. The countries of South America gained independence from Spain and Portugal in the 19th century. However, in Asia and Africa more lands were coming under foreign–that is, European–rulers.

Above **Big factories appeared during the Industrial Revolution.**

Right **The spinning jenny was one of the machines that made cloth-making into a huge industry.**

Below **Garibaldi's "redshirts'" conquest of Sicily led to the union of Italy in 1861.**

THE DOMINANCE OF THE WEST

One effect of the Industrial Revolution was to make the West (Europe and North America) much richer and stronger than the rest of the world. By the end of the 19th century, most of Africa and much of Asia was ruled by Europeans. The biggest empire belonged to Britain, the leading nation in the Industrial Revolution, whose navy was unchallenged on any ocean in the world. France held huge regions of Africa and south-east Asia. Several other European countries had colonies much larger than themselves.

Capitalism

European power and influence was not restricted to its own colonies. In every continent, European wealth turned peasants into factory workers, built railways and dockyards, financed mines and factories. London was the financial capital of the world and sterling was the chief international currency.

The new capitalist system had serious drawbacks. It created undreamed-of wealth

for some people, but the mass of the people, even in the industrialized countries, remained poor.

Social welfare

In the later 19th century governments began to enforce greater control. Efforts were made to protect ordinary people by social reforms such as sickness benefits and old-age pensions. It became illegal to send young children to work; they had to go to school. Working conditions in industry improved, and working hours were shortened. Public health measures – clean water and proper drains – ended the terrible epidemics of typhoid and cholera. In the industrial countries the standard of living was rising by 1900, and Europe was fairly peaceful in the last half of the 19th century. But the peace was soon to be shattered.

Left **A painting showing the Mughal emperor handing over control of** Bengal to the British general, Robert Clive, in 1765.

Left **The First World War was fought mainly in a small area. Artillery and machine guns prevented infantry advancing.**

Right **Battles were also fought in the air.**

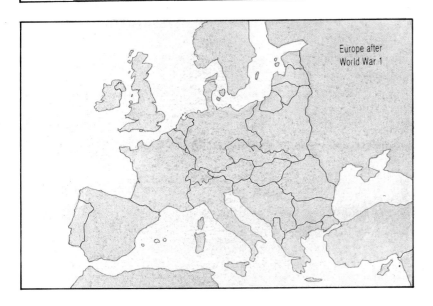

Allies
Central Powers
Neutrals

Europe during World War 1

Europe after World War 1

THE FIRST WORLD WAR

The rise of the German empire destroyed the old balance of power among the European nations. Europe became divided into two armed camps, with Britain, France and Russia on one side and Germany and Austria-Hungary on the other.

The First World War, mainly a European war in spite of its name, was waged from 1914–18. On the Western Front a stalemate soon developed with both sides dug into trenches, and thousands of men sacrificed for a few yards advance.

In 1917 the United States entered the war against Germany, helping to force a German surrender. Europe was left in a bad way: poor, battered and unstable. Both the Ottoman empire and the Austrian empire had disappeared, and German ambitions were checked. The only true victor in the war was the United States, which after 1918 was clearly the most powerful country in the world.

THE RUSSIAN REVOLUTION

Russia withdrew from the war in 1917 as a result of a revolution in which the government of the tsar was overthrown. The Bolsheviks, led by Lenin, gained control and set up the first Communist state – the Union of Soviet Socialist Republics. The USSR was an international outcast, shunned by other governments and torn by civil war.

The Bolsheviks had expected the revolution to spread, but the war proved that nationalism was a stronger force than the international brotherhood of the working class.

Dans la lutte actuelle, je vois du côté fasciste les forces périmées, de l'autre côté le peuple dont les immenses ressources créatrices donneront à l'Espagne un élan qui étonnera le monde. Miró.

COMMUNISTS AND FASCISTS

The First World War settlement, agreed at Versailles, pleased almost no one. The Germans were especially angry. They were unwilling to accept the verdict that they were responsible for the war and ought to pay for it. The Versailles meeting also set up the League of Nations, the forerunner of the United Nations. It had little influence on big international conflicts.

On paper, the Treaty of Versailles seemed to be a victory for nationalism and democracy. An independent republic of Czechoslovakia was one result. But a strong reaction soon set in. In the Soviet Union, the Communist system under Stalin was changed into a brutal dictatorship, in which all opposition was crushed. In Italy the reaction took the form of fascism, a crude, power-loving, racist system which worshipped force and disdained justice.

Aggressive fascist dictators also arose in Hungary, Spain and, above all, in Germany, where the Nazis, under Adolf Hitler, came to power in 1933.

Sowing seeds of conflict

Democratic governments like those of France and Spain appeared weak and helpless compared with the vigorous dictatorships of Hitler, Mussolini (in Italy) or Franco, victor in the Spanish Civil War. One exception was the United States, where President Roosevelt's New Deal programme helped overcome the depression.

Since the First World War, the United States had tried to stay out of Europe's dangerous affairs. The Americans were more concerned with Japan, their chief rival in the Pacific region. Japan had adopted a policy of aggressively nationalistic empire-building which made it the natural ally of Hitler's Germany.

Above left **Over 15 million were unemployed in the United States at the height of the Great Depression, in 1932. People queued for free food at "soup kitchens".**

Above **A poster by the Spanish artist Joan Miró supporting the Republican side in the Spanish Civil War. The right-wing, "Nationalist" rebels won the war with aid from Fascist Italy and Nazi Germany.**

THE SECOND WORLD WAR

Below **After the Second World War, Europe was divided into two military groups – the Warsaw Pact countries, led by the Soviet Union, and NATO (North Atlantic Treaty Organization), led by the United States.**

Bottom **German tank columns in the Second World War. The speed and ferocity of these panzer divisions took Europe by surprise.**

The immediate cause of the Second World War was the aggressive actions of the fascist dictators, including a Japanese attack on China, an Italian attack on Ethiopia and a German attack on Poland. It was Hitler's invasion of Poland, that finally provoked Britain and France to declare war.

Escalation of the war

As in 1914, the war began as a European war. By 1941, Hitler had conquered most of Europe, and Britain, supported by the Commonwealth, was his last serious opponent.

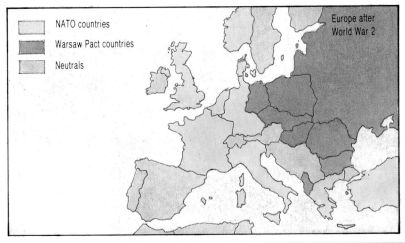

NATO countries

Warsaw Pact countries

Neutrals

Europe after World War 2

But in 1941 things changed. Hitler attacked the Soviet Union despite a no-war pact, and Japan attacked (without warning) the main US naval base in the Pacific.

With the Soviet Union and the United States caught up in the war, the Nazis and their allies were bound for defeat, but at great cost in terms of lives lost. The Japanese surrendered only after atomic bombs had blasted two cities.

The United States and the Soviet Union were in every respect the true winners. The old European powers were reduced to second-class states in the world-power league, and Germany was split in two.

THE COLD WAR

The former allies soon fell out. The Russians and the Americans distrusted and feared each other, and an "iron curtain" descended on Europe, shutting off the Soviet Union and its allies. During this cold war, a third world war, which would be fought with nuclear weapons, often looked probable. There were many crises, but gradually the prospects improved as both superpowers recognized that in the next war, if it happened, there could be no winners.

84

THE THIRD WORLD

Above **The Ayatollah Khomeini, who inspired the Shi'ite revolution in Iran in 1979.**

Below **The General Assembly of the United Nations.**

Below right **Testing a nuclear bomb.**

One result of the Second World War was the end of imperialism. Former colonies of the European powers in Africa and Asia gained political independence, though sometimes after violent struggle. The membership of the United Nations, the international organization set up before the end of the war, expanded (see page 206). The member-states could be divided roughly into three groups: the democratic West (North America, western Europe), the Communist bloc (the Soviet Union and its allies or "satellites"), and the Third World (mainly poor, new states of Africa, Asia and South America). China, where a long period of civil war ended in Communist victory in 1949, was not admitted until 1971.

An enormous contrast existed between the industrialized West and the Third World. Already wealthy in the 1940s, the West (including Japan, Australia and New Zealand) grew more and more prosperous between the 1940s and 1980s, in spite of economic slumps and unemployment. Japan rose to challenge the United States as the world's richest country.

The less-developed Third World countries, where most people were fully occupied growing enough food to feed themselves, remained poor. Efforts to industrialize them were mainly unsuccessful. Another problem was the population explosion. In many poor countries, although the economy might grow fast, the population grew even faster.

In the 1970s a "fuel crisis", a shortage of oil, brought difficulties to all countries. Many people in poor Third World countries were troubled by a different "fuel crisis" – not enough firewood for cooking.

UNITY AND CONFLICT

Developments in transport and communications have made the world seem a smaller place in the late 20th century. Besides the United Nations many organizations, such as the EEC (European Economic Community), were formed to draw countries closer together, economically and politically (see page 207).

And yet there were more small wars and other conflicts between the 1950s and 1980s than in any other period. None took place in Europe or North America, but the superpowers and their allies were usually involved, directly or indirectly.

The first big clash between Communism and Democracy was the Korean War (1950–53). South Korea's independence was preserved against Communist attack from the North by US-led forces. In Vietnam the United States tried to play the same part, assisting the South against the Communist North, but there the Communists won and in 1975 the United States was forced to withdraw. In a similar way, the Soviet Union became involved in a long struggle in Afghanistan in support of an unpopular pro-Soviet government. But by 1988, with new leadership in Russia, the climate had changed, and peace plans were being made

for a withdrawal of Soviet troops from Afghanistan.

Another troublespot was the Middle East. The creation of the Jewish state of Israel in Palestine in 1948 resulted in a series of wars with hostile Arab neighbours, but with US backing the Israelis enlarged their territory at Arab expense.

Top **Israeli tanks advance across the desert. Some Arab land won by Israel has not been returned.**

Above **A concert by Western pop musicians to raise money for famine relief in Africa.**

World Events

Historical Events

Ancient Civilizations

BC

3000 Civilization begins in Egypt and Mesopotamia
2500 Cities built in Indus valley
2300 First Chinese dynasty
1200 Israelite Exodus from Egypt
1100 Assyrian Empire founded
814 Carthage founded by Phoenicians
538 Cyrus the Great of Persia conquers Babylon
509 Roman republic founded
490 Greeks defeat Persians at Marathon
404 Greek war ends in defeat of Athens
335–323 Alexander the Great creates Greek empire
202 Han dynasty founded in China
146 Romans destroy Carthage
58–51 Caesar conquers Gaul
27 Octavian becomes the Roman Emperor Augustus
5 Birth of Jesus Christ

AD

29 Crucifixion of Jesus
43 Roman conquest of Britain
320 Gupta empire founded in India
476 Fall of Rome

The Middle Ages

622 Muhammad's *Hejira* (flight) from Mecca to Medina
624 T'ang dynasty founded in China
711 Muslim conquest of Spain
800 Charlemagne crowned Holy Roman Emperor
886 Alfred defeats Danes in Britain
1066 Normans defeat English at Hastings
1071 Normans conquer Byzantine Italy
1095 First Crusade begins
1100 Inca empire established in South America
1187 Saladin captures Jerusalem
1210 Mongol invasion of China
1250 Death of Emperor Frederick II
1305 Pope moves residence from Rome to Avignon
1337 Hundred Years' War between England and France begins
1348 The Black Death kills one-third of Europe's people
1368 Ming dynasty founded in China
1398 Tamerlane invades India
1453 Ottoman Turks capture Constantinople
1455–85 Wars of the Roses in England
1492 Last Muslim kingdom in Spain conquered

Dawn of the Modern Age

1502 Safavid dynasty established in Iran
1521 Cortés conquers Aztecs in Mexico
1526 Mughal empire founded in India
1529 Turks besiege Vienna
1533 Ivan the Terrible accedes to the Russian throne
1533 Pizarro conquers Incas in Peru
1571 Christians defeat Turks at Lepanto
1572 Dutch revolt against Spain
1588 Spanish Armada defeated by English
1598 Edict of Nantes ends French religious wars
1608 Quebec founded by the French
1609 Netherlands wins independence from Spain
1613 Romanov dynasty founded in Russia
1614–48 Thirty Years' War in Europe
1620 *Mayflower* carries first colonists to New England
1642–46 English Civil War
1644 Manchus found Ch'ing dynasty in China

Arts, Sciences and Learning

BC

2600 Great Pyramid built at Giza, Egypt
1700 Minoan palace of Crete built
1500 *Rig Veda*, Indian scriptures, composed
1100 Alphabet developed by Phoenicians
960 Temple built at Jerusalem
850 *Iliad* and *Odyssey* composed
776 First Olympic Games
600 Iron used in China
488 Death of Buddha
460 Parthenon built in Athens
399 Death of Socrates
390 Plato writes *The Republic*
215 Building of Great Wall of China begun
10–20 Virgil writes *Aeneid*

AD

114 Trajan's Column erected in Rome
413 Augustine writes *The City of God*
500 Mayan city of Chichen Itzá completed

552 Buddhism reaches Japan
788 Great Mosque at Cordoba built
850 Brick city of Zimbabwe built
900 Building of Angkor Wat (Khmer Empire)
969 Cairo founded
1000 Scandinavian settlement in Newfoundland
1050 Omar Khayyam writes his *Rubaiyat*
1194 Building of Chartres cathedral begins
1271 Marco Polo reaches court of Kublai Khan
1280 Invention of eye glasses
1314 Dante writes his *Divine Comedy*
1325 Aztecs built Tenochtitlan (now Mexico City)
1388 Chaucer writes his *Canterbury Tales*
1405 Chinese ships reach East Africa
1454 Gutenberg sets up his printing press in Germany
1492 Columbus discovers the West Indies
1497 Cabot discovers Newfoundland
1498 Vasco da Gama reaches India

1503 Leonardo paints *Mona Lisa*
1508 Michelangelo paints Sistine Chapel
1513 Machiavelli writes *The Prince*
1517 Luther attacks Church, beginning Protestant Reformation
1519–22 Magellan sails around the world
1534 Loyola founds Jesuit order
1543 Copernicus publishes his theory of the universe
1582 Gregorian calender adopted
1586 Beginning of *kabuki* theatre in Japan
1590 Galileo publishes his law of falling bodies
1615 Cervantes writes *Don Quixote*
1616 Death of Shakespeare
1628 Harvey discovers circulation of the blood
1632–54 Taj Mahal built in India
1645 Council of Trent signals start of Counter-Reformation
1661 Versailles palace begun near Paris
1669 Death of Rembrandt

1652 Cape Colony (South Africa) founded by the Dutch	**1687** Newton publishes law of gravity
1654 Portuguese capture Brazil	**1750** Descartes' *Encyclopedia* published
1701–13 War of the Spanish Succession	**1750** Death of J.S. Bach
1707 Union of England and Scotland	**1752** Franklin invents lightning conductor
1740–48 War of the Austrian Succession	**1765** Watt improves steam engine
1756–63 Seven Years' War	**1777** Lavoisier discovers nature of oxygen
1776 US Declaration of Independence	**1791** Death of Mozart
1789 French Revolution	**1793** Eli Whitney invents cotton gin
1789 Washington elected US president	**1819** First steamship crossing of Atlantic
1804 Napoleon becomes emperor of France	**1825** Stockton-Darlington railway opens
1812 Napoleon invades Russia	**1827** Death of Beethoven
1815 Napoleon's final defeat at Waterloo	**1832** Telegraph invented
1835–37 Great Trek of Boers in South Africa	**1848** *Communist Manifesto* published
1848 Revolutions in Europe	**1853–56** Livingstone crosses Africa
1854–6 Crimean War	**1855** Bessemer invents his steelmaking process
1857 Indian revolt against British	**1859** Darwin publishes his *Origin of Species*
1860 Italy united	**1865–69** Tolstoy writes *War and Peace*
1861–65 American Civil War	**1869** Opening of Suez Canal
1867 Canada becomes a Dominion	**1870** First performance of Wagner's *Ring* cycle
1870–71 War between France and Prussia	**1874** First exhibition of Impressionist painters, Paris
1871 German Empire proclaimed	**1876** Telephone invented by Bell
1894–95 Chinese-Japanese War	**1895** Marconi invents the wireless
1898 Spanish-American War	**1895** Freud publishes his *Studies of Hysteria*
1899–1902 Boer War in South Africa	**1896** First modern Olympic Games

The Twentieth Century

1905 First Revolution in Russia	**1900** Planck publishes his Quantum Theory
1911 Revolution in China under Sun Yat-sen	**1903** Wright brothers make first flight in man-powered aircraft
1912–13 Balkan Wars	**1905** Einstein publishes his Special Theory of Relativity
1914–18 First World War	**1906** Cubist movement in art
1917 Russian Revolution	**1909** Peary reaches North Pole
1917 USA enters the War	**1911** Amundsen reaches South Pole
1919 Treaty of Versailles	**1914** Opening of Panama Canal
1923 Turkish republic founded	**1916** Dada movement founded
1929 Stock Market crash begins Great Depression	**1918** Bauhaus school of design founded
1931 Japan occupies Manchuria	**1919** Rutherford splits atom
1933 Hitler gains power in Germany	**1922** Eliot publishes *The Waste Land*
1936–39 Spanish Civil War	**1922** Joyce publishes *Ulysses*
1939–45 Second World War	**1924** Breton publishes first *Surrealist Manifesto*
1940 Battle of Britain	**1925** Television invented
1941 Japan attacks Pearl Harbor: USA enters War	**1928** First "talkies" (sound films)
1943 Germans halted at Stalingrad, Soviet Union	**1931** Empire State Building opened in New York
1944 "D-Day" landings in Normandy	**1937** Picasso paints *Guernica*
1945 First atom bombs dropped on Japan	**1947** Discovery of Dead Sea scrolls
1945 United Nations founded	**1948** Transistor developed
1947 India and Pakistan gain independence	**1949** Orwell's *1984* published
1948 State of Israel founded	**1953** Hilary and Tensing climb Mount Everest
1948 Mahatma Gandhi assassinated	**1953** Molecular structure of DNA discovered
1949 Communist republic established in China	**1954** Salk develops anti-polio vaccine
1950–53 Korean War	**1957** Soviet Union launches first space satellite
1953 Death of Stalin	**1961** Gagarin becomes first man in space
1956 Suez Canal crisis	**1962** Beatles make their first disc
1956 Soviet troops crush Hungarian Rising	**1962** Rachel Carson writes *Silent Spring*
1957 European Econonic Community founded	**1967** First heart transplant operation
1959 Cuban Revolution	**1969** Armstrong walks on the Moon
1961 Berlin Wall built	**1970** Solzhenitsyn awarded Nobel Prize for Literature
1962 Cuban missile crisis	**1976** First flight of *Concorde*
1963 US President Kennedy assassinated	**1981** First flight of US space shuttle
1967–70 Nigerian Civil War	**1986** Soviet nuclear reactor at Chernobyl explodes
1968 Soviet troops invade Czechoslovakia	
1974 US President Nixon forced to resign over Watergate	
1975 End of Vietnam war	
1976 Death of Mao Tse-tung	
1978 Polish cardinal elected Pope John Paul II	
1979 Revolution in Iran	
1979 Soviet Union invades Afghanistan	
1980 Iran-Iraq War begins	
1982 British-Argentine war in Falkland Islands	
1982 Israel expels PLO from Lebanon	
1985 Gorbachev becomes Soviet leader	

The Living World

PREHISTORIC LIFE

Life on Earth began about 3,500 million years ago. It evolved very slowly. The first living things were one-celled organisms called bacteria. The first true plants and animals did not appear until about 2,000 million years later.

During the next 1,000 million years one-celled animals gave rise to many different kinds of many-celled animals. We know very little about these creatures. When they died, their soft bodies decayed quickly, leaving little or no trace. Sometimes scientists find impressions of their bodies or tracks preserved in rocks.

About 570 million years ago, a number of animals developed shells or outer skeletons. They did this to provide themselves with a defence against predators. When the animals died, their shells or skeletons were often buried in sand or silt. Such hard coverings do not decay quickly and later they became included in the rocks as fossils. A fossil is simply the remains of a plant or animal preserved in rock.

We know this period of time as the Cambrian period. It marks the beginning of what we call the Geological Time scale, shown on pages 128–29 as a chart. It is divided into a number of periods, grouped together into three main eras. These are the Palaeozoic ("ancient life"), Mesozoic ("middle life") and Cenozoic ("new life") eras.

During the Cambrian period, Earth's seas abounded with all kinds of creatures such as snails, corals and primitive relatives of modern sea urchins. One very common group of animals – the trilobites – were related to modern insects and crabs.

Below **Evolutionary "trees" of the animal and plant kingdoms.**

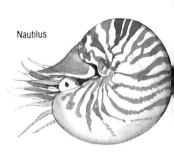

Nautilus

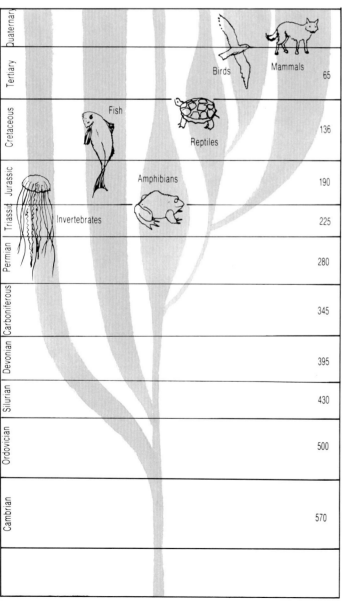

Millions of years ago

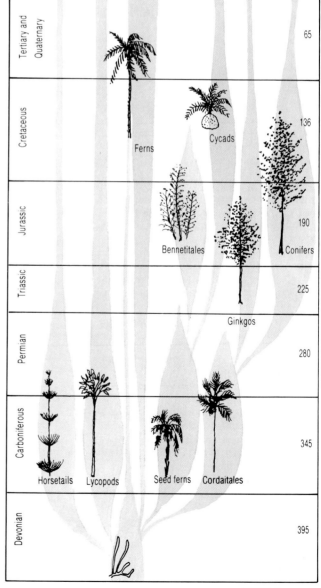

Millions of years ago

Stegosaurus

Pteranodon

Tylosaurus

Eryops

Animals with backbones

Cambrian animals were all creatures without spines or backbones. The first animals with backbones appeared about 500 million years ago. These were jawless fishes that sucked up their food from the sea bottom. By 400 million years ago huge, heavily armoured fishes existed. They had fearsome jaws for preying on other sea animals. They soon died out and were replaced by the first sharks, which had skeletons made of cartilage. At the same time the ancestors of modern bony fishes appeared.

Life on land

By this time plants were becoming established on land. They provided food for land animals. Among the first of these were early insects. In turn, these provided food for larger animals. The first amphibians evolved from fishes about 350 million years ago. Animals became established on land with the appearance of the first reptiles about 300 million years ago. 75 million years later there were many kinds, and reptiles dominated the world for about 150 million years. The Mesozoic era was the age of the dinosaurs, sea reptiles and flying reptiles.

Birds first appeared about 200 million years ago. When the flying reptiles died out, they had the skies to themselves, and many kinds evolved during the Cenozoic era. The first mammals evolved from reptiles about 200 million years ago. While dinosaurs ruled they could not evolve, but when the dinosaurs disappeared 65 million years ago, mammals spread. Many different kinds evolved. The first humans appeared about four million years ago.

Top **Some of the animals that formerly lived on planet Earth. Most are now extinct, but the mollusc *Nautilus* still exists.**

Above **Many plants have been preserved in coal.**

Left **The sea anemone uses its tentacles to catch a fish, and kills it by stinging it.**

Below **Invertebrate animals form a large part of the animal kingdom. Many live in water, and most of these are found in the sea.**

THE ANIMAL KINGDOM

There are over 1,300,000 different kinds of animal in the animal kingdom. Some have backbones, or spines, and we call such animals vertebrates. Vertebrate animals include the fishes, amphibians (frogs, toads and newts), reptiles, birds and the mammals, the group to which we ourselves belong.

On the other hand there are many animals that do not have backbones. These are the invertebrates. Invertebrates include an even larger number of very different animal groups. They range from simple, one-celled animals to quite complex ones, such as insects and octopuses.

Animals without backbones

All animals and plants are built up of tiny units called cells. An animal cell consists of a membrane around a liquid material called cytoplasm. Floating in the cytoplasm are tiny structures, or organelles, that carry out the work of the cell.

A plant cell differs from an animal cell in that it usually has a stiff cell wall. This is made of the chemical called cellulose. Plant cells are generally green, because they contain a green substance called chlorophyll. This is a special chemical that enables plants to use the energy contained in sunlight to make their own food (see page 116).

One-celled life
Organisms that consist of just one cell are among the simplest forms of life. Some of

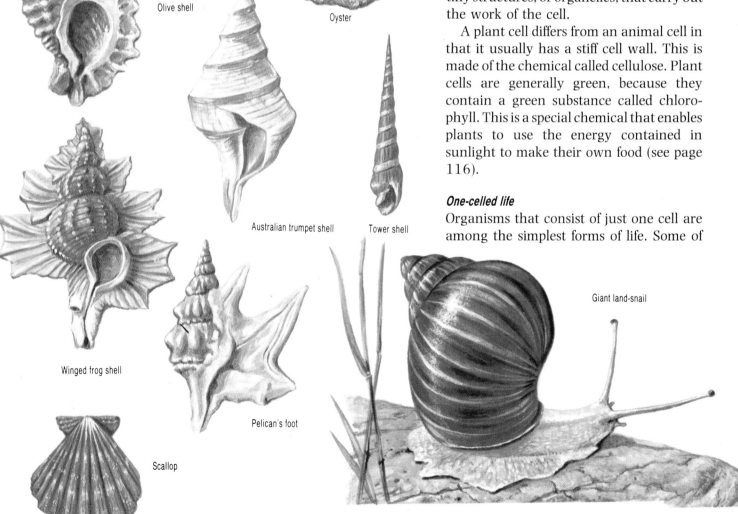

Squid

Drill

Olive shell

Oyster

Australian trumpet shell

Tower shell

Winged frog shell

Pelican's foot

Scallop

Giant land-snail

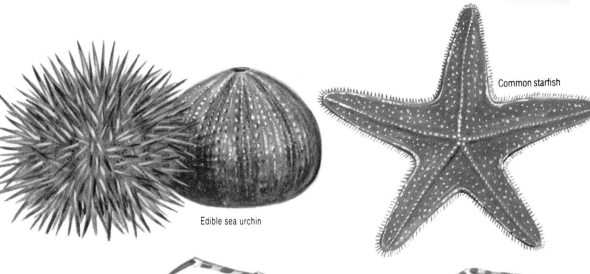

Right **Sea urchins and starfish belong to the group known as the Echinoderms, or "spiny-skins".**

Below right **Crustaceans are members of the arthropod ("jointed leg") group. They include crabs and lobsters.**

Edible sea urchin

Common starfish

Giant Japanese spider crab

Edible crab

Lobster

these organisms are animals. Examples include the swimming *Paramecium* and the amoebas. Other one-celled organisms contain chlorophyll and can therefore be thought of as plants. However, it is not always easy to tell the difference between an animal and a plant and there are some one-celled organisms with both plant and animal features.

Some scientists therefore classify one-celled organisms in a group by themselves, separate from the plant and animal kingdoms. This group is known as the Protista. Bacteria and fungi, which have neither plant nor animal characteristics, are also sometimes included in this group.

Sponges and corals

Animals that consist of more than one cell vary from very simple types to very complex ones. Among the simplest animals are the sponges. These are sea animals that live attached to rocks or the sea bed. The body of a sponge consists of a group of cells that more or less work together.

The animals that belong to the group known as the coelenterates have more organized bodies. They include such creatures as sea anemones, corals and jellyfish. Their tube-like bodies have only one opening, the mouth. Many coelenterates are equipped with special stinging cells for killing prey.

Worms

The animal kingdom contains an enormous variety of worms and worm-like animals. The group known as the platyhelminths contains the flatworms and several kinds of parasite (see page 121), such as tapeworms and liverflukes. The annelid, or segmented, worms include earthworms and leeches, as well as a number of sea worms, such as lugworms, ragworms and fan worms.

Other worms include the ribbon worms, the thorny-headed worms, the peanut worms and the acorn worms. Roundworms are probably more numerous than any other kind of animal. Many are parasites, others live free in the soil or in water. In the sea alone it is thought that there may be over 40 million million million million roundworms!

Spiny animals

The echinoderms, or "spiny skinned" animals form another important group of invertebrates. This group includes the sea urchins, starfish, sea cucumbers and brittlestars. Echinoderms have bodies built on a five-sided plan. Although invertebrates, they have a hard, chalk-like skeleton that lies buried within the skin.

Molluscs

The molluscs form the second largest group of invertebrates (the largest includes the insects, spiders and crabs). Molluscs are mostly shelled animals, with snails and slugs forming the largest part of the group. A typical snail has a spiral shell into which it can retreat when danger threatens. It can close off the opening with a hard "lid" called

an operculum. Snails are found on land and in fresh water. Examples include the common garden snail and the pond snails.

There are also many different kinds of sea snail, such as whelks, topshells and periwinkles. Some members of this group have uncoiled shells. Examples include limpets, slipper limpets, ormers and cowries. Slugs and sea slugs have small, almost invisible shells, or lack shells completely.

The bivalves form another group of molluscs. Among these are many familiar seaside animals, such as cockles, clams, mussels, venus shells, razor shells, oysters

Above **The casts produced by lugworms can often be seen on sandy beaches.**

Opposite **Spiders, scorpions, ticks and mites belong to the group known as the arachnids.**

Below **A cross-section through a spider. To make silk, a sticky liquid is forced out through the spinnarets.**

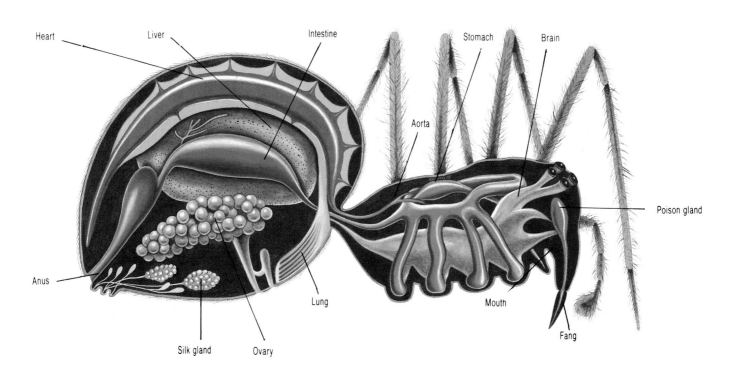

and scallops. Many bivalves spend their lives buried in the sand. Mussels and oysters attach themselves to rock surfaces, while the shipworm bores holes in wood.

The last group of molluscs contains the squids and octopuses. These all have tentacles surrounding the head. They use them for catching prey. Squids have internal shells and ten tentacles. They often live in large groups, or shoals and can change colour very rapidly. Octopuses have eight tentacles and generally live alone. Both squids and octopuses can squirt out clouds of ink to confuse attackers.

Animals with jointed legs

The largest invertebrate group is called the arthropods, which means "jointed legs". Among the arthropods are the millipedes, centipedes, crustaceans (crabs and their relatives), arachnids (spiders and their relatives) and the insects. All these animals have hard outer skeletons. Their legs are made up of several jointed, tube-like sections.

Centipedes are fast-moving creatures that prey on other small animals. Millipedes are slow movers and feed on plant material. The crustaceans include the shrimps, prawns, crabs and lobsters. Barnacles and a number of small shrimp-like animals also belong to this group. Most crustaceans live in the sea. A few, such as the water flea, are found in fresh water and some, such as the beach flea and the woodlouse, live on land.

As well as spiders, the arachnids include the scorpions, mites, ticks and harvestmen. All arachnids live on land. They have eight legs and their bodies are divided into two distinct parts. Most arachnids are carnivores, preying on insects or other animals.

Spiders are well-known for their use of silk. Many spiders build webs to trap their prey. Orb-web spiders, such as the garden spider, build elaborate cartwheel-like webs with sticky threads to catch flying insects. A bolas spider swings a sticky blob on the end of a silk line in order to catch them.

Some spiders do not use silk. Brightly coloured crab spiders sit camouflaged in flowers, lying in wait for unsuspecting insects. Wolf spiders catch prey animals simply by chasing them and the so-called bird-eating spiders of South America catch small animals in the same way.

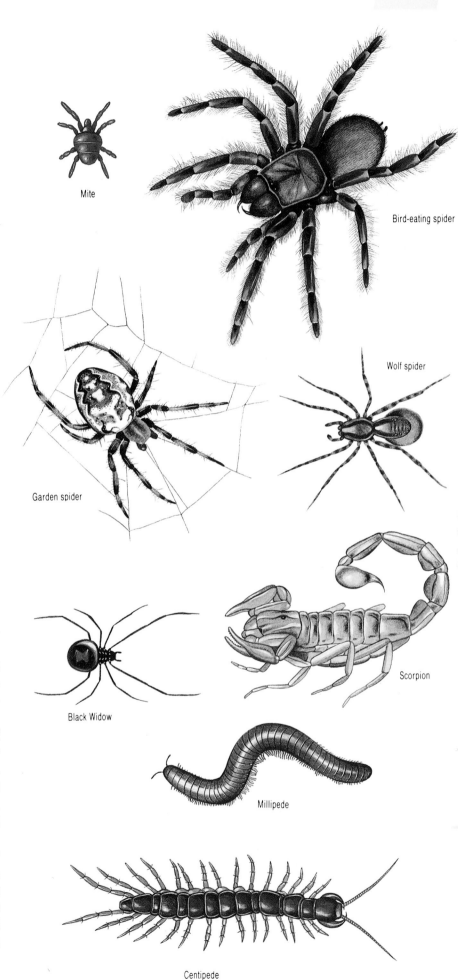

Mite

Bird-eating spider

Wolf spider

Garden spider

Black Widow

Scorpion

Millipede

Centipede

INSECTS

More than 85 per cent of all the known animals in the world are insects. About one million species have been identified so far. Scientists believe that there may be another four million that have yet to be discovered. An insect's body is divided into three parts: head, thorax ("chest") and abdomen ("stomach"). It has six legs attached to its thorax.

A few kinds of insect are wingless, but most have one or two pairs of wings. Winged insects belong to two main groups. In one group the young hatch out from their eggs in forms that resemble miniature adults. These are known as nymphs. As they grow, they moult (shed their skin) at intervals. At each moult the nymphs become more like their parents. Insects belonging to this group include dragonflies, termites, grasshoppers, cockroaches, earwigs, stick insects, lice and bugs.

On the other hand, a number of insects have young that are completely different from their parents. The young hatch out from the eggs as larvae, such as caterpillars and grubs. For a time, the larva feeds and grows. Many larvae eat an enormous amount of food, often causing damage to crops or buildings. When it is fully grown it undergoes a dramatic change and becomes a pupa inside a tough case. It looks lifeless, but the animal's tissues are being completely reorganized within it. When this is complete, the insect emerges as the familiar adult. Insects that have this kind of life cycle include butterflies, moths, flies, caddisflies, beetles, bees, wasps and ants.

Below **Many termites build huge nests of earth, cemented together with saliva and dung. Some nests are 3 m high.**

Below **Worker wood ants carry a cocoon. There is normally only one queen, but there may be several million workers.**

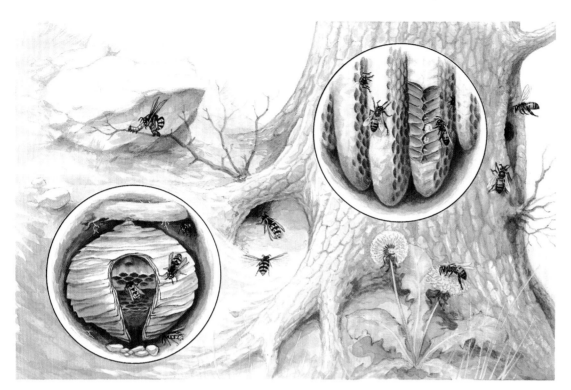

Left **A wasp nest consists of many tiny six-sided chambers, arranged in several storeys, or levels. The upper level is begun by the queen in spring, but when the first workers hatch, they take over the task of nest-building.**

Below **The creature that hatches from a butterfly egg is a caterpillar. When this reaches full size it becomes a pupa. After a few weeks or months the pupa breaks open and an adult butterfly emerges.**

Social insects

Most kinds of insect live by themselves. They join others of their own kind only in order to mate. However, a few insects live in highly organized colonies. Each member of the colony belongs to a particular social group, or caste. Each caste has a particular task to perform for the good of the colony as a whole.

Among the most familiar social insects are the honey bees, which have three castes: workers, drones and queen bees. The worker bees, which are sterile females, construct the wax nest of six-sided chambers, or cells. During the summer, they forage in flowers for pollen and nectar which they carry back to the nest.

Younger workers convert the nectar into honey and store it. They also feed the developing grubs on a mixture of pollen and honey, and tend the queen bee. Each nest has only one queen, whose task is to lay the eggs that hatch into grubs. She mates with one of the drone, or male, bees of the colony, who do no other work.

Several kinds of wasp also live in colonies, as do all ants and termites. Wasps build underground nests of paper, made from chewed-up wood. The young grubs are fed on insects.

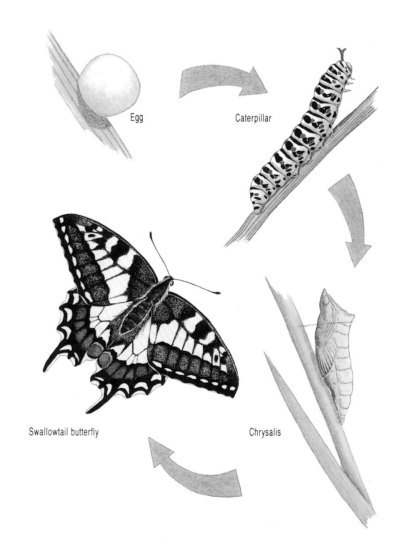

Egg

Caterpillar

Swallowtail butterfly

Chrysalis

FISHES

Below **Many different kinds of fish inhabit the world's oceans, lakes and rivers. Like all animals fish need oxygen to live. They get this oxygen from the water around them, using organs called gills. These have blood vessels very close to the surface and are specially designed for extracting oxygen from water. The water is taken in through the mouth, which then closes. The water is then forced out over the gills and through the gill opening.**

Fishes are the simplest vertebrates. Most have skeletons made of bone, but some fishes have skeletons made of a softer material called cartilage. The most primitive fishes are the lampreys and hags, which have very simple skeletons without proper backbones and with no jaws. Lampreys are parasites (see page 121). A lamprey uses its sucker-like mouth to cling on to other fish and feed on their blood and flesh. Hags live buried in mud, feeding on worms, shrimps and dead fish.

Sharks and rays

Sharks, dogfish, skates and rays have skeletons made of cartilage. They have jaws that allow them to open and close their mouths.

Cartilage is lighter than bone, but even so these fish cannot float in the water like bony fish, which have an air sac inside. Instead, the body and fins of a cartilaginous fish act like wings to lift the fish up from the sea bed as it swims along. Thus most cartilaginous fishes have to keep swimming to stop themselves from sinking.

Sharks and dogfish have streamlined, torpedo-like bodies for fast swimming. They are covered in small, pointed scales and, in the mouth, these scales often become fearsome teeth. They are used for catching, holding and tearing prey. Some sharks are dangerous creatures; the most notorious is the great white shark. But most do not attack people. The largest sharks – the whale shark and the basking shark – are gentle animals that feed by scooping up plankton: the masses of tiny animals and plants that float in the water.

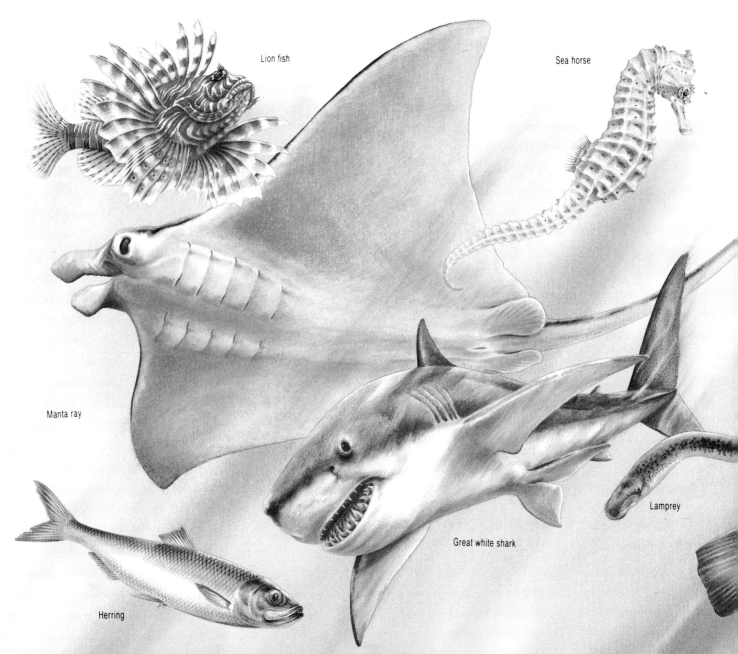

Lion fish

Sea horse

Manta ray

Great white shark

Lamprey

Herring

Rays and skates have flattened bodies, with large "wings" at the sides. Most feed on shrimps and other crustaceans. But the huge manta ray also scoops up plankton as it glides along.

Bony fishes

Bony fishes are the masters of the world's oceans. They can be found at all depths and in every kind of living area, or habitat. Two important features have made this success possible. First, a bony fish has a swim bladder inside its body. This is a gas-filled bag that allows the fish to float in the water at any depth. Second, the jaws of a bony fish are made up of many tiny bones. Also, the mouth points forwards. This makes it possible for a bony fish to nibble food rather than tear at it like a shark. Bony fishes are therefore able to eat many different kinds of food.

A typical bony fish has a streamlined body which it flexes from side to side as it swims, using its tail as a propeller. The fins on its sides and back are used for steering and braking. Among the many examples of such fishes are herring, cod and tuna. However, bony fishes have also developed an enormous number of variations on the basic plan, to adapt to different lifestyles. A number of fishes use their fins rather than their bodies to propel themselves along; examples include pipe fish, sea horses, puffer fish and wrasse. The fishes with some of the strangest adaptations are found in the deepest parts of the oceans, where it is always dark and food is less abundant.

Above **The Sargassum fish is a master of camouflage. Its colouring and leaf-like outgrowths make it almost invisible among the sargassum seaweed in which it lives.**

Piranha

Perch

Catfish

FROGS, TOADS AND NEWTS

Frogs, toads, newts and salamanders belong to the group we call amphibians. Generally, these are animals that have adapted to a life spent partly in water and partly on land. They have legs for moving about and most amphibians have lungs for breathing air. They also take in oxygen through their skins and the lining of the mouth. However, some amphibians spend all their lives in water. Frogs and toads are not only the largest group of amphibians, they are also the best adapted to living on land.

From egg to adult

Female amphibians produce soft, delicate eggs that must be laid in water. Thus all amphibians have to find water in order to breed. Frogs mate in water, producing the large masses of eggs we call frogspawn. Toads produce "ropes" of eggs. The eggs hatch into tadpole larvae, which in many amphibians look very different from the adults. A tadpole has a long tail and no legs. It gets oxygen through feathery gills on the outside of its body. After about a month it loses these and develops internal gills instead. A month later, it starts to grow legs. It also develops a lung and comes to the surface to breathe air. In limbed amphibians, the body now starts to change very dramatically. Its tail disappears, the hind legs become longer and its mouth gets larger. Within another month it becomes a miniature adult.

Newts and salamanders

Newts and salamanders form a group called the urodeles. They have long bodies with weak legs and long tails. The tadpole larvae are often very like the adults. Some species of salamander, such as the mud puppy and the Mexican axolotl, never lose their larval features.

Many newts and salamanders are strik-

Bottom **A frog's egg hatches out into a tadpole after about two weeks. Over the next two months, it loses its fish-like features, developing lungs and back legs to replace the gills and tail-fin. An adult frog of three months is able to live in water or on land.**

Common frog

European tree frog

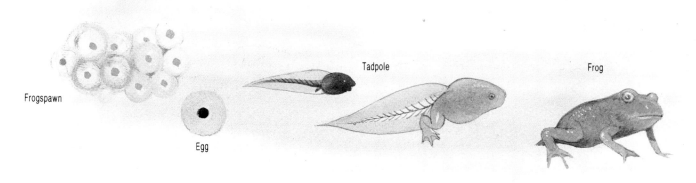
Frogspawn   Egg   Tadpole   Frog

Below **Amphibians are all animals that must return to water at some stage in their lives in order to breed. Some, such as the axolotl, remain like larvae all their lives and never leave water. And those that do leave the water need moist conditions to prevent their skins drying out.**

ingly coloured; the yellow and black fire salamander is an example. Some male newts develop crests and bright colours during the breeding season to attract the females. Mating usually takes place in water and the females lay their eggs singly on the leaves of underwater plants.

The European fire salamander lives in woods sheltering under logs. So the myth grew that salamanders were born in fire: when the logs were burned, the unseen salamanders appeared.

Unlike newts, salamanders do not hibernate because they generally live in warmer climates.

Frogs and toads

Frogs and toads belong to a group called the anurans. They have short bodies and powerful hind legs, which are used for jumping and swimming. True frogs are slender animals with large eyes, and in most cases they are more agile than toads. True toads, on the other hand, are generally rather heavy and clumsy. They also have warty skins that can produce an irritating or poisonous slime.

Tree and water dwellers

The anurans are a varied group: they include the tree frogs, which cling to the tree bark using suckers on their toes. Asian tree frogs lay their eggs in foam nests they make in the trees. When the tadpoles hatch they drop into the water below. Flying frogs have an interesting adaptation – large, webbed feet that they use like parachutes for gliding from tree to tree.

Another group, known as the pipids, includes the South African clawed frog and the Surinam toad, which spend nearly all their lives in water. They are excellent swimmers, having flattened bodies and large, webbed, hind feet. The Surinam toad is one of a few species that look after their young; the males carry the developing tadpoles on their backs.

Toads mating

Crested newt

European fire salamander

Axolotl

REPTILES

Whereas amphibians must have moist or wet surroundings, reptiles can live in much drier conditions. They have tough, scaly skins that stop them drying out and they lay hard-shelled eggs that can survive without water. Thus reptiles are true land animals.

Snakes and lizards

A lizard is a typical example of a reptile. It walks on four legs held out sideways from the body. Many lizards walk with their bellies touching the ground. This is to save energy; the position of the legs means that lifting the body off the ground is hard work. Most lizards can run very fast and some even run on their hind legs.

Lizards include the chameleons, geckos, skinks, agamas and iguanas. The largest is the Komodo dragon, which can be up to a metre (3 ft 3 in) long. The Gila monster and the beaded lizard are the only two poisonous kinds.

Snakes are closely related to the lizards. However, there are some major differences between them; snakes have no legs, and they are unable to close their eyelids. Most snakes move by throwing their bodies into backward-moving waves. These push against the stones and plants on the ground, moving the snake forward.

Snakes prey on other animals. The grass snake catches small animals simply by seizing them in its teeth. Some large snakes kill their victims by coiling round them and squeezing them to death. Such snakes are called constrictors; examples include the pythons and the boas. Most snakes, how-

Below **An American side-necked turtle.**

Bottom **The distinguishing feature of a crocodile is that the fourth tooth in its lower jaw remains visible when the mouth is closed. An alligator's tooth disappears into a pit in the upper jaw.**

Crocodile

Alligator

ever kill their prey using fangs to inject poison.

Bull snake

Python

Crocodiles and alligators

Although crocodiles and alligators are reptiles, they are usually to be found in or near water. Their eyes, ears and nostrils are arranged so that they can lie almost completely submerged. They can also remain underwater without breathing for up to five hours. They feed mainly on fish, but large kinds sometimes prey on mammals, such as deer, coming to drink.

Like all reptiles, crocodiles and alligators lay their eggs on land, deep inside nests. A female alligator tends her nest and helps to dig her young out when they hatch.

Turtles and tortoises

Turtles and tortoises evolved about 200 million years ago and they have changed very little since they first appeared. The most obvious feature of a turtle or tortoise is its shell, which covers most of the body. This is made up of bony plates, fused together and covered with a horny material. The top is attached to the animal's backbone.

Tortoises live on land. The largest are the giant tortoises of the Galapagos Islands and the Indian Ocean island of Aldabra, some of which weigh over 180 kg (396 lb). Many turtles, on the other hand, have returned to the water. The large sea turtles include the green turtle and the loggerhead turtle. Leatherback turtles sometimes measure over 2.5 m (8 ft) in length and may weigh over 800 kg (1,763 lb).

Above **The bull snake uses poison to kill its prey. Pythons squeeze their victims to death.**

Below **Lizards have tough, scaly skins. The frilled lizard is harmless, but can scare away potential attackers by raising its frill and hissing.**

Green lizard

Frilled lizard

Hummingbird

Fulmar

Condor

BIRDS

The birds are the masters of the air. Although they evolved from reptiles about 150 million years ago, their bodies soon became covered with feathers rather than scales. Instead of front legs they developed wings, which most birds now use for flying. Birds succeed in flying by being as light as possible. They have hollow bones, small skulls without teeth, and rigid skeletons that need few muscles. The wings are operated by large, powerful flight muscles.

Unlike reptiles, birds are warm-blooded.

A reptile's body temperature tends to change with the temperature of the surroundings; most reptiles use the sun's heat to warm them up during the day. A bird, however, keeps its body temperature the same, regardless of the temperature of the air outside. It does this by using its body processes to generate heat. Its feathers insulate it, helping to keep this heat in.

There are more than 8,600 different kinds of bird. The largest group is made up of the so-called perching birds. Among these are swallows, warblers, sparrows, finches, crows, flycatchers, bunting,

Above **A fulmar has long thin wings for fast, gliding flight low over the sea. A condor uses its broader wings for high, soaring flight. A hummingbird's wings are for hovering.**

Right **The ostrich and cassowary cannot fly. The penguin "flies" underwater.**

lyrebirds, weaver birds and many others. The remaining major groups of birds include the woodpeckers, owls, parrots, pigeons, gulls and waders, pheasants and grouse, birds of prey, geese and ducks, swifts and hummingbirds, cuckoos, pelicans, divers, herons, kingfishers and the albatrosses. A few birds have lost the ability to fly; examples include the ostrich, the emu and the kiwis. Penguins use their wings to "fly" underwater.

How birds fly

A bird's wing is shaped a bit like the wing of an aeroplane. It is slightly curved so that air passes more quickly over the top than it does underneath. When the wing travels forward through the air, this shape produces an upward force known as lift. The bird therefore rises up in the air.

In an aeroplane, the forward movement, or thrust, is usually produced by one or more engines. A bird, however, uses its wings to produce both the lift and the

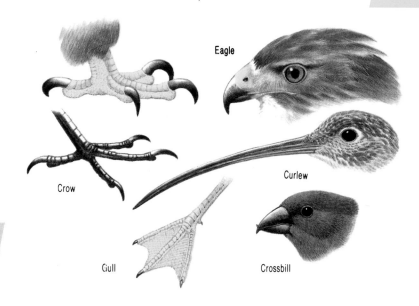

Above **The hooked beak and talons of an eagle show that it is a carnivore. The curlew probes the ground for its food. The crossbill uses its beak for picking seeds out of pine cones.**

thrust. It does this by beating the wings up and down. On each downbeat the feathers at the tips of the wings twist. They act like propellers to push the bird forward through the air.

The shapes of bird's wings show how they fly. Birds like albatrosses, which fly long distances low over the sea, have long thin wings with a massive span for fast, gliding flight. Swifts also have thin, swept back wings for high-speed flight. A vulture, on the other hand, has large, broad wings for slow soaring high in the air. Woodland birds often have short, broad wings that enable them to take off rapidly and manoeuvre easily.

Meat eaters

Bird's beaks are adapted for making use of different kinds of food. For example, birds of prey can be recognized by their large hooked beaks. They use these for tearing the flesh of their victims. Their claws are sharp talons for catching and holding on to their victims. Owls have similar beaks and talons.

Insect eaters

Many birds prey on insects. Birds with short beaks, such as larks, flycatchers, thrushes and warblers, catch insects among the leaves of trees or on the ground. Treecreepers have slightly longer beaks for prizing insects out of the rough bark of trees. A woodpecker drills a hole into the bark,

then uses its incredibly long tongue to reach insects underneath. A woodcock has a long beak to help it find worms and insects in the soil. Swallows and swifts catch insects in the air. To help them do this they have mouths that open very wide.

Water feeders

Many birds feed on water animals. Wading birds have long legs and long bills for finding small animals in shallow water. Flamingos use their bills like sieves to strain their food from the water. Other birds catch fish in a variety of ways. Penguins and puffins chase fish underwater, while pelicans catch them by dipping their huge, scoop-like beaks into the water. Cormorants, herons and kingfishers also prey on fish.

Plant eaters

Plant materials are preferred food for a number of birds. Geese, swans and many ducks have flat beaks for grazing on water plants and grass. Finches and buntings use their short, stout beaks for cracking open seeds. Parrots have downward curving beaks for dealing with tropical fruits while the beautiful hummingbirds have very long, delicate beaks for drinking nectar from flowers.

Mixed feeders

Some birds eat a variety of foods. Pigeons eat many kinds of plant food. Tits, starlings and blackbirds eat insects, worms and plant material. Crows and gulls scavenge for what they can find. The kookaburra of Australia is said to eat absolutely anything; it is famous for its ability to catch snakes.

Courtship

Birds lay hard-shelled eggs in nests. Before this happens, male and female birds often go through a period of courtship. Courtship is like a special language. A bird calls and displays in order to attract the attention of a possible mate. Sometimes both birds display, but in many cases it is the male that displays to the female. Therefore, male birds are often much more brightly coloured than the females. The male's display may also

Below **A male frigatebird displays to his mate by half opening his wings and inflating his bright red throat pouch. At the same time he shivers and rattles his feathers. After mating the female lays a single egg, which both parents take turns to look after. The egg hatches after 55 days.**

Below **The peregrine falcon is a bird of prey. Its wings are designed for very fast flying. In level flight it can chase other birds at 80 km/h (50 mph). It may reach speeds of up to 290 km/h (180 mph) when it folds its wings and dives, or "stoops", on a victim. This peregrine is on the point of catching a goldfinch. One blow from the peregrine's talons will kill it.**

serve to warn off other males and can also indicate a possible nesting site to his intended mate.

Nesting and nestlings

When a male and female have established a bond between them, they mate. They may share the task of building a nest, but often the female does this by herself. Some birds build elaborate, cosy nests of moss and feathers, bound together with mud and saliva. Others build rough nests of twigs. Ducks and game birds, such as grouse and pheasants, build nests on the ground.

The female may lay just one egg or several. These are kept warm, or incubated, while the chicks develop inside. After they hatch, the chicks of many birds are naked, blind and helpless. They have to be fed and looked after by their parents for some time. The chicks of ground-nesting birds, on the other hand, are covered in downy feathers. Within a day or two, they can run about and find their own food.

Penguins are amongst the most endearing of birds. The one egg the female lays is passed over to the male. He tucks it under a fold of skin on his belly, on top of his feet, so keeping the egg warm and off the ice.

Below **A robin feeding a young cuckoo. The cuckoo's own parent substituted its egg for one of the robin's eggs and on hatching, the cuckoo chick threw out the remainder.**

MAMMALS

Mammals, like birds, are warm-blooded animals. They usually have a covering of fur, which helps to prevent too much heat being lost. All mammals suckle their young with milk after they are born, and many mammals care for their offspring for some time.

Egg-layers and pouches

Most mammals give birth to active young. However, there are a few that still lay eggs, like their reptile ancestors. These are the duckbilled-platypus and the five kinds of spiny anteater, or echidnas. Together these animals are known as the monotremes. They are found only in Australasia – Australia, Tasmania and New Guinea.

The pouched mammals, or marsupials, do not lay eggs. However, a young marsupial is born when it is still very tiny and poorly developed. It immediately crawls up its mother's belly and into her pouch. There it fastens on to one of her teats and begins to suckle, remaining permanently attached until it is quite well developed. A few marsupials do not have pouches, and in these kinds, the newborn young cling to the mother's fur.

Most marsupials are found in Australasia. Only the opossums live in the Americas. The best known Australasian marsupials are the kangaroos and wallabies. They have enormously powerful hind legs that they use for leaping across the ground. A large kangaroo can make leaps of over 10 m (32 ft).

Other marsupials include a number of animals that live in trees, such as the koala, the honey possum and the gliding possums. On the ground there are the bandicoot,

Below **The strange duck-billed platypus of eastern Australia is an egg-laying mammal.**

Hedgehog

Mole

Rabbit

Flying squirrel

Shrew

Rat

Capybara

Elephants

The largest living land animal is the African elephant, which may weigh over six tonnes and stand about three and a half metres (over eleven feet) at the shoulder. It and the slightly smaller Asian elephant form a mammal group by themselves. The elephant's trunk is a long tube made up of the nose and upper lip. It is used to smell, to pass food into the mouth and to suck up water, which is then squirted into the mouth or over the elephant's back.

Below **Hooved mammals are common in all parts of the world.**

Opposite **Hedgehogs, moles and shrews are insectivores. Flying squirrels, rats and the capybara are rodents.**

Above **Of the two kinds of elephant, the African** (right) **is larger than the Indian.**

wombat and marsupial mole. Marsupial carnivores (flesh-eaters) include the Tasmanian devil and the so-called native cats.

Hooved mammals

Many of the world's plant-eating mammals, or herbivores, walk on the tips of their toes, which have become hooves. There are two groups of hooved mammals. The perissodactyls have an odd number of toes on each foot. This group includes the horses, rhinoceroses and tapirs. The artiodactyls have an even number of toes. Hippopotamuses have four toes on each foot. The rest have two toes and are often known as cloven-hooved animals. They include the pigs, camels, giraffe and deer. The largest artiodactyl group is the cattle family, which includes many kinds of antelope, goats, sheep and cattle.

Placental mammals

Most of the world's mammals belong to the group known as the placentals. A young placental mammal remains within its mother's body for some time before being born. There it is nourished by means of a special organ called a placenta.

Zebra

Indian buffalo

Wild boar

Arabian camel

Elk

Giraffe

Rhinoceros

Rodents

The rodents form the largest group of placental mammals. They are gnawing animals that have a pair of chisel-like cutting teeth at the front of each jaw. They live mainly on plant material. Rodents include rats, mice, voles, hamsters, dormice, lemmings, gerbils, jerboas, porcupines and beavers. Also rodents are squirrels, chipmunks, marmots and prairie dogs. Rabbits and hares, although similar to rodents, belong to a separate group.

Sea mammals

One group of placental mammals has returned to the sea. They have streamlined bodies, and paddles and tail fins instead of legs. These are the whales, or cetaceans, of which there are two main kinds.

Toothed whales include the dolphins, porpoises and the sperm whale. They use their teeth for catching prey, such as fish or squid. Whalebone whales have huge filtering systems for straining tonnes of shrimp-like creatures from the water.

Above **Wolves, hyenas, lions, bears and seals belong to the carnivore family.**

Below **The whale group includes the dolphins and porpoises, and the huge baleen whales.**

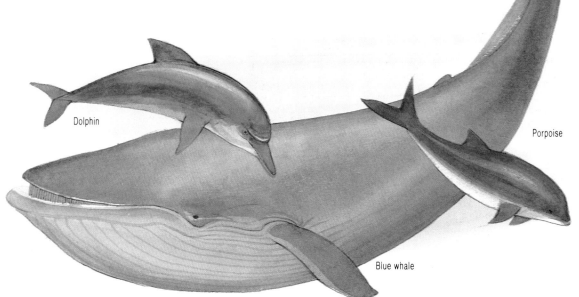

Mandrill

Gibbon

Orang-utan

Spider monkey

Gorilla   Baboon

Lemur

Chimpanzee

Primates

The group known as the primates covers the monkeys, apes and humans. Primitive primates include the tree shrews of south-east Asia, the lemurs and sifakas of Mada-gascar, the bushbabies of Africa and the lorises of south-east Asia.

Monkeys are divided into two groups. The Old World monkeys of Africa and Asia include the colobus monkeys, guenons, langurs, macaques, baboons and mandrills. Unlike most monkeys, these last two species spend their days on the ground. The New World Monkeys of the Americas have broader, flatter noses, with nostrils set wide apart. Many of them can use their tails to grasp the branches of trees. New World monkeys include the capuchins, howler monkeys, spider monkeys, tamarins and marmosets.

The apes are divided into two families. The first contains the gibbons, which use their long arms for swinging from branch to branch. The other contains the great apes – the orang-utan, the gorilla and the chimpanzee. These are among the most intelligent animals in the world and chim-panzees are probably the closest living relatives of human beings.

Carnivores

The group called the carnivores includes all of the world's flesh-eating mammals. The cat family covers the big cats, such as the lion, tiger and leopard, together with a number of small cats. The wolf, coyote, dingo and many foxes are members of the dog family. Polecats, badgers, sable, mink and stoats (as well as the weasel) make up the weasel family. Bears, raccoons, civets, mongooses and seals are all carnivores too.

Insectivores

The most primitive mammals belong to the group called the insectivores. This includes shrews, moles and hedgehogs. Shrews are very numerous, feeding mainly on insects, snails and worms. Moles spend their time tunnelling underground, where they eat earthworms. Hedgehogs, frequently found in fields and hedgerows, eat insects, slugs and snails. Bats are the only mammals that actually fly. Others, such as flying squirrels, can only glide. Most small bats feed on insects that they catch in the air. Some large bats feed on fruit. Vampire bats drink the blood of other animals.

Above **The primates include all the monkeys, apes – and humans. All these have five fingers. Their hands, and often their feet, can generally be used for grasping. Most have flat faces, with forward-pointing eyes, which give excellent vision.**

THE LOWER PLANTS

The plant kingdom is divided into several groups. The lower plants is the combined name given to three of these groups: the algae, the mosses and liverworts, and the ferns.

Seaweeds and other algae

Algae are plants that have no stems, roots, or leaves. Nearly all live in water, and the simplest kinds consist of just one cell. Other algae consist of a number of cells linked together. The pondweed *Spirogyra*, for example, is made up of long strings of cells.

The green seaweed known as sea lettuce has a "leaf" made up of two flat layers of cells. Others have more complicated structures. The most familiar algae are the brown seaweeds, such as the kelps and wracks.

Mosses and liverworts

Mosses and liverworts form a plant group known as the bryophytes. They have leaves and many have thin stems but they do not have true roots. Instead they cling on to the ground or to rocks by means of root-like threads called rhizoids.

Liverworts live in moist surroundings because they tend to dry out very easily. The simplest kinds have flat, sprawling plant bodies. Others have thin, filmy leaves on delicate stems. Mosses have distinct leaves arranged on stems. They form mats or small cushions on rocks, moist banks, trees and in bogs.

Liverworts and mosses reproduce with the help of spores. These are formed in capsules on the ends of long stalks. When each capsule is ripe, it splits open, releasing the thousands of spores inside. Spores that land in suitable places grow into new plants.

Ferns

Ferns have well-developed stems and leaves, but unlike mosses, they have true roots. However, these are generally quite

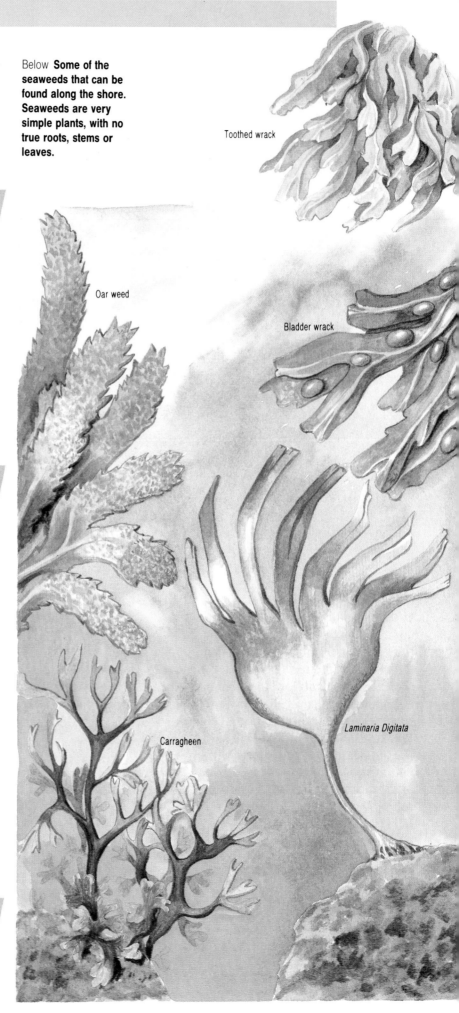

Below **Some of the seaweeds that can be found along the shore. Seaweeds are very simple plants, with no true roots, stems or leaves.**

Toothed wrack

Oar weed

Bladder wrack

Laminaria Digitata

Carragheen

Moss pixy cap

Chanterelle

Inkcap

Boletus

Amethyst agaric

Cup fungus

Earth ball

Death cap

small; a fern's main underground organ is a creeping stem called a rhizome. The leaves of some ferns are very simple, such as the strap-like leaf of the hart's tongue fern, while others have leaves that are divided into many small leaflets, or fronds. Most ferns are fairly small plants, but some tropical tree ferns reach heights of 2 m (6¾ ft). Close relatives of the ferns include the clubmosses and horsetails.

Ferns also reproduce using spores which are usually formed on the undersides of the leaves.

Bacteria and fungi

Bacteria and fungi are often grouped among the plants. However, these organisms have no plant features. For example, the cell walls are not made of cellulose and they do not contain the green material chlorophyll.

Bacteria are one-celled organisms. Some are round, others are rod-shaped, comma-shaped or form spirals. There are types of bacteria that can cause diseases. However, many more feed harmlessly on dead plant and animal material. In doing so, they release chemicals into the soil that can then be re-used by plants.

Some fungi also feed off decaying plant and animal matter. Others live off living organisms and cause disease. The most familiar fungi are those that produce large fruiting bodies, such as toadstools. Other fungi include moulds, mildews and yeasts.

Some fungi, such as mushrooms, can be eaten. Others are poisonous. Anyone eating the death cap is almost sure to die.

Above and right
Toadstools are the fruiting bodies of fungi.

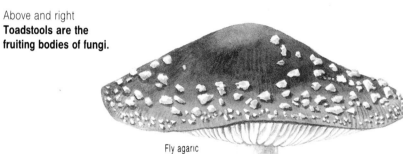

Fly agaric

Below **One type of fungus causes brown rot in apples.**

Bottom **Some different kinds of bacteria as viewed under the microscope.**

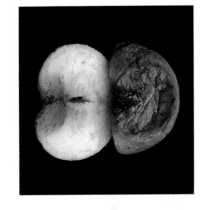

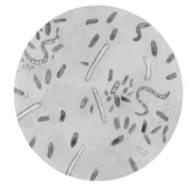

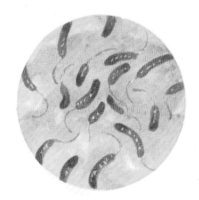

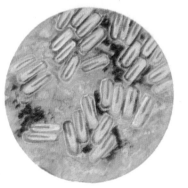

CONE-BEARING PLANTS

The higher plants all reproduce with the help of seeds. Cone-bearing plants, or conifers, produce their seeds in cones. These seeds are not enclosed in fruits as are those of flowering plants; they lie exposed to the air on the scales of the cones. Conifers are therefore included in the group of plants known as the gymnosperms. This name simply means "naked seed".

Conifers

A typical conifer has small needle-like leaves. They are tough and leathery and able to survive wind and frost. They also help to conserve water. Conifers therefore often grow where water is scarce. They can survive on very poor soils.

Most of the world's conifers are found in a broad band of forest below the Arctic Circle. The main trees of this forest are pines, spruces, firs and larches. Except for the larches, all these are evergreen trees. This does not mean that their leaves never die; in fact, each leaf actually lives for only three or four years. It is just that the leaves of a conifer do not all die at once. They are shed continually and there are living leaves present all the time.

Farther south, in Europe and Asia, grow such trees as the Mediterranean pine, the cedars and the cypresses. The cypress family includes the junipers, which have small blue cones that look like berries.

North American conifers include the coast redwoods. These are the world's tallest trees, reaching over 100 m (328 ft) in height. The giant redwoods are the world's largest trees; the largest is believed to weigh

Cypress

Larch

Scots pine

Douglas fir

about 2,030 tonnes (1,998 tons). North America also has the world's oldest trees – the bristlecone pines of the White Mountains in California. One of these is 4,600 years old.

Only a few conifers are found in the southern hemisphere. The monkey puzzle tree, for example, grows naturally in Chile.

Conifers actually produce two kinds of cones; male and female. The male cones produce a dust-like material called pollen. This contains special male sex cells. When the cone is ripe, it opens and releases clouds of pollen into the air. The process of transferring pollen from a male cone to a female cone is called pollination. Conifers depend on wind for pollination.

The female cones open up to receive the pollen and then close up again. Inside, the male cells from the pollen fuse with female cells. On each scale of the female cone two winged seeds develop. Two years later the cone opens to release its seeds.

Conifer relations

Several other plants are included among the gymnosperms. Yews have leaves that look like those of conifers. But their seeds develop partly enclosed by a red, fleshy "fruit".

The maidenhair tree is a native of China. It is the only living member of a group that flourished 130 million years ago. It has fan-shaped leaves and male and female flowers grow on separate trees. The hard seeds develop on the ends of stalks.

Cycads are palm-like, tropical trees. They also have separate male and female plants. Seeds develop in a large cone in the centre of a female tree.

Far left **The giant redwoods of California are the world's largest trees.**

Below left **Each kind of conifer can be easily recognized by the shape of the tree and its cones.**

Below **Conifers can survive extreme cold and poor soils. Thus they are often found in places where broadleaved trees cannot grow.**

FLOWERING PLANTS

Flowering plants are the most advanced group of plants. They are also the most successful. Scientists know of over 360,000 different kinds of plant in the world and 220,000 of these are flowering plants. Flowering plants produce seeds enclosed in fruits.

Biologists divide flowering plants into two main groups; the monocotyledons (or monocots) and the dicotyledons (or dicots). These names refer to the number of seed leaves, or cotyledons, that are present in the seeds.

Monocots

There are about 55,000 species of monocots. The adult plants generally have long thin leaves and flowers with either three or six petals.

The grasses form the largest and most important family of monocots. There are about 8,000 different kinds and they are found all over the world. We grow several grasses as important cereal crops, including wheat, rice, maize, barley, rye, oats and millet. Other monocots include such plants as orchids, lilies and daffodils. Tropical monocots include the palms and bananas.

Dicots

The dicots, or broadleaved plants, are a much larger group. Scientists know of more than 170,000 different kinds and they are divided into about 340 different families. Important families include the buttercups, cabbages, carrots (or umbellifers), daisies (or composites), peas, pinks, roses, heaths and lipped flowers (labiates).

Stems and growth

Most flowering plants are green-stemmed, or herbaceous, plants. In places where winters are cold, the stems and leaves of such plants generally die off in the autumn. Annual plants die off completely. Perennial plants produce new shoots in the following

Right **Many flowers are pollinated by bees. When a bee visits a flower, pollen from the anthers sticks to its body. This pollen may be deposited on the stigma of the next flower that the bee visits.**

Below **Wind-pollinated plants have large anthers and produce huge quantities of pollen. In some cases the anthers are produced in special male groups of flowers known as catkins. The female flowers develop separately.**

Rye grass

Hazel

Willow

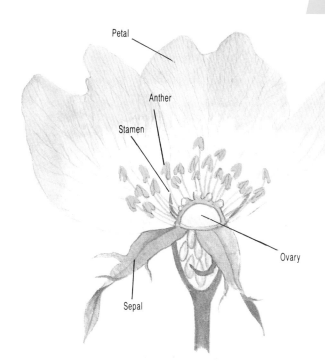

Petal

Anther

Stamen

Ovary

Sepal

spring. Many monocots grow new shoots from bulbs, corms or rhizomes. These are underground buds and stems which are used as special food stores.

Shrubs and trees are perennial plants with tough, woody stems. The wood is formed from water-conducting cells in the stem. Each year the stem, or trunk increases in size as new wood cells are laid down. This growth produces the annual rings that can be seen in a log or a tree stump. Dicot trees include the willows, birches, beeches, oaks and maples.

Flowers and pollen

The purpose of a flower is to produce seeds. Flowers contain the plant's male and female sex organs. Around these there is often a ring of petals, surrounded by another ring of green, leaf-like sepals. The male organs are the stamens. Each of these has a long stalk, at the end of which are bags of tiny pollen grains called the anthers. The female organs are called the carpels. Each one contains an ovary and has a pollen-receiving area called a stigma.

The first stage in seed production is called pollination. Pollen from a stamen has to be transferred to the stigma of a carpel. Ideally, pollen should be transferred to a different flower, or even a different plant. This is

Right **The bee orchid is pollinated by male bees that try to mate with the flower.**

Below **To prevent self-pollination, the primrose has two kinds of flower, with stamens and stigma in different positions.**

called cross-pollination. It helps to ensure that the new plants will be strong.

Wind pollination

Many flowers, such as those of grasses, are pollinated by the wind. Such flowers are generally small and not brightly coloured. They produce enormous amounts of pollen and have large, feathery or sticky stigmas. In some species the stigmas ripen only after the stamens have shed all their pollen. In others, the male and female flowers are separate and may even be on different plants. Both these features help to bring about cross-pollination.

Insect pollination

Flowers that are pollinated by insects tend to be brightly coloured, in order to attract them. Sweet nectar lures the insects to the flower's centre. Many insect-pollinated plants prevent self-pollination in the same way as wind-pollinated plants.

Spreading seeds

After pollination has been achieved seeds develop in the ovary. At the same time, the

Above **Attracted by nectar deep inside, a hummingbird pollinates a brightly-coloured tropical flower.**

Below **The flowers of the baobab tree are pollinated by bats.**

ovary wall becomes a fruit. The purpose of the fruit is to help spread the seeds as far as possible from the parent plant.

Many fruits and seeds are carried away by the wind. Orchids have tiny seeds that are easily blown away. Feathery parachutes or plumes carry away the fruits of dandelions and old man's beard. Fruits of birch, ash and sycamore trees have wings that help them drift away from the parent tree as they fall to the ground.

Birds and mammals also disperse seeds. They eat brightly-coloured, juicy fruits and the tough seeds pass through their bodies unharmed. Squirrels take nuts and acorns away and store them in underground stores. Some of these stores are then forgotten. Other fruits, such as those of goosegrass and burdock, are equipped with tiny hooks that cling on to the fur of animals.

Many plants disperse their own seeds. Some have fruits which are capsules that open up when they are dry, allowing the seeds to be shaken out. Others have pods or other containers that burst open when they dry.

Making food

Plants do not feed like animals. Instead they make their own food. They do this by using

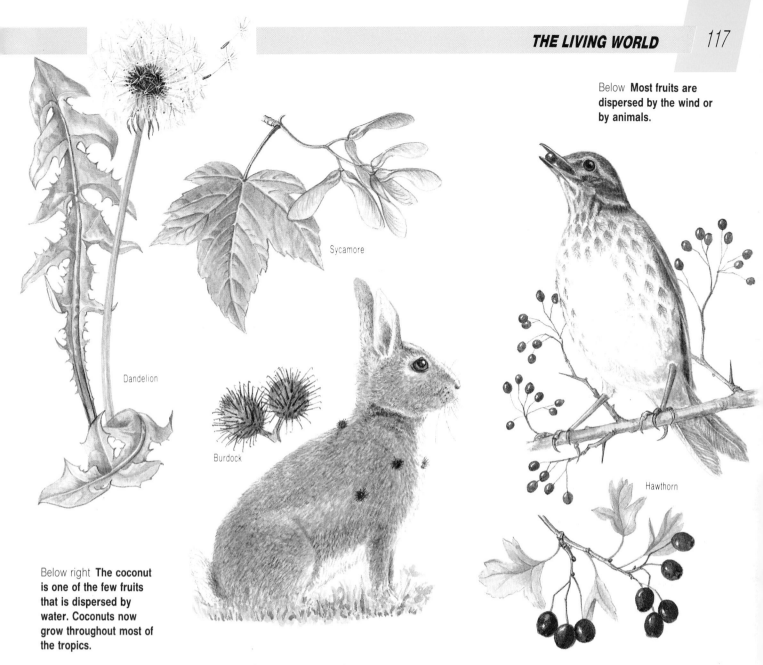

Below **Most fruits are dispersed by the wind or by animals.**

Sycamore

Dandelion

Burdock

Hawthorn

Below right **The coconut is one of the few fruits that is dispersed by water. Coconuts now grow throughout most of the tropics.**

sunlight to help them make sugar. This process is called photosynthesis.

Plants contain the green chemical chlorophyll. This performs a very special task; it turns the light energy from the sun into chemical energy, which is used to power a chemical reaction. The reaction takes place in the plant cells. There, carbon dioxide gas combines with water to form sugar and oxygen. The sugar may be turned into starch and stored. Or it may be converted into cellulose, the chemical from which plant cell walls are made.

Photosynthesis usually takes place in the leaves of a plant. Carbon dioxide from the air enters a leaf through tiny pores on the undersides. At the same time oxygen is released into the air. Therefore, plants not only make food but they also replenish the supply of oxygen in the air which is vital to all other forms of life as well.

SURVIVAL

Survival in the natural world is seldom easy. Animals are involved in a constant battle both to find food and avoid being eaten themselves. Also, plants and animals may have to find ways of coping with harsh conditions. Many have developed clever ways of ensuring their own survival.

Camouflage and disguise

Some animals disguise themselves in order to avoid being seen. Both predators (animals that prey on other animals) and prey are often coloured so that they merge with the background. This kind of colouring is known as camouflage. A lion, for example, is difficult to see in the dry grass of the savannah grasslands of central Africa. Green caterpillars are almost invisible as they feed on the leaves of plants. A female grouse can sit unnoticed on her nest in the heather because of her mottled brown colouring. A flatfish has a pebbly or sandy appearance that enables it to blend in with the sea bed where it lies.

Patterns often seem to break up the smooth outline of an animal's body. Some moths have wing patterns that allow them to "disappear" when they land on lichen-covered trees. Sometimes the outline of the body really is disguised. The sargassum fish, for example, which lives among sargassum seaweed, has many long outgrowths making it very hard to see.

Some animals go further and actually disguise themselves as pieces of plant material. There are caterpillars that look like short, winter twigs. Stick insects could be twigs or pieces of dead grass. A few insects look exactly like leaves; "chewed" edges and brown "blemishes" add to the illusion.

Below **Even "the king of the beasts" can merge astonishingly well into the background.**

Warning signs and bluffs

Many prey animals contain substances that make them unpleasant to eat. To advertise this fact, they are brightly coloured to warn off possible predators. A bird that eats a cinnabar moth or a monarch butterfly is promptly sick. Thereafter the bird avoids these creatures, recognizing them by their bright colours. Other animals with warning colours include bees and wasps, skunks, arrow poison frogs and many poisonous snakes.

Sometimes several different animals have the same warning colours. This makes it easier for predators to learn to avoid them all. For example, the well-known black and yellow stripes of the common wasp are also seen on several other harmful insects, including the caterpillar of the cinnabar moth. Yet other insects cheat. They copy the warning colours of other animals even though they themselves are quite harmless. Hoverflies, for example, have the same yellow and black markings as a wasp. As a result, birds avoid eating them.

A number of animals, particularly insects, attempt to bluff their way out of trouble with large eyespot markings. When these are suddenly exposed, a would-be attacker may be confused into thinking that it has disturbed a much larger animal.

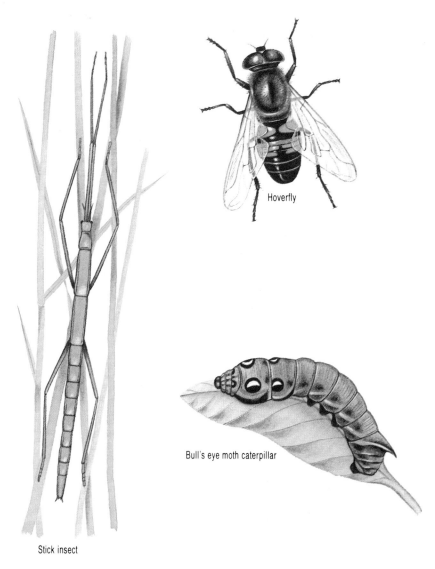

Hoverfly

Bull's eye moth caterpillar

Stick insect

Above **Three different ways of surviving attack. The stick insect resembles pieces of grass and avoids detection. The harmless hoverfly mimics a wasp. The bull's eye moth larva startles a predator with the owl-like "eyes" on its body.**

Left **The stink bug's bright colouring is a warning to predators. When attacked, it produces a foul-smelling liquid.**

Taking partners

Some animals and plants improve their chances of survival by teaming up with others. Such a relationship benefits both partners and is called a symbiosis. In some cases the two partners rely on each other completely for their survival.

Plant partners
A number of plants form close associations with fungi. An example is a lichen, which is not a single plant despite appearances. It is actually a combination of fungus and a one-celled alga. The fungus protects the alga and supplies it with water and minerals. In return it receives food that the alga makes by photosynthesis.

Left **Common dodder is a parasite of several kinds of plant, particularly members of the pea and heather families.**

Below **A lichen is a close partnership between a fungus and an alga. Lichens are often found on rocks or the bark of trees.**

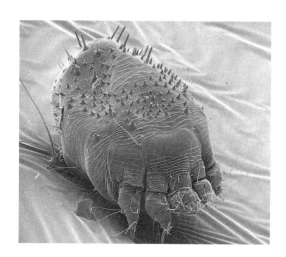

Left **Some mites are blood-sucking parasites, others do no harm to their hosts, and yet others are free-living.**

Below **A cleaner wrasse at work, cleaning parasites and dead skin from a client fish.**

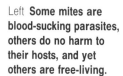

Sometimes plants and animals form relationships. For example, the spiny whistling thorns of Africa provide homes for ants. They live in large bulbs at the bases of some of the spines. In return, the ants defend the thorn trees against animals that try to eat the leaves.

Animal partners
There are also associations between animals. In many cases one partner is a "hitch-hiker". For example, some mites cling on to birds or insects in order to get about; they neither harm nor benefit their hosts. Other hitch-hikers provide some benefit: sea anemones, for example. The hermit crabs that carry sea anemones on their shells get some protection because the anemones have stinging tentacles. The anemones on the move probably get more food than they would attached to a rock.

Oxpeckers are African birds that ride on the backs of hooved animals, such as antelopes and zebra. They help to keep their hosts clean by feeding on ticks and other parasites that attack the skin.

Parasites

In some partnerships the relationship is more one-sided. Animals and plants that live on or in other animals or plants without giving anything in return are called parasites. They do not benefit their hosts in any way and may actually cause them considerable harm.

Parasitic plants include the mistletoes, dodders, broomrapes and toothworts. Many fungi are also parasites. *Rafflesia* is a parasite of tropical vines.

Parasitic animals

There are an enormous number of parasitic animals, most of which are invertebrates. Parasitic one-celled animals include those that cause the human diseases malaria and sleeping sickness. Tapeworms and liver-flukes are parasitic flatworms. Blood-suckers, such as mosquitoes, fleas and lice, are parasitic. In the case of ichneumon wasps it is the larvae that are parasitic, feeding on the bodies of other insects. Ticks and mites are parasitic kinds of arachnid and there are also many kinds of parasitic roundworms, molluscs and crustaceans.

Very few vertebrates are parasites. The only parasitic fishes are the lampreys, whereas among the birds there are about 100 kinds that lay their eggs in the nests of other birds. Such birds are called brood parasites; the cuckoo is the best known example. A female cuckoo removes one of the host bird's eggs and replaces it with one of her own. She then leaves the owners of the nest to hatch out the egg and feed the cuckoo chick.

Above **Oxpeckers perform a cleaning service for grazing animals by eating parasites.**

Below **In this partnership, the sea anemone helps protect the hermit crab from attackers. In return, it gets more food.**

Arabian came

Lanner falcon

Kit fox

Addax

Rattlesnake

Scorpion

Road runner

Desert Jerboa

Above **Cacti store water in their stems.**

Left **Desert animals deal with drought in several ways. Many of them never drink; they get water from their food.**

SURVIVING EXTREMES

Some regions of the world are gripped by icy cold for a large part of the year. Others are baked dry by the heat of the sun. Yet many plants and animals have found ways of surviving such inhospitable conditions.

Coping with cold and heat

The world's coldest places are the Arctic tundra and high mountains. Summers are very short and in winter there are biting winds, ice and snow. Plants living there are mostly low-growing, cushion-forming varieties. Many of them flower and seed very rapidly during the brief summer.

Animals in such regions often have a thick layer of fat under the skin. An extra thick winter coat of fur also helps to keep them warm. They generally have small ears and tails to reduce the area through which heat can be lost. Many of the large animals move to warmer regions during the winter. Some smaller animals hibernate; that is, they go into a sort of deep winter sleep in a sheltered spot. Others manage to remain alive under the snow, where they are protected from the extreme cold outside.

Desert animals and plants have very different problems. Water is vital to all living things, but in deserts it is scarce. In between the few rainstorms are long periods of drought. Some plants avoid such times altogether: their seeds lie inactive in the ground through dry periods. After a rainstorm, they quickly germinate, grow and flower. Within a few weeks they produce new seeds.

Other plants are able to tolerate dry conditions. Many store water in fleshy stems, leaves or roots. Some plants have roots that reach deep into the ground in search of moisture.

Desert plants lose very little water

Lemmin

Arctic fox

through their leaves. Cacti have no leaves at all. Their leaves have become spines.

In ordinary conditions, most animals lose excess heat by panting or sweating. But this involves losing water, so generally desert animals do not sweat. Large animals sweat only if their bodies get very hot. Desert foxes have adapted in a different way. They have large ears which not only help them detect prey but also help them to lose heat.

Migration

Even in more temperate climates, life can be difficult. Animals often migrate from one place to another in order to find food and avoid harsh conditions. Huge herds of grazing mammals, such as wildebeest and gazelles, migrate around the plains of Africa in search of fresh grass.

Most migrations are connected with the breeding habits of animals. They need to find the best conditions in which to raise their young. Birds are the best known migrators. In the north many insect-eating birds move south as their food becomes scarce in autumn. In spring they return to their breeding areas where they can be sure of an abundant supply of insects to feed their young.

Above **Mountain animals have adapted to living in harsh conditions.**

Below **Polar animals generally have a thick covering of fur or fat to keep out the cold.**

Migration is usually an ingrained part of an animal's way of life. Some animals always return to the same place to breed every year. To do this they often have to travel very long distances. The Arctic tern travels 17,700 km (11,000 miles) from the Antarctic in order to breed in the Arctic in summer while a female sea turtle may swim thousands of kilometres to lay her eggs always on the same beach.

Left **Many animals live all year round in the tundra.**

Below **Albatrosses travel all round the world, but always breed on the same islands each year.**

COMMUNITIES

Animals and plants do not live in isolation. They live as members of a delicately balanced population, or community. The world's largest communities are known as biomes. Each one contains an entirely different type of plant life. And the plant life that an area can support depends on the climate.

The world's biomes

The names of biomes reflect the type of plant life they contain. The coldest biomes are those of the Arctic tundra and mountain regions. They have small plants that can tolerate cold. Coniferous forest occurs in slightly warmer regions. In warmer areas still, the conifers give way to deciduous forest, with oak, ash, maple and other trees. Deciduous means that these trees shed their leaves in the autumn. They do this to avoid being damaged by frost in winter. Food is plentiful in deciduous forest, which therefore supports a large number of animals.

Deciduous trees need a fairly high rainfall so in drier areas the forest is replaced by grassland, such as the American prairies and the dry, tropical grasslands (savannah) of Africa. Grasslands are home to herds of grazing animals and the meat-eaters that prey on them. Very dry areas become deserts, where only specially adapted desert plants can survive. Tropical regions with a very high rainfall grow luxuriant rainforest. Tropical rainforest is the most productive biome and contains an enormously rich variety of wildlife.

Communities, food and energy

Within any biome there are an enormous number of smaller communities. Biologists call these ecosystems. An ecosystem is any self-contained community of animals and

Far right **A simple food chain forms part of a never ending cycle. Eventually, all waste material returns to the soil, where it can be taken up by plants.**

Below right **A deciduous woodland contains a rich variety of wildlife.**

Below **Each of the world's plant biomes is determined by climate – the average conditions of rainfall, wind and temperature that prevail in a particular region.**

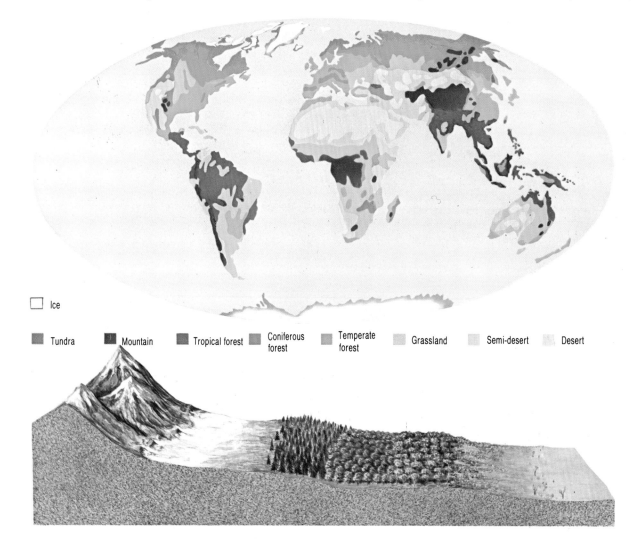

☐ Ice

■ Tundra   ■ Mountain   ■ Tropical forest   Coniferous forest   Temperate forest   Grassland   Semi-desert   Desert

plants living in a particular environment. A woodland is such a community. It may contain a wide variety of animals and plants, but the lives of all of them are interrelated.

Each animal in an ecosystem eats other living things. It may also be eaten itself by another animal. Thus it forms part of a food chain. However, most animals eat several kinds of food and as a result, several food chains combine to form a more complicated food web.

At the bottom of a food web are the plants. These are the producers in the ecosystem. They capture energy from the sun and store it in the form of food. Animals are consumers. When they eat plants or other animals, they use some of the stored energy to build up their own bodies. But only about a tenth of the energy is used in this way. The rest is used for such things as keeping warm and moving about. In the end, all the energy stored by plants returns to the environment as heat energy. The ecosystem also contains organisms known as decomposers – mostly bacteria and fungi. They break down animal wastes and the bodies of dead animals, supplying essential nutrients to the plants.

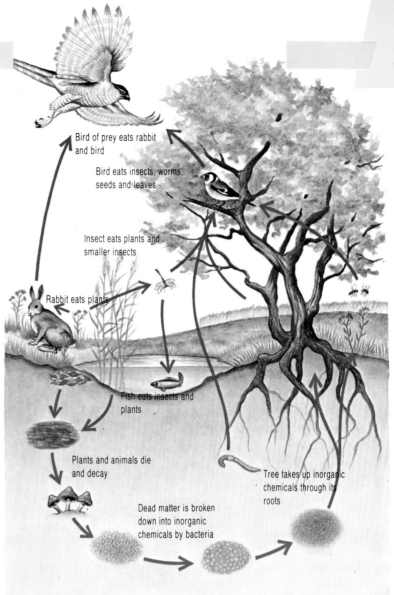

Bird of prey eats rabbit and bird

Bird eats insects, worms, seeds and leaves

Insect eats plants and smaller insects

Rabbit eats plants

Fish eats insects and plants

Plants and animals die and decay

Dead matter is broken down into inorganic chemicals by bacteria

Tree takes up inorganic chemicals through its roots

CONSERVATION

Throughout the history of life on Earth animals and plants have become extinct. This usually seems to happen because they cannot adapt to changes in their environment. Today, however, our own activities are causing animals and plants to disappear at an unusually fast rate. Many animals and plants have already died out; others are now close to extinction; and yet more seem to be extremely vulnerable.

Causes of extinction

Three human activities cause animals to decline in numbers. Many animals are hunted for food or for parts of their bodies, such as furs, skins, horns, tusks and shells, which man desires as trophies or as fashion items, such as fur coats. Food can be obtained without causing animals to become endangered, but unfortunately, humans are greedy and many animals are overhunted. Examples include several kinds of deer, cats, rhinoceroses, otter, whales and turtles.

Another way in which we endanger animals and plants is by introducing new kinds of animals into places where they did not exist before. This is often a problem on islands where native animals and plants may have evolved without having to deal with competitors or predators. In such

Above **The Serengeti National Park in Tanzania. Such places are a refuge for wildlife.**

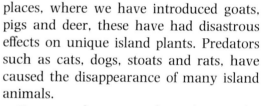

Below **An appreciation of our natural environment is an important first lesson in conservation.**

places, where we have introduced goats, pigs and deer, these have had disastrous effects on unique island plants. Predators such as cats, dogs, stoats and rats, have caused the disappearance of many island animals.

However, the activity that is having the most devastating effect on animals and plants is the destruction of their habitats – the places where they live. Without their preferred habitats plants and animals cannot survive. Over two-thirds of our endangered animals and plants have been brought to this state at least partly by habitat destruction.

This process has been going on for some 9,000 years, since man first started to clear land for farming and timber. In the process new habitats, such as moorland, were often created. But today we have the technology to destroy natural habitats at an ever increasing rate. Woodland, wetland and even moorland is fast disappearing to make room for more farmland, roads, factories and houses.

However, it is the speed at which the world's rainforests are being destroyed that is the cause of major concern to many people. No one really knows how fast these forests are being cut down, but since 1950 over half the world's rainforests have disappeared.

Conserving wildlife

We need to preserve the world's animals and plants for many reasons. They offer a potentially inexhaustible supply of raw materials. Without wildlife, this planet will become a barren place. Our own existence may be threatened if we wipe out too many plants and animals.

Fortunately, there are a number of organizations dedicated to conserving the environment and the wildlife it contains. International organizations, such as the World Wildlife Fund, operate throughout the world. Others are organized within particular countries. Anyone can play a part by joining a local conservation group.

Such organizations aim to teach people the value of wildlife and how to look after their own part of the environment. Very often, drastic measures have to be taken to conserve endangered species or habitats, and sometimes such measures are successful. For example, the Arabian oryx and the American alligator have, for the time being, been saved from extinction. But for many others help may come too late and they will disappear.

Giant panda

Indian tiger

American alligator

Above **The American alligator and the Indian tiger have, for the moment, been saved from extinction. The giant panda has become the symbol of conservation all over the world. But it is threatened with extinction because the bamboo forests on which it depends are disappearing.**

Left **Cutting down rainforest in Brazil to make room for beef cattle.**

Living World Factfinder

Adaptation A characteristic developed by a plant or animal which helps it live in its environment.

Algae Very simple plants which live in or near water. Most algae are very small but some, like certain seaweeds, are large.

Amoeba A tiny jelly-like animal which consists of one cell only. It reproduces by splitting into two.

Amphibian A cold-blooded animal which lives on land but breeds in water. Frogs and toads are amphibians.

Arachnid A class of arthropod animals which includes spiders and scorpions.

Arthropods A large group of invertebrates (animals without spines), which make up 80 per cent of known species. They have external skeletons and jointed legs, and include all insects.

Bacteria Tiny organisms with only one cell, usually classified as plants. Many feed on decaying plants and animals, and some spread disease.

Biome A large community of organisms living in a particular habitat, such as a desert, rain forest or grassland.

Botany The study of plants.

Carapace The external skeleton or shield of an animal. The shell of a tortoise is its carapace.

Carnivore An animal that feeds mainly on the flesh of other animals. Lions and tigers are carnivores.

Carpel The organ in the centre of a flower which is concerned with reproduction.

Cartilage Tough tissue which connects and protects bones in vertebrates. Some animals, such as sharks, have skeletons made of cartilage, not bone.

Cell The smallest unit of an organism, consisting of jelly-like protoplasm with a nucleus. All living things are made up of at least one cell.

Cereals Plants belonging to the grass family, which bear grains. They are an important source of food. Wheat, rice, maize, barley, oats and rye are cereals.

Chlorophyll The green pigment (colouring) in plants which enables them to use the energy from sunlight for photosynthesis.

Conifer A tree which bears cones containing its seeds. Most conifers are evergreen.

Convergence The resemblance between animals of different species which has developed because they have adapted to the same kind of life in different parts of the world. For example, the Australian spiny anteater has habits like the European hedgehog and looks very similar.

Coral The product of small sea animals called polyps which grow a hard, chalky exoskeleton. They often live in huge colonies and their remains form coral reefs.

Cotyledon A seed leaf of a plant. It is the first leaf, or pair of leaves, inside the seed, and contains food for the plant to grow.

Crustacean A class of animals belonging to the arthropods. Most crustaceans, such as crabs and shrimps, live in water, and have a carapace hardened with lime.

Deciduous plant A tree or shrub that sheds its leaves at the end of its growing season, usually in the autumn.

Dicotyledon A plant which has two seed leaves in each seed.

Dinosaur A prehistoric reptile known only from fossils. Dinosaurs of many kinds were the chief land animals between about 205 and 65 million years ago.

Ecosystem All living things and their habitat in a particular place. An ecosystem is studied as a single unit, like a body made up of many different parts.

Edentate A group of placental mammals, including sloths, anteaters and armadilloes which have no teeth or have very undeveloped teeth.

Embryo A young organism in the first stage of development, such as a bird before it hatches from the egg or the beginnings of a plant inside the seed.

Evergreen A tree or shrub that does not lose its leaves in winter. Evergreens do shed their leaves, but not all at once nor during one season.

Evolution The process by which species of animals and plants develop and change from more primitive forms over a long period of time.

Exoskeleton A skeleton which covers the outside of the body of an animal, such as the shell of a crab.

Family Part of an order of animals which are related and more or less alike. For example, lions, tigers and pet cats all belong to the cat family.

Food chain The way in which energy, which is obtained from food, passes from one living organism to another, beginning always with plants.

Fossil The remains or traces of an organism found in rocks. When plants or animals die, they are often buried in soil, which eventually turns to rock. Some remains of the dead organism may also turn to rock, or leave an impression in the rock.

Fungus One of a large group of non-flowering plants, including mushrooms and toadstools. They have no chlorophyll, stem or roots and cannot make their own food. Many are parasites.

Genus A group of different but very closely related species. A family of animals is divided into genera (plural of genus).

Germination The beginning of growth in the seed of a plant.

Habitat The type of place in which particular species of animals or plants live, such as the seashore, a pine forest, etc.

Herbaceous plant A plant with a soft, not woody, stem, which dies off above the ground at the end of the growing season.

Herbivore An animal that eats only plants, not meat.

Hermaphrodite An organism that has both male and female reproductive organs. Many plants are

Precambrian period

DEVELOPMENT OF LIFE
ON EARTH

Devonian period

Permian period

Triassic period

Mesozoic era

Jurassic period

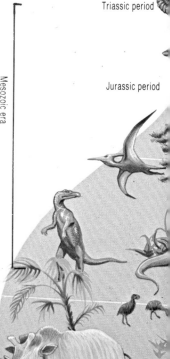

Quaternary period

ambrian period

Ordovician period

Silurian period

us period

Palaeozoic era

Cretaceous period

Cainozoic era

Tertiary period

hermaphrodites, and so are some simple animals, such as earthworms.

Hibernation Sleeping during winter. Hibernating animals use little energy and therefore need little food. Most reptiles and amphibians, and many mammals, hibernate.

Humus Decaying organic matter (remains of dead plants and animals) in the soil.

Larva A stage in the development of insects and some other animals, between hatching and becoming an adult. They are usually very unlike their adult form. For example, the larva of a butterfly is a caterpillar.

Mammals The dominant class of animals on Earth, to which human beings belong. They are warm-blooded animals with spines. Mammals feed their young with milk produced by the mother.

Marsupials An order of mammals which have a pouch for carrying their young which are still very undeveloped when born. They are especially common in Australia and include kangaroos, wombats and opposums.

Metamorphosis A complete change of form, as when a larva becomes an adult insect, or a tadpole a frog.

Molluscs A large group of invertebrate animals which usually, but not always, have a hard shell. They include snails and octopuses.

Monocotyledon A plant which has a single seed leaf in the seed.

Monotremes A group of mammals which lay eggs instead of giving birth to live young. The duck-billed platypus is a well-known monotreme.

Nectar A sweet liquid produced by plants to attract insects which help with pollination.

Nocturnal Active at night. Owls and bats are almost entirely nocturnal.

Order One of the divisions in which animals and plants are classified. An order belongs to a class and is divided into families.

Organism Any living thing, plant or animal.

Palaeontology The study of life on Earth in pre-historic times, based on the evidence of fossils.

Parasite A plant or animal that depends on another (known as its host) for its food.

Pelagic Living in the upper waters of the open sea.

Perennial A plant that lives for a number of years, unlike annuals or biennials.

Photosynthesis The process by which green plants absorb energy from sunlight to make the materials for growth – their food.

Placental mammals Mammals whose young are well developed inside the mother before they are born. (The placenta is the organ which supplies the unborn baby with food.)

Pollination The transfer of pollen from the stamen to the stigma, the tip of the carpel, in a flowering plant.

Predator A carnivorous animal which gets its food by hunting and killing other animals.

Primates The most highly developed order of mammals. They usually have flexible hands and feet (with five fingers and toes), large brains and good eye-sight. Apes, monkeys and human beings are primates.

Pupa A stage in the development of some insects which comes between the larva and the adult insect. The pupa is enclosed in a hard case while great changes take place inside. The pupa of a butterfly is called a chrysalis.

Rainforest Dense forest in parts of the tropics, where the temperature is always warm and there is heavy rainfall. Rainforest trees are mostly evergreen.

Reptiles A class of vertebrates which are cold-blooded and have tough horny-plated or scaly skins. Most reptiles lay eggs, and most are land animals.

Rodents An order of mammals which have sharp front teeth for gnawing. They are the largest order of mammals but most species, such as mice and squirrels, are small.

Scavenger An animal that feeds on the flesh of animals that have died or been killed. Jackals and vultures are scavengers.

Shrub A plant which has a woody stem but no main trunk and does not grow to a great height.

Skeleton The hard parts of an animal. In vertebrates, the skeleton is a framework of bone which supports and protects the soft parts of the body. In many invertebrates, the skeleton is outside. *See* Exoskeleton.

Spawn Eggs without hard shells that are laid in very large quantities by fish, amphibians or molluscs.

Species The smallest group into which organisms are classified. Parents of one species produce young like themselves, which in turn produce more young of the same kind.

Spore A single cell with a protective coat produced by certain plants, such as fungi, instead of seeds. Spores have no embryo and can grow into new plants without being fertilized.

Stamen The male part of a flower, which produces pollen. They are thin stalks or filaments bearing a sac of pollen, the anther.

Territoriality The behaviour of a particular animal which treats a certain area as its own property for feeding or mating. It will try to drive off another male of the same species.

Tuber A fleshy underground stem in certain plants, such as potatoes, used to store food for the plant.

Ungulate A herbivorous mammal with hooves. Horses and cows are ungulates.

Vertebrate An animal with a spine. All mammals, reptiles, amphibians, fishes and birds are vertebrates.

Zoology The study of animals and their way of life.

Zooplankton Tiny animals, mostly crustaceans and fish larvae, that drift in large masses near the surface of oceans and lakes.

An Introduction to Science

NATURE'S BUILDING BLOCKS

The world is made up of many different substances. A list would be huge and include things like rocks, lava, minerals, iron, dirt, bricks, wood, plastics, air, water, gas, oil, flesh, blood, and so on. All these things are different forms of matter, and matter is the stuff the world and the whole universe is made of.

Although there are millions of different forms of matter, they are made up from only about 90 basic "building blocks". These building blocks are known as the chemical elements.

Most things are made up of just a few chemical elements combined together. Water is made up of two elements, hydrogen and oxygen, while gold is made up of just one element, gold. Chalk is made up of three elements: calcium, carbon and oxy-

Below **Water appears in all of its three states in the world around us. As well as in its liquid state, it can also be solid ice, or gaseous water vapour, which then condenses to form clouds.**

gen. Chemists, the scientists who study the elements, call chalk calcium carbonate. This is its chemical name. The chemical name of a substance is made up from the elements it contains.

Elements and atoms

All elements are made up of extremely tiny particles called atoms. If an atom were broken open all that would be found is mainly empty space! In the centre is a piece of matter called the nucleus. It is made up of two kinds of particles, called protons and neutrons. Even tinier particles called electrons circle around the nucleus. The number of protons is the same as the number of electrons. The electrons and protons each have a tiny electric charge. They attract one another, and this keeps the atom together.

The atoms of most elements never change, no matter what is done to them. But some atoms can be made to split up. This is called fission or nuclear fission. When it occurs, enormous energy is given out. This energy is used in nuclear power stations to create electricity (see page 151). The element used for this nuclear fission is called uranium.

Solids, liquids and gases

All the many different kinds of matter come in just three different forms, or states. They can be a solid, like rock; a liquid, like water; or a gas, like air.

Solids have a definite size and shape. They are stiff, or rigid. The minerals that make up the rocks are solids. They sometimes form into the most beautiful shapes called crystals.

Liquids are not rigid. They flow, or move about. They take the shape of any container they are in. Water is the most important liquid of all. It covers more than seven-tenths of the Earth's surface. The human body is also made up of seven-tenths water.

Gases also flow, but they have no size or shape. They fill completely any container they are in. Air is the best known gas. Actually it is a mixture of gases, mainly oxygen and nitrogen. Most living things must breathe oxygen to live.

When the temperature changes, matter may change its state. This can be seen with water. If water is heated up enough, it changes from a liquid into gas (steam). If water is cooled enough, it changes from a liquid into a solid, known as ice.

Most materials will change state in this way if they are heated or cooled enough. For example, if gases are cooled long enough, they will change into liquids. The very cold liquid gases hydrogen and oxygen are used as fuels in the US space shuttle.

Below **A sugar lump is made up of many tiny sugar crystals pressed together. But inside each crystal are millions of these sugar molecules. Each sugar molecule contains 12 carbon atoms (black), 11 oxygen atoms (yellow) and 22 hydrogen atoms (red).**

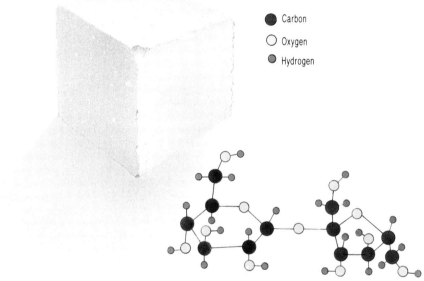

- ● Carbon
- ○ Oxygen
- ◓ Hydrogen

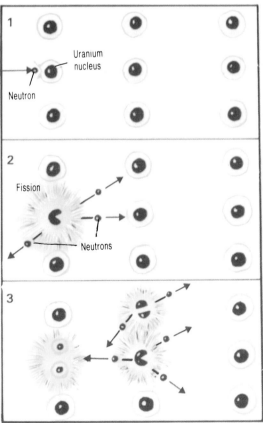

Left **Nuclear fission.**
1 Inside a reactor uranium atoms break apart when struck by neutrons.
2 Each atom then produces more neutrons which strike more uranium atoms.
3 These atoms in turn break apart and produce yet more neutrons. This chain reaction produces large amounts of heat.

FORCES OF THE UNIVERSE

When an apple is ripe, what happens? It falls from the tree. Why does this happen? Something pulls the apple back down to the ground. It is the Earth's pull, known as the force of gravity.

Gravity is one of the great forces of the universe. Every body in space – the Earth, the Moon, the planets and the stars – has gravity. The bigger it is, the greater is its pull. The Moon is a much smaller body than the Earth, and it has only one-sixth of the Earth's pull. This means that on the Moon anyone could clear at least 4 m (13 ft) in the high jump! But if this was tried on the giant planet Jupiter, the same jump would be only 25 cm (10 in), because its gravity is so great.

A rocket has to overcome the Earth's gravity to get into space. It does this by speed. But it must travel very fast indeed to beat gravity. Then it can go into orbit, travelling round the Earth. A strange thing happens in orbit – the pull of gravity is so reduced that astronauts and everything else became virtually weightless.

Below **Astronauts in a rocket notice that the pull of gravity begins to get weaker as they go further from the Earth. They can eventually float around the cabin. They can also do this in orbit around the Earth because the pull of the Earth is balanced by the centrifugal force.**

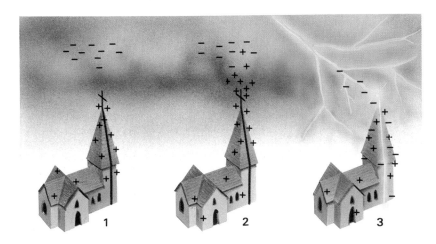

Left 1 **In a thunderstorm, large negative electric charges build up in the clouds and large positive charges on the ground. If the two charges become very strong, the negative charge suddenly moves towards the ground to neutralize the positive charge. As the charge moves through the air, it** heats the air so much that a flash of lightning occurs. It may also set fire to any object it strikes on the ground.
2 **A lightning conductor e.g. on a church steeple helps to neutralize the charges so that lightning does not strike.**
3 **If it does, the lightning strikes the conductor and not the building.**

Magnetism

When reading a compass, another force of the universe is being used – magnetism. The compass works because of the attraction between a big magnet and a little magnet. The little magnet is the compass needle. The big magnet is the Earth. The Earth acts as if it is a magnet, with one end near the North Pole and one end near the South Pole. The north end of the Earth-magnet attracts the N end of the compass needle. That is why the needle always points north. Other planets and the stars also have magnetism.

Electricity

Sometimes when you comb your hair, it crackles. If you then hold the comb above your hair, your hair will stand up. These things happen because combing has made your hair electric! Scientists say it has given your hair an electric charge. It has also given the comb an electric charge. The charge on the comb is different from the charge on the hair. We say one is a positive charge, the other a negative charge. And the positive charge attracts the negative charge, making your hair stand up.

Here is another force, between positive and negative electric charges. It is truly a force of the universe, because it is what keeps every atom together! Atoms are held together by the attraction between the protons (positive charge) and the electrons (negative charge).

The electricity of electric charges is known as static (fixed) electricity because the charges do not move easily. Ordinary

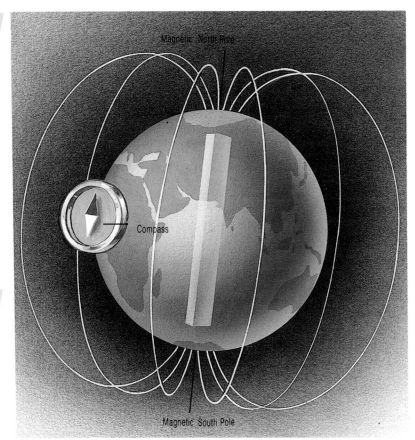

Above **The Earth acts as if it has a huge magnet inside and its magnetic field extends all over the world. The magnetic poles are near the North Pole and the South Pole, and a compass needle points towards the north because it contains a small magnet.**

electricity from a battery flows easily through wires.

Electromagnetic waves

Electricity and magnetism are not just found here and there in the universe. They are found everywhere in the form of waves. These are called electromagnetic waves.

Some of these waves can be seen. They are called light rays. The different colours in light are different kinds of electromagnetic waves. X-rays and radio waves are different kinds of electromagnetic waves that cannot be seen.

ELECTRONS AT WORK

When an electric light is switched on, the bulb starts to glow. The light comes from a thin coil of wire inside the bulb. The wire glows because electricity is passing through it and heating it up. Many other things in the house work when electricity flows through them – the vacuum cleaner, electric drill, hair dryer, TV set, and so on.

Electricity is a form of energy. It is very useful as it can be sent through wires to where it is needed. The electricity that flows into homes all round the country comes from the public electricity supply. This is called the mains. The mains electricity is made in power stations and travels through wires to the home.

Torches, calculators and personal stereos also work by electricity. But they get their electricity from batteries. In batteries the electricity is made by chemicals. The electricity from batteries is not very strong, but the mains electricity is very powerful, and if used carelessly can kill.

Electric currents

What exactly is electricity? Scientists say it is a flow of electrons. They are the tiny particles found in every atom. In some materials the electrons can be made to move about from atom to atom. And this is

what makes an electric current. Electric current flows best through metals. Metals are called good conductors of electricity. When metals are connected to a battery, power from the battery supplies a kind of "pressure" to start the current flowing. This electric pressure is called voltage.

Electric currents can do simple things, such as light a bulb or power a hair dryer. They can also be used to do more complicated things, such as carry conversations, music, messages, and TV pictures.

Electric currents carry conversations along telephone lines. In the telephone mouthpiece is a device called a microphone. This changes the pattern of sounds in the voice into a pattern of electrical currents.

Above **Modern electronic devices, such as computers, use tiny electrical circuits, called silicon chips.**

Below **A torch battery is a rod of carbon surrounded by chemicals. When the rod is connected to the bulb, the chemicals produce electrons.**

Below left **When a wire is connected to a source of electricity, the electrons begin to move in one direction and an electric current flows along the wire.**

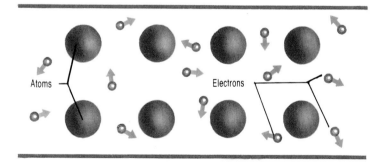

Atoms   Electrons

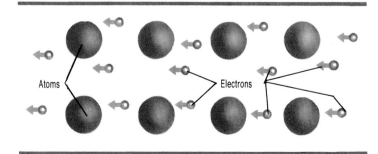

Atoms   Electrons

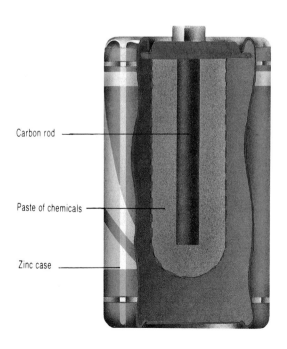

Carbon rod

Paste of chemicals

Zinc case

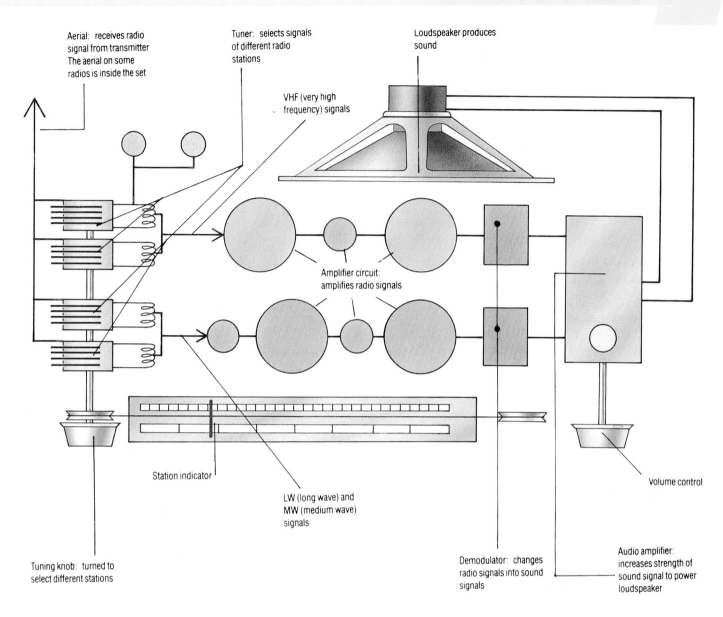

Aerial: receives radio signal from transmitter The aerial on some radios is inside the set

Tuner: selects signals of different radio stations

Loudspeaker produces sound

VHF (very high frequency) signals

Amplifier circuit: amplifies radio signals

Station indicator

LW (long wave) and MW (medium wave) signals

Tuning knob: turned to select different stations

Demodulator: changes radio signals into sound signals

Volume control

Audio amplifier: increases strength of sound signal to power loudspeaker

They flow through the telephone wires to the person you are calling. In that person's earpiece the pattern of currents make a little disc vibrate and make sound waves. These sounds are just like the words spoken into the mouthpiece.

In a similar way music can be changed into a pattern of electric currents. Then this pattern can be recorded on disc or tape. When the disc or tape is played, the pattern of currents is brought back and fed to a loudspeaker. The loudspeaker changes them back into the sounds of music.

Crystal chips

Electricity can also flow through empty space, gases and certain crystals, as well as through wires. The study of this branch of electricity is called electronics. This science

led to the invention of the pocket calculator and the home computer.

The most important part of each of these clever devices is a very thin wafer of crystal, smaller than a postage stamp. This crystal is made of silicon, and usually is called a silicon chip. The chip is made up of thousand upon thousand of electrical paths, or circuits. These are so tiny that a microscope is needed to see them. Scientists can design these tiny circuits so that they can count and do arithmetic. Then they can be used in watches, calculators and computers.

A much bigger and more familiar electronic device is the tube in the TV set. Inside the tube an electron "gun" fires a beam of electrons at the screen. Where the beam hits the screen, they make it glow. The picture is built up as the beam moves back and forth across the screen in a series of lines. The lines can be seen if you look at it closely.

Above **A radio uses an electric current to convert radio signals to sounds we can hear. When the radio waves strike the metal of the aerial, they make a weak electric signal flow along the aerial. This signal is amplified and then fed to the loudspeaker in the radio. The loudspeaker converts the electric signals into sound waves.**

Science Factfinder

Absolute zero The coldest temperature possible, $-273.15°C$. It is only possible in theory, but scientists have recorded temperatures one-millionth of a degree above it.

Acceleration The rate at which velocity changes with time. Acceleration is measured by the change of speed divided by the time taken.

Acid A substance which produces hydrogen ions when dissolved in water. The hydrogen can be replaced by a metal to form a salt.

Alkali A base which is a soluble metal hydroxide. Alkalis neutralize acids to form salts.

Archimedes (287–212 BC) Greek mathematician. He proved that the weight lost by a body in water is the same as the weight of an equal volume of water. He also invented a pump that worked on the principle of a screw.

Atmosphere The band of air around the Earth. The highest layer, called the ionosphere, extends roughly 400 km above the surface.

Atom The smallest part of an element that can exist. *See* molecule.

Biology The study of living things. It includes botany (plants) and zoology (animals).

Boiling point The temperature at which a liquid boils and turns from liquid into gas. The boiling point of water is 100°C at sea level. Other liquids have different boiling points..

Catalyst A substance which speeds up a chemical change without being changed itself. For example, platinum speeds up the oxidization of ammonia to nitric acid.

Centrifugal force The force that makes an object, which is travelling in a circle, move outwards. (A bucket of water swung around the head does not spill.)

Chemistry The science of the composition of things. Organic chemistry is concerned with carbon compounds (mostly in living things), inorganic chemistry with all other compounds.

Colour A quality, of any object, which can only be seen by the eye. The eye receives different wavelengths of the spectrum of light, and the colour of an object depends on which parts of the spectrum are not absorbed.

Combustion Another word for "burning". This is a chemical reaction, caused when a substance combines with oxygen and gives off heat and light.

Compound A substance consisting of two or more elements in a fixed proportion, which can be stated by a formula. For example. Water (H_2O) is a compound of hydrogen and oxygen.

Condensation The changing of a gas into a liquid. It is caused by cooling or by pressure. For example, steam condenses to water on a cold surface.

Conductor A substance that allows electricity to flow through it. All metals are electrical conductors.

Crystal A solid made up of groups of atoms or molecules in a fixed, regular pattern. Each grain of common salt is a crystal.

Curie, Marie (1867–1934) Polish physicist. Her research in radioactivity led to the discovery of radium.

Density The mass of a substance in relation to its volume. It is usually stated as kilograms per cubic metre, or pounds per cubic foot.

Distillation A method for purifying or separating liquids. The mixture is heated until vaporized, and the vapour is condensed. As liquids have different boiling points, they can be separated by this method.

Einstein, Albert (1879–1955) German physicist. His Theory of Relativity was the greatest scientific development of this century and changed our understanding of the universe.

Electricity A basic feature of nature which can be regarded as both a force, like magnetism, and a substance, containing electrons and protons.

Electrode A metal piece into and out of which an electric current passes, such as the terminals of a battery. The negative electrode is called the cathode, the positive electrode the anode.

Electromagnetism The related effects of electricity and magnetism. Electric currents have magnetic effects, and magnetic fields can produce electric currents.

Electronics A branch of physics dealing with the use of electrons. They are tiny particles circling the nucleus of an atom, and have a negative electric charge. Electrons can be set free by themselves, as in a cathode-ray tube.

Element A substance made up of atoms all of which are exactly the same. There are 92 elements in nature. All other natural substances are compounds.

Energy The ability to do work. There are many forms of energy, such as heat, light or electrical energy. One form of energy can be changed into another form, but energy cannot be lost or gained.

Evaporation A process in which liquid turns to vapour without reaching a boiling point. A little water left to stand in a saucer eventually "dries up": it evaporates.

Faraday, Michael (1791–1867) British scientist. Among many discoveries, he proved that a magnet can produce electricity – the principle of electromagnetic induction, which led to the invention of the electrical generator.

Fission Another word for "splitting". In nuclear fission, the nucleus of an atom splits in two, releasing nuclear energy.

Fluorescence The glow caused when light is absorbed at one wavelength and sent out at another. In a neon tube, ultraviolet light is turned into visible light by flourescent substances in the tube.

Force An invisible power which makes an object move, or change shape or direction. Examples are gravity and magnetism, and also wind and muscle power.

Frequency The number of times something is repeated in a set time. In the movement of waves

Top **A thermograph, showing body temperature. White areas are hottest, then red. Blue areas are coolest.**

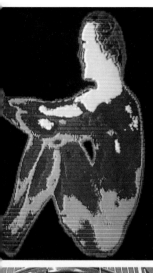

Above **An electron microscope. It achieves huge magnifications by focusing a stream of electrons instead of ordinary light.**

such as radio waves, the frequency of vibrations or peaks in the wave is measured in hertz (the number of cycles per second).

Friction The force that makes touching surfaces "stick". It is friction that makes a rolling ball slow down and stop.

Fusion The joining of two things as one. In a nuclear fusion (thermonuclear) reaction, such as the explosion of a hydrogen bomb, the nuclei of two atoms join together, releasing nuclear energy.

Gas A substance that spreads itself out to take up all the space available. A gas has no volume and no shape.

Gravity The force that draws any two bodies together. Gravity depends on mass. The large mass of the Earth creates strong gravitational force, so objects fall downwards. But gravity decreases with distance.

Heat A form of energy. When an object is heated, its atoms or molecules move faster than they did when it was cold. This causes a rise in temperature.

Ion An atom, or group of atoms, which carry an electric charge. This results from a loss of electrons (giving a positive charge) or a gain (giving a negative charge).

Lavoisier, Antoine (1743–94) French scientist, the "father of chemistry". He discovered oxygen and its function in breathing and combustion, and as a compound with metals.

Light Electromagnetic radiation which affects the eyes, making them "see". Some light waves, such as ultraviolet, are invisible, however.

Litmus A substance obtained from plants. In contact with an acid it turns red; with an alkali it turns blue.

Magnet An object which attracts iron and attracts or repels other magnets. When free to move, it points north and south, as in a compass. A magnet (or an electric current) is surrounded by a magnetic field with poles at north and south.

Mass The amount of matter in an object. Mass is different from weight because weight depends on gravity but mass is always the same. (You weigh less on the Moon, but your mass is unchanged.)

Molecule The smallest part of a chemical substance, consisting of one or more atoms. It cannot be divided any further and remain the same substance.

Neutron A particle found in the nucleus of all atoms (except hydrogen). Unlike protons and electrons, it has no electric charge.

Newton, Isaac (1642–1727) British scientist. His discovery of the laws of gravity was one of the most important single events in the history of science. His second great discovery was that white light really consists of many colours.

Nucleus The centre of an atom. It is a positively charged region, containing protons and neutrons, about which electrons orbit.

Ozone A form of oxygen which has three atoms in each molecule instead of two. The ozone layer in the atmosphere protects the Earth from too much ultraviolet radiation.

Particle A very small piece of a material. In modern physics the word is used to describe the components of the atom, such as protons or neutrons.

Physics The science of the study of matter and forces of nature, such has heat, light and motion.

Phosphorescence Light sent out by certain substances, as a result of a chemical reaction. Phosphorescence is different from fluorescence because it does not stop when the outside source of light ceases.

Pressure The force or weight acting on a unit area of surface. Atmospheric pressure is the pressure of the air on the Earth's surface.

Proton A particle found in the nucleus of all atoms. It has a positive electrical charge equal to the negative charge in an electron.

Radiation The spreading of energy by electromagnetic waves, such as light, radio, X-rays, etc. Heat radiation is the transfer of heat by waves, which is how the Earth is warmed by the Sun.

Radioactivity Radiation of gamma rays and alpha and beta rays. This is caused by the splitting of the nuclei of atoms in an unstable element, such as radium, as it breaks up.

Reflection The bouncing back of light or other rays from a surface.

Refraction The bending of light rays as they pass from one medium to another. It is easily seen by putting a straw in a glass of water.

Resistance The force acting against a change in motion, as water "resists" a ship. Electrical resistance is the force acting against the flow of current through a conductor.

Rutherford, Ernest (1871–1937) New Zealand physicist. His theory of the disintegrating (breaking-up) atom caused a revolution in physics by upsetting the old law that matter cannot be destroyed.

Silicon The substance used for making microchips (silicon chips), used in computers, etc. A huge number of complicated circuits can be carried by one tiny "chip".

Superconductor A substance which loses its electrical resistance at very low temperatures. Superconductors are usually metals. Researchers today are seeking other superconducting substances which do not require such extreme temperatures.

Thermodynamics A branch of science concerned with heat and mechanical energy, and how one is changed into the other.

Vacuum An empty space. As it contains no matter, there is no pressure. A *perfect* vacuum, however, is impossible in practice.

Waves Regular disturbances caused by movement. Sound waves make the molecules of the air vibrate, just as molecules of water vibrate when disturbed by a ripple.

X-rays Electromagnetic waves of very short wavelength. They can pass through matter (depending on its density) and can also affect a photographic plate.

Technology at Work

METALS AND ALLOYS

The most important of all the materials used are the metals. They are part of everyday life: bridges and skyscrapers, jet planes, cars, machines and engines could not be built without them.

Most of the metals used are strong and hard. They are also easy to shape, and they conduct, or pass on, heat and electricity well. But each metal has different properties, which make it useful for a certain job.

Iron is the most useful metal of all because it can be made into steel. Steel is very strong and quite cheap to make. That is why it is used to build machines and vehicles and to make tools and cutlery.

Aluminium is another very useful metal. It is strong and is much lighter than steel, but it is more expensive. It is used to build planes and spacecraft, which need to be strong but light. In the house, aluminium is used to make saucepans because it conducts heat very well. Copper is one of the best conductors of electricity. That is why it is used for most electrical wiring in the home and everywhere else. Quite a lot of tin

Below **A steel foundry is a hot and noisy place. The steel is heated until it is white-hot so that it can be forged into any shape required. The molten steel flows into moulds, and sets into bars. The hot bars are fed into huge machines which press them into steel girders, wires, rods, plates, and many other kinds of objects.**

Right **Steel is made in huge fiery furnaces. A mixture of iron ore, limestone and coke is fed into the top of a high, tower-like furnace called a blast furnace. As it descends through the furnace it is heated with a roaring blast of hot air. At the bottom, a white-hot molten mixture of iron and carbon called pig iron runs into enormous buckets called ladles. Then oxygen gas is blown over it, which burns off some of the carbon and turns the pig iron into steel.**

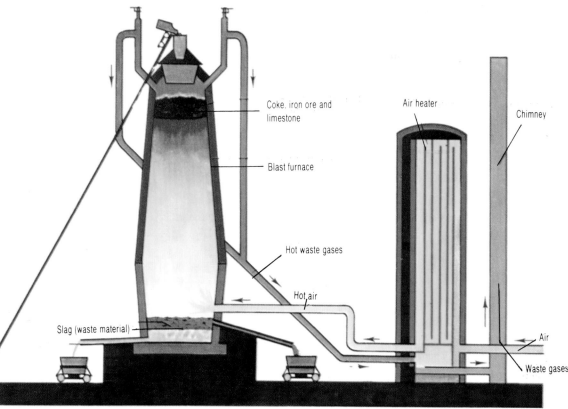

Coke, iron ore and limestone

Blast furnace

Air heater

Chimney

Hot waste gases

Hot air

Slag (waste material)

Loading truck

Air

Waste gases

is also used in the home, in the form of tin cans. Actually they are not made from solid tin, but from steel coated with a layer of tin.

Steel, one of the most useful metals, is an alloy of iron. This means it is a mixture of iron with small amounts of other metals and carbon. We use many metals in the form of alloys. Coins are made of alloys. "Copper" coins are actually made of bronze, a mixture of copper and tin. "Silver" coins are made from cupronickel, a mixture of copper and nickel.

Smelting and refining

Only a few metals are found in their pure form in the ground. The precious metals gold and silver are two of them. Most other metals are found in the form of minerals. These are often earthy substances that look nothing like metals at all. In a mineral the metal is combined with other chemical elements. Therefore the mineral has to be treated in some way to remove the metal. Minerals from which metals can be obtained are called ores.

Most of the iron used comes from ores called iron oxides, in which the iron is combined with oxygen. The iron is removed by smelting, or roasting, the ores in a blast furnace with coke and limestone. It is called a blast furnace because hot air is blasted through to make the coke burn fiercely, at temperatures up to 1,500°C (2,732°F). At such temperatures the iron melts and collects in the bottom of the furnace. But the iron is not very pure, and so it has to be refined, or made pure, in another furnace.

Shaping metals

Molten metals from the furnace are often poured into moulds and allowed to cool. They set into blocks or slabs. These can then be shaped in a number of ways, such as by forging (hammering) or rolling.

Molten metal may be shaped by casting. It is poured into a mould of the right shape, and takes that shape when it cools. This is just how a jelly is shaped in a jelly mould. The most common things made by casting are the engine blocks of cars. They are made of cast iron.

A variety of things made of metal. Steel is used to make girders and tools. Aluminium is also extremely important in making machinery, aircraft bodies (below) and kitchen utensils. Copper and brass are used in electrical fittings and cables. Copper is also used in coins, together with such other metals as zinc and nickel. Mercury is used in thermometers and other instruments.

PLASTICS

After metals, plastics have become the most important of the materials used in manufacturing. Plastics are found everywhere, especially in the home. Here are just a few of the things that are often made of plastic: bowls, buckets, cups, plates, heat-proof surfaces, washable wallpaper, squeezy bottles, flooring, insulation, shoes, boots, telephones, pens, guttering, light fittings, record discs, toys, carpets and clothes. And most items nowadays are packed in plastic bags.

There are many different kinds of plastics, but they are alike in a number of ways: they are all shaped by heating; they are usually

plastics also begin with "poly-". This is because of the way they are made. They are made in a process which joins together many small molecules into big long ones. "Poly-" means many.

Most plastics are shaped by moulding. They are heated until they melt, and then they are put in moulds. When they cool, they become solid and take the shape of the moulds. Some plastics are pumped into moulds under pressure. Some are pressed in moulds. Others are blown into moulds – this makes bottles.

Plastic film for bags is made by forcing the molten plastic through a thin slit. Heat-proof surfaces are made from thin layers of

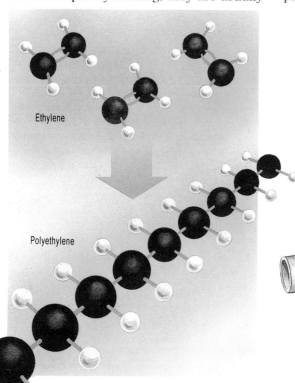

Ethylene

Polyethylene

made from chemicals that we get from oil; and they all are made up of long molecules. This means that their atoms are joined together in long "chains". This is what makes plastics special. Most other materials are made up of short molecules.

Plastics of many parts

Polythene and polystyrene are two of the most common plastics. Polythene is used to make see-through plastic bags; polystyrene is used to make the light white foam packing. The names of some of the other

Below left **Polyethylene is used to make plastic bottles and bowls. It is made from the gas ethylene, which has small molecules containing only six atoms. In polyethylene, the carbon atoms join to form molecules containing chains of thousands of atoms.**

Below **Two types of plastic moulding machines, producing plastic tubing** (top) **and combs** (bottom).

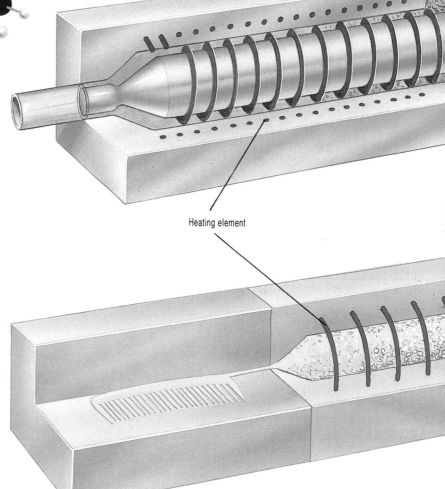

Heating element

Right **The hull of a boat made from fibre-glass. The combination of plastic and glass is very tough and hard-wearing – ideal for withstanding rough seas.**

Bottom **A bath shaped in plastic is being checked at a factory.**

plastics. Sometimes plastics are strengthened with other materials. Fibreglass is plastic strengthened by thin strands of glass. It is very tough and hardwearing, and is used to make things like suitcases and boat hulls.

Some plastics make really good glues, or adhesives. They are even used in the aircraft industry to stick parts of planes together! In the home we use them to mend plates and other objects that get broken. The latest plastic "superglues" are very strong and stick anything instantly, including fingers!

Synthetic fibres

Nylon is another very useful plastic, and is used for making toys and many machine parts. It is also used in the form of fibres to make carpets, curtains, socks and shirts. Nylon is called a synthetic fibre. "Synthetic" means "made from chemicals".

To make nylon fibres, lumps of nylon plastic are melted in a small furnace. Then the liquid plastic is forced through the tiny holes of a cap called a spinneret. The nylon comes out as thin streams, which harden into long threads.

There are other synthetic fibres such as polyesters and acrylics. They are made in a slightly different way from nylon. All the synthetic fibres are much stronger than natural fibres such as cotton and wool. Also they do not absorb water. This means that they "drip-dry" quickly. Another important use of polyester is in the manufacture of plastic bottles for soft drinks.

MANUFACTURING

These days most of the clothes worn, the goods used and the vehicles used for transportation are made in factories. In the factories, people use machines to make materials such as fibres, metals and plastics into the products we buy. This process is known as manufacturing.

The word "manufacturing" actually means "making by hand". Many years ago most goods were made by hand, but today they are mostly made by machines. Machines work faster than human beings, and do not get tired.

People started using machines in their work just over 200 years ago, in the spinning industry. Mill owners put many spinning machines in a building and paid people to work them. These were the first factories. They brought about what is called the Industrial Revolution (see page 79), and set the pattern for manufacturing that has been followed ever since.

Accurate parts

Most of the articles used today are made by joining together a number of parts. For example, a bicycle is made up of two wheels, a frame, handlebars, pedals, a chain, and so on. In the bike factory workers put together, or assemble, all these pieces into complete bikes. To do this, all the parts must fit together exactly. If they did not fit together properly they would soon fall apart.

All the parts are made using accurate machines called machine tools. These machines have powerful motors and sharp tools. The tools cut, drill and grind each metal part until it is exactly the right shape and size, so that it will fit the other parts exactly.

In some factories each worker makes a complete product themselves, by fitting together all the various parts. In other factories each worker only fits one part of the product. The product is built up bit by bit as it passes along a line of workers. This is called an assembly line. Because the workers each have to do the same thing time and time and time again, they can do it very quickly. This means that the products can be made much faster.

Above **Spinning yarn in a factory. Automatic machines now do the work hundreds of workers used to carry out.**

Below **A motor cycle assembly line in Japan. The machines are mounted on a conveyor belt which runs past the workers. They each perform a task before the finished product emerges at the end of the line.**

Right **A robot can be programmed to make a variety of movements. The arm can move in and out, the "shoulder" allows the arm to be raised and lowered, and the "waist" action allows the robot to swing from side to side. The "hand" can move in lots of different ways, too. Robots can be programmed to make a sequence of movements and so can be used on assembly lines to do repetitive jobs.**

Below right **Robots at work in a car factory. Their actions are controlled by a computer.**

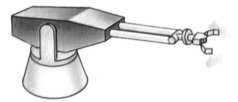

Most cars are made on an assembly line. They start off as a skeleton frame. Workers then add parts to this frame – engine, wheels, doors, brakes – as it is carried past them on a conveyor. By the time the car has reached the end of the assembly line, it is complete, ready for the road. In recent years robots have started working on assembly lines, side by side with human workers. They carry out unpleasant jobs such as welding and paint spraying.

Automation

Most of the robots used in industry work automatically without a human operator. So do many of the other machines, and sometimes even whole factories! These automatic machines are looked after by computer. The computer checks everything they do and corrects them if they start going wrong. Using automatic machines on a large scale is known as automation.

One of the best examples of automation is found at an oil refinery. Here there are many tanks, pipes and tall towers. But there is hardly anyone around – only a few people in a control room, watching lots of instruments, lights and dials.

THE CONSTRUCTION INDUSTRY

Human beings have been changing the face of the Earth for thousands of years, and are still doing so today. The landscape is changed by constructing, or building all kinds of things to improve our lives in one way or another. Roads are built to make it easier to travel from place to place. Bridges are built to take our roads and railways across streams and valleys, while tunnels take them under rivers or through mountains. Dams are constructed across rivers to make lakes and provide hydroelectricity (see p. 150). Enormous "skyscraper" office blocks are built to make the most of the limited building space in our cities. Almost everywhere you look, new homes are being built.

Preparing the ground

In most construction projects one of the biggest tasks is earth-moving. The construction site has to be cleared of trees, rocks and other obstacles, and the ground then has to be dug out, or excavated. To do this work, engineers use all kinds of powerful machines. They use bulldozers to level the ground, uproot trees and clear rocks. They use scrapers to move large amounts of soil.

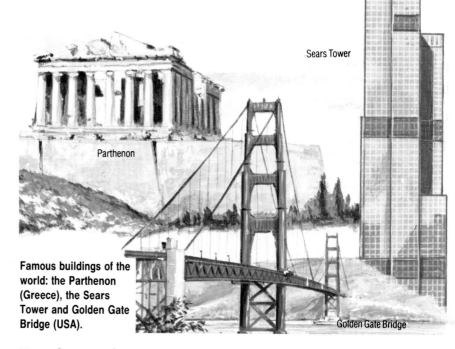

Famous buildings of the world: the Parthenon (Greece), the Sears Tower and Golden Gate Bridge (USA).

Sears Tower

Parthenon

Golden Gate Bridge

You often see these machines at work in roadbuilding, scooping up the soil in their huge bowls.

Different types of excavators are used for digging. Some remove the soil using buckets, which they drag over the ground by cable. Others have their digging buckets on the end of hinged arms. These excavators and the bulldozers mentioned earlier usually run on caterpillar tracks. These are endless belts of flat plates. They help the machines move more easily over rough and wet ground.

Below **The workers have dug deeply into the ground to make the foundations for a new building.**

Below **A dramatic shot of a motorway flyover under construction.**

Below right **A skyscraper being built using steel and concrete.**

One reason for excavating the ground on a construction site is to lay foundations, the solid base on which a structure can safely be built. A huge structure like a skyscraper needs very strong foundations, otherwise it will sink into the ground.

If possible, engineers like to build directly onto solid rock, which makes the strongest foundations. But this is not often possible. So they usually build concrete foundations instead. This is a large block of concrete, which is reinforced (made stronger) with steel rods.

Building the structure

The most common materials used in construction work are steel and concrete. They are often used together to make a material that is strong and hard and can stand up to the weather. Skyscrapers are built with a steel frame, which is then covered with concrete. In this way buildings can be constructed hundreds of metres high. The biggest at present is the Sears Tower in Chicago, which soars to a height of 443 m (1,453 ft). It has 110 storeys.

The strength of steel also makes it possible to build huge bridges. In a suspension bridge the deck, or roadway, of the bridge hangs from a pair of thick steel cables. The cables drop down from two tall towers.

The strength of dams usually comes from their great weight. This stops the water behind them from pushing them over. Dams certainly are heavy. The Grand Coulee dam in North America weighs no less than 20 million tonnes (19.6 million tons)! It is made of reinforced concrete.

FUEL AND POWER

Everyday the world uses large amounts of energy, or power. At home power is used every time the lights or the television are switched on, the central heating is turned up, or a hot meal is prepared on the cooker. Cars, buses, trains and other vehicles use power to keep moving. Machines in our factories, in our mines and on our farms use power to produce the goods we need and the food we eat.

Where does all this power come from? Most of it comes in one way or another from burning fuels. When fuels burn, they give out energy as heat. This energy is then used to make electricity or to drive machines. The first fuel people used long ago was wood. But today the main fuels are coal, oil and gas. These fuels give out a lot of heat when they burn. They are found underground in various parts of the world and are removed by mining or drilling.

Getting the coal

Coal is a fossil fuel. It is the remains of giant trees and ferns that have rotted and been compressed over millions of years.

We reach the coal seams (layers) by mining. In places the seams lie near the surface. Then they can be worked by surface, or opencast mining. Huge dragline excavators first strip off any soil. Then power shovels move in to break up and load the coal into trucks or railway wagons. Some of the excavators are massive: the largest, called Big Muskie, weighs 12,000 tonnes (11,785 tons). Its digging bucket is larger than a dumper truck!

Going underground

In many countries coal is found hundreds of metres underground. An underground coal mine is also called a pit. To reach the coal, miners first bore shafts (holes) into the ground down to the coal seam. Then they dig tunnels along the seam, removing the coal as they go. In many mines a number of seams are worked at different levels. The miners travel along these tunnels to the coal face by railway.

At the coal face, the miners work with powerful cutting machines called shearers and trepanners. These machines slice away the coal as they travel along the coal face. The roof of the area in which they are working is held up by steel supports, or props. The props are moved forward after each pass of the cutting machine.

The miners travel to and from the various levels in the mine in lifts or cages. Other cages carry the coal that has been cut up to the surface. The coal is carried to these cages by long moving conveyor belts or by railway wagons.

Above **When oil was formed in the rocks, so was gas. And this is another valuable fuel. Often it is called natural gas, because it occurs naturally. Some of it comes up with the oil in oil wells, but most is found by itself and in vast amounts. We can tap this gas by drilling in the same way as with oil. Some of the world's largest gas fields are also in the North sea.**

Left **Oil is a fossil fuel, like coal. It is the remains of tiny plants and animals that lived millions of years ago in the seas. These plants and animals died, fell to the bottom of the sea and started to rot. They were then covered in mud and sand and turned into slime. Over millions of years the mud and sand became rock, and the slime became oil. The oil then became trapped in various places in the rocks.**

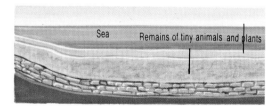
Sea — Remains of tiny animals and plants

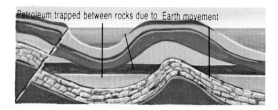
Petroleum trapped between rocks due to Earth movement

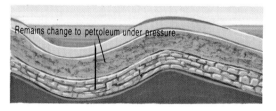
Remains change to petroleum under pressure

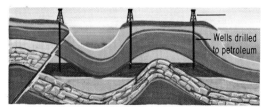
Wells drilled to petroleum

Oil and gas

Coal used to be the world's most important fuel. But now oil is more important. Also called petroleum (rock oil), some 5,000 million litres (1,100 million gallons) of it is used every day worldwide.

This is about 1 litre (1.6 pints) for every man, woman and child on the Earth! Most of the oil is used as fuel for cars, buses, trucks and aircraft. The rest is used to make chemicals. These chemicals are then made into such things as plastics, drugs, dyes, insecticides and explosives.

Drilling the wells

Oil engineers "mine" the oil by drilling holes down to it. But first they have to find it, which is often very difficult. They use various methods to look for the kinds of rocks that trap oil. In one method they use explosives to send shock waves through the rocks. Then they record how these shock waves bounce back from the rock layers.

When they think that oil may be trapped below, they drill into the ground from a tall steel tower, or drilling rig. They drill using a cutting bit, which turns on the end of long lengths of pipe joined together. Sometimes they drill several kilometres deep and find

nothing. But if they are lucky, they find, or "strike" oil. The oil bubbles up to the surface through the hole they have drilled.

Drilling for oil takes place at sea as well as on land. Some of the world's biggest oilfields are found offshore, for example, in the North Sea. Drilling for oil at sea is even more difficult, and has to be done from ships or special floating rigs. When oil is found, a production platform has to be built on the seabed. This may be made of steel or concrete. Above this, on the surface, is the production rig.

Transporting and refining

From the oilfields, the oil is carried in various ways to where it is needed. It is pumped through pipelines on the seabed and overland. Overseas it is carried by huge oil tankers. These are among the largest ships afloat. Some can carry half a million tonnes of oil in their tanks!

By pipeline or tanker, the oil arrives at a refinery. This is the place where the oil is turned into useful products. By itself it is a thick, blackish goo, of little use. But the refinery turns it into petrol (for cars), diesel fuel (for buses, lorries and cars) kerosene (for aircraft) and heating oil (for home heating). The refinery also changes it into hundreds of chemicals for use in industry.

Above **This pipeline in Alaska carries oil from the remote oilfields to terminals, from where it is transported overseas by tankers.**

Below **In modern coal-mines, the coal is cut from the face by special machines called shearers. Explosives are sometimes used to break up the face. As the coal is cut, it is carried back to the shaft on a conveyor belt or in small trucks that run on rails. The coal is then taken up to the surface in the lift.**

FUEL AND POWER – ENGINES

The world is full of machines. To work, these machines need an engine. An engine is a machine that can use the energy in a fuel to produce movement. This movement can then be used to drive another machine, an electricity generator for example.

Petrol and diesel engines

The petrol engine used in cars is a complicated machine made up of some 150 moving parts. But the way in which it works can be explained quite simply. The engine is made up of a number of cylinders (tubes), in which pistons (solid cylinders) move up and down. Petrol is mixed with air to form an explosive vapour (gas). This is then sucked into the top of the cylinders above the pistons.

Electric sparks explode the petrol vapour to produce hot gases. These gases force the pistons down the cylinders. This movement turns round a shaft called a crankshaft. The crankshaft then connects with other shafts in the car's transmission, which turn the wheels.

Different systems, or groups of parts, work together to make the engine go. For example, the ignition system produces the sparks to explode the fuel. It uses the electricity from the car's battery. The car engine becomes hot as the fuel burns. So it has a cooling system to keep it cool. Water is pumped through the engine to take away the heat. It is cooled by the car's radiator, and pumped back through again. The engine also has a lubrication system, which keeps the moving parts oiled. Without oil, the parts would grind together and stop the engine.

A diesel engine works much like the petrol engine. But it uses a light oil for fuel. The other main difference is that sparks are not used to explode the oil. The oil burns when it is injected into hot air in the cylinders.

Turbines

Other kinds of engines produce power from fuels in a different way. They burn fuel to produce hot gases, and then let the gases pass through turbines. As they pass through, the gases make the turbines spin. Turbines are rather like pinwheels, which spin when blown on.

In industry, gas turbines are used to drive machinery. Other kinds of gas turbines are used to power aircraft. In a turboprop aircraft engine, the turbines drive a propeller. A jet aircraft engine is rather different. It has a turbine, but its driving power comes from the jet of gases that stream from it.

Some of the most powerful engines on land are steam turbines. These are modern versions of the steam engine, which was the first engine to be used widely in industry. In a steam turbine, steam produced in a boiler forces its way through the turbine wheels and spins them round. In a steam ship, the turbine turns a shaft carrying the propeller. In power stations, the turbine turns a generator, a machine that produces electricity. Hydroelectric power stations, on the other hand, use water turbines to spin the generators.

Right **The petrol engine is the form of internal combustion engine most used in cars. It relies on a lubrication system (shown in green) using engine oil, to prevent friction between moving parts. A cooling system, in which water (red for hot, blue for cold) circulates through the engine, is also essential, to stop the engine over-heating.**

Below right **Diesel engines are often used in railway locomotives. In this cutaway diagram, the diesel engine is shown in position. It drives an electric generator which, in turn, produces electric power that drives motors situated in the wheels.**

Below left **Inside the jet engine of an airliner, burning fuel heats air passing through the engine. This makes the air expand, raising the air pressure inside the engine. The hot high-pressure air forces the engine forward as it streaks from the exhaust.**

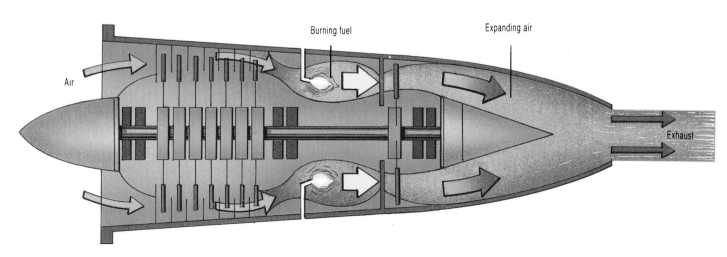

Air   Burning fuel   Expanding air   Exhaust

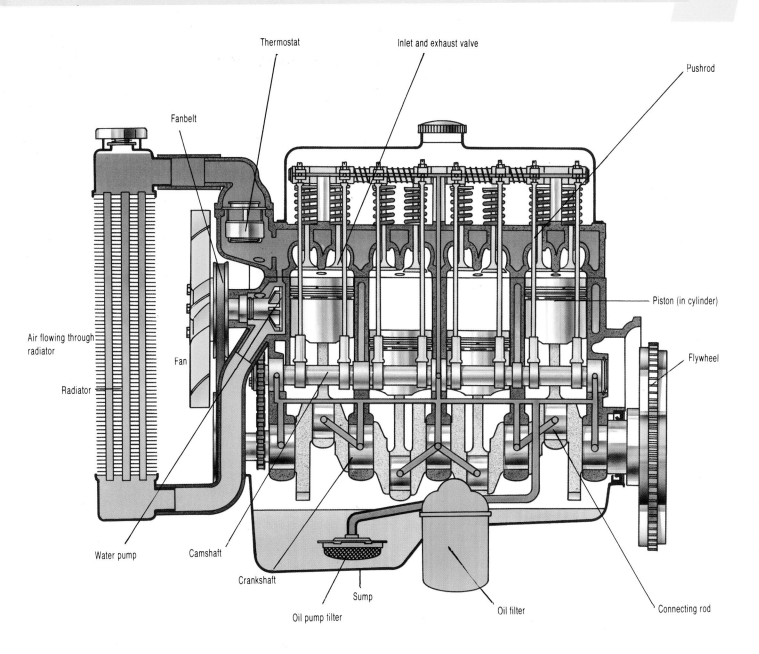

Thermostat

Inlet and exhaust valve

Pushrod

Fanbelt

Air flowing through radiator

Radiator

Fan

Piston (in cylinder)

Flywheel

Water pump

Camshaft

Crankshaft

Oil pump filter

Sump

Oil filter

Connecting rod

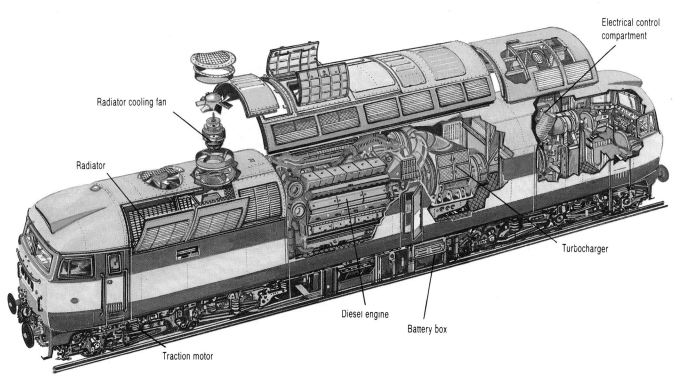

Electrical control compartment

Radiator cooling fan

Radiator

Turbocharger

Traction motor

Diesel engine

Battery box

150

ALTERNATIVE ENERGY

Oil was formed in the rocks millions of years ago, and is now our most important fuel. But so much is being used that it could soon run out. This could happen in the next 50 years. Natural gas will not last for much longer. And in time coal will run out too. What will provide power when this happens?

An alternative is the power provided in nature. Past generations harnessed the power of water flowing in the rivers and of wind blowing in the air. It may also be possible to harness the energy of the Sun and the heat locked up in underground rocks. A certain amount of water, wind and solar power is already in use, especially in those countries where fossil fuels are in short supply. Nuclear energy is also another source of power.

Running water

In the old days people tapped the energy of flowing water with waterwheels. Today, engineers use water turbines, which look rather like a ship's propeller. They direct the water through the turbines, and connect the turbines to electricity generators. The water spins the turbines, the turbines turn the generators, and the generators produce electricity. Electricity generated in this way is called hydroelectricity ("water-electricity"). The water to run hydroelectric power stations comes from great storage lakes, or reservoirs. The reservoirs are usually made by building dams across river valleys (see page 145).

Another kind of hydroelectric scheme uses the rise and fall of the tides to produce power. Water is trapped at high tide (high water level). At low tide water is let out through the turbines. A tidal power plant like this has been working successfully on the River Rance in north-western France since 1966.

Wind and wave power

The power blowing in the wind can be harnessed with wind turbines. These are the modern version of the old windmills,

Right **Wind power can be harnessed, using wind turbines. Modern designs use propellers carried on steel towers. The combined energy of hundreds of turbines can generate a considerable amount of electricity.**

Bottom **Satellites carry large solar panels. These trap solar energy in space, which is used to power them in orbit.**

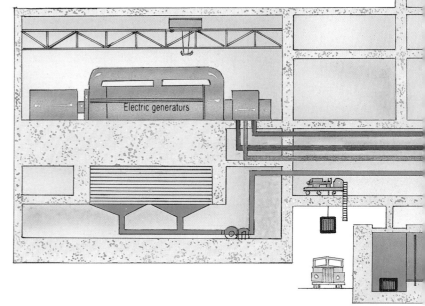

Electric generators

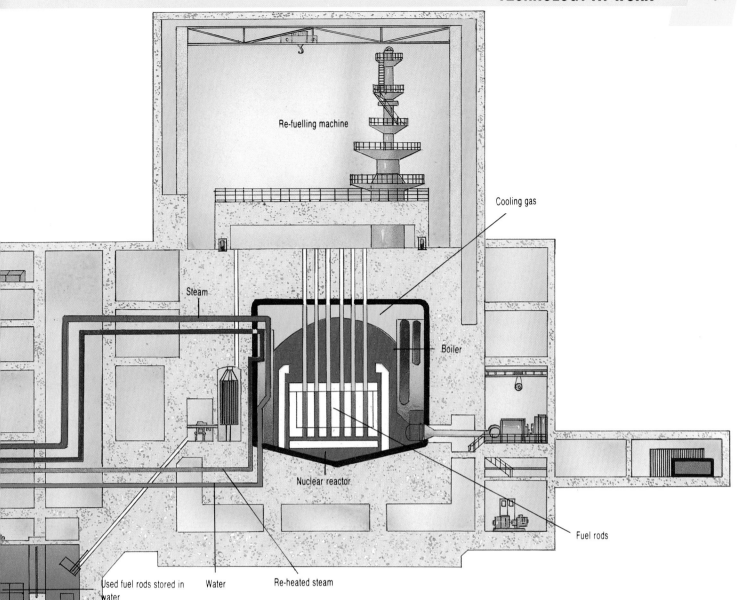

Re-fuelling machine

Cooling gas

Steam

Boiler

Nuclear reactor

Fuel rods

Used fuel rods stored in water

Water

Re-heated steam

which used to grind grain into flour. Some of the latest wind turbines have propellers, carried on top of a steel tower. The wind also helps whip up the waves at sea. Several machines are being tested to harness wave power.

Solar power

The Sun pours plenty of energy down on the Earth, and many homes now use this energy to heat their water. It is difficult and expensive to trap solar energy on a large scale. But in some sunny parts of the world scientists have built experimental solar "power-towers" to do this. Hundreds of mirrors reflect sunlight onto a boiler on top of a tower. This heats up water in the boiler into steam, which can then be used to turn electricity generators.

Nuclear power

Many countries now have nuclear power stations. These use a rare metal called uranium as a kind of fuel. The energy comes from inside the nucleus (centre) of the atoms that make up the metal.

Under certain conditions, the nucleus of uranium atoms can be made to split. This is called fission. When this happens, fantastic amounts of energy are given out. This is the energy the power stations tap. One of the main drawbacks with a nuclear power station is that it produces dangerous waste. It is dangerous because it gives out radiation (rays) that can harm most living things. Nuclear engineers have to make very sure that none of the radiation escapes, either from the reactor (where fission takes place) or the waste.

Above **The nuclear reactor in a nuclear power station produces heat that is changed into electricity. Metal fuel rods are fed into the reactor and heat up. A cooling liquid or gas flows through the reactor to take the heat away. It goes to a boiler where it boils water to produce steam. The hot steam powers electric generators to make electricity.**

FOOD AND FARMING – CROPS

Farming is the oldest industry in the world. People began farming about 10,000 years ago. Before then they simply gathered the grains and fruits that grew in nature. Also they hunted wild animals for meat. Then they started growing crops and keeping animals, such as sheep and goats.

Today farming is truly an industry. Farmers use many machines to help them plant and harvest the crops they grow. They raise animals, or livestock, in huge numbers, rather like factories produce goods in huge numbers.

Farmers use other things to help them produce bigger and better crops. They use chemical fertilizers, which put back into the soil the goodness that growing plants take out. Farmers also treat their crops with pesticides. These are chemicals that kill insect pests and cure diseases. The trouble is that they can cause pollution if they are not used carefully.

The variety of crops

By far the most important crops farmers grow are cereals. In North America and

Above **Efficient factory farming, can produce a huge output of crops. Here, a huge mountain of grain collects at a store in South Dakota, USA.**

Above right **In poorer parts of the world, slash-and-burn cultivation is common in the forests. Crops are grown in the ash of burnt trees. Clearing the forest, however, can lead to soil erosion.**

Left **Spraying cacao trees in Ghana. This protects the trees against disease and insects.**

Right **A modern combine harvester gathers a cereal crop quickly and efficiently.**

Europe, wheat, maize (corn), barley, rye and oats are the cereals most widely grown. Wheat is particularly valuable because it can be ground into flour to make bread. In Asia rice is the most common cereal grown. It is the main food of hundreds of millions of people.

Root crops are also widely grown on farms. They include potatoes, turnips, carrots and sugar beet. Sugar beet is grown to make sugar. Some root crops are grown as animal feed. Grass is also grown to feed animals. It is grown for grazing and also for hay and silage. Hay is grass that is cut and then stored dry. Silage is cut grass that is stored moist in a tower or silo.

Fruit and vegetable farmers grow many other kinds of crops. In the "fruit and veg" department of any supermarket can be seen the enormous variety of crops grown locally and all over the world.

The farmer's machines

Of all the machines the farmer uses, the tractor is the most important. It pulls wagons, ploughs, harrows, seed drills, rollers and mowers. The farmer uses the plough to dig up the ground before sowing seeds. The plough has a number of curved blades that bite into, and turn over the soil. This buries the weeds.

After ploughing, the farmer pulls the harrow over the ground. This smoothes out the ridges in the ground produced by ploughing. The seed drill comes next, sowing the seeds just beneath the surface of the soil. Later, when the crop is finished and the stubble burnt, the ground may be rolled with a heavy roller.

Most crops can now be harvested by machines – even fruit crops. But the most important harvesting machine is the combine harvester, which is used mainly for cereal crops. The combine harvester is so-called because it combines jobs – reaping, threshing and winnowing. Reaping means cutting the crop. Threshing means knocking the grain from the seed heads. Winnowing means freeing the grain from the chaff by means of wind or fanned air. Some of the latest combine harvesters are huge and can cut a swathe nearly 10 m (33 feet) wide.

LIVESTOCK FARMING

Farmers raise animals, or livestock, on the farm for several reasons. For example, they keep cows for their milk or meat, pigs for their meat, sheep for their wool or meat, and chickens for their meat and eggs. Hundreds of millions of these animals are raised throughout the world. Australian farmers alone raise nearly 200 million sheep!

Farmers started taming wild animals and keeping them in herds about 10,000 years ago. Over the years they gradually improved their herds by selective breeding. This means they bred only from their best animals. For example, they bred from the meatiest and strongest bulls and from the cows that gave the most milk. Farmers still do this today. They raise carefully selected breeds, which are the best producers.

Outdoors and indoors

On most farms throughout the world the livestock are kept outside. Cattle and sheep graze on grass in the open fields. On the big cattle ranches in the United States and the sheep stations in Australia, the livestock roam free over vast areas of land. In South Australia, cattle stations can cover as much as 30,000 sq km (nearly 12,000 sq miles). This is nearly a quarter the size of England!

On such large farms the livestock are mostly left alone, but are rounded up from time to time. On hill farms, for example, sheep are usually brought down to lower ground in the winter for shearing. The cattle that roam free on the stations are beef cattle, bred for their meat. Dairy cattle, bred for their milk, are kept near the farm because they have to be milked twice a day. Pigs and poultry are also kept close by and they require shelter.

Some farmers now raise pigs and chickens entirely under cover in specially designed sheds. In these sheds thousands of animals are kept in carefully controlled conditions. The temperature is just right, the light is good, and the air is kept fresh. The animals are fed the right amount of food at the right time. Everything is done automatically, like in a factory. This method of raising animals is often called factory farming.

Above **A cattle station in Australia. The livestock roam free over vast areas of land, sometimes hundreds of miles from the homestead.**

Right **A sheep is sheared to remove its fleece. To make woollen cloth, the fleece is then gathered and combed in machines.**

Dairy products

The milk produced by dairy cattle is drunk in many countries as a wholesome food. In some countries people drink the milk of other animals, such as goats and camels. Cows give milk after they have had a calf. Some of the best dairy breeds are Friesians, Jerseys and Guernseys. Friesians produce the most milk – as much as 10 tonnes (9.8 tons) a year.

Large amounts of milk are made into other dairy products. Butter is made from the cream which settles on top of milk when it stands. It is made by churning or turning the cream over and over in a drum, or churn. Cheese is made by adding substances to milk to make it curdle. The solid curd is then left for some time to ripen, when it develops its cheesy flavour.

Above and right **The cows on most dairy farms these days are milked by machine. The milking machine draws off the milk by a gentle sucking action. From the farm, the milk goes by tanker lorry, or sometimes a pipeline, to the dairy. There it is heated for a short while and then cooled. This kills any germs in it. Then it is put into cartons or bottled, ready for delivery to the shops or our homes.**

ROAD TRANSPORT

The Romans made the first roads. They built good, straight roads so that soldiers could travel quickly to where they were needed. But when the Romans returned to Rome, no one bothered to repair the roads. This meant that there were only rough tracks between towns. Horses were used to carry goods from town to town.

In towns, where there were roads, wagons were used to carry goods. Rich people travelled in a sedan chair. This was a chair in a box. It was carried by servants using long poles at the front and the back. About 350 years ago, carriages were built to carry people. These had springs to give a smooth ride over the rough roads.

The "horseless carriage"

Slowly the roads between towns improved. In about 1700 the first stage coach appeared. Stage coaches carried mail as well as people. For many years, they were the main way people travelled on land. Then the "horseless carriage" was invented. The first of these carriages had steam engines, inside which coal or wood was burnt. The heat of the engine turned water into steam, and the steam was used to move the carriage. The first steam carriage was built in 1769 by a Frenchman called Nicolas Cugnot.

Bicycles

About this time bicycles began to appear on the roads. The first bicycle was simply two wheels joined by a bar that carried a seat. The rider walked along while sitting on the seat. The "penny-farthing" bicycle was invented in 1871. It had a large front wheel and a small back wheel and soon became very popular in spite of being difficult to ride. The Rover safety bicycle, which had

Below **A selection of early bicycles and cars. Cugnot's steam wagon** (bottom right) **ran on three large, wooden cartwheels. The body was made of thick wooden beams. A large boiler was at the front. The car built by Karl Benz** (top left) **was built like a three-wheeled bicycle. Its frame was of steel tube, and the wheels had wire spokes. The 1790 Walk-along** (bottom left) **was an early type of bicycle. The rider sat on the frame and pushed on the ground with the feet. Progress was slow, except going down hills. The penny-farthing bicycle** (top right) **of the 1870s was hard to ride. The pedals were at the centre of the large front wheel. The front wheel was turned to steer the bicycle.**

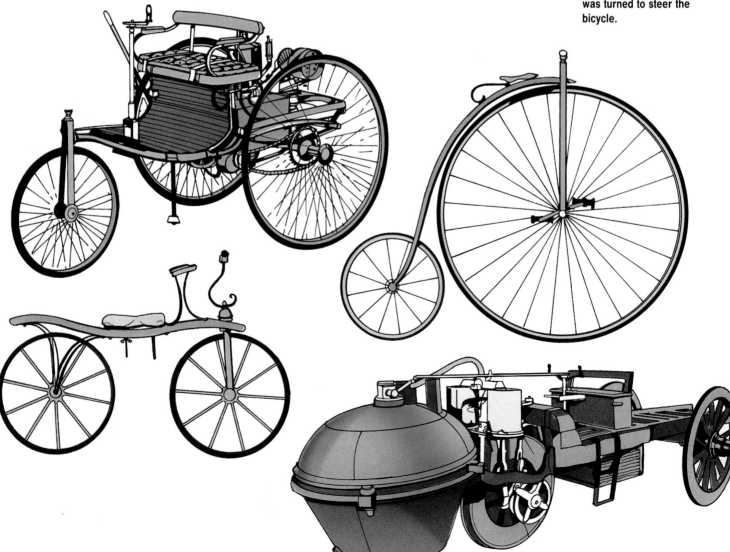

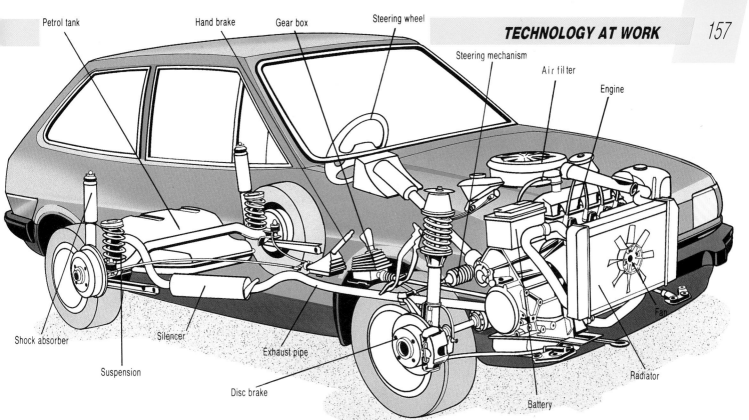

Petrol tank   Hand brake   Gear box   Steering wheel

Steering mechanism

Air filter

Engine

Shock absorber

Silencer

Suspension

Exhaust pipe

Disc brake

Fan

Radiator

Battery

solid rubber tyres, and was much more comfortable, appeared in 1885.

The first cars

In 1876, a German called Nicholas Otto invented a new kind of engine for the horseless carriage. It used gas as a fuel. Another German, Gottlieb Daimler, improved the Otto engine by using petrol as the fuel (see page 148). He drove his first petrol-driven car around the town of Cannstatt in 1886. At about the same time, Karl Benz also made a car that used petrol. The first person to make a large number of cars was Henry Ford of the United States, who made over 15 million of the Model T. It was so cheap that many people could afford to buy one. Soon the car, or automobile, was the most popular way to travel.

Below **An automobile engine usually has four cylinders inside which petrol is exploded. The pistons are pushed up and down by the** explosions. As they move up and down, they turn the camshaft around. This turns a drive shaft that makes the wheels go round.

Top **A cutaway diagram of a motor car.**

Above **A Ford Model T, the world's first mass-produced automobile.**

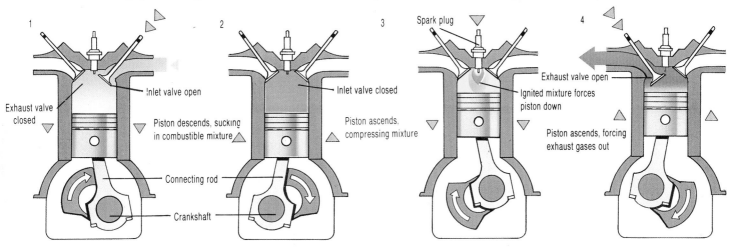

1   Exhaust valve closed   Inlet valve open   Piston descends, sucking in combustible mixture   Connecting rod   Crankshaft

2   Inlet valve closed   Piston ascends, compressing mixture

3   Spark plug

4   Exhaust valve open   Ignited mixture forces piston down   Piston ascends, forcing exhaust gases out

RAIL TRANSPORT

The first railways were used in coal mines. They had tracks made of wood and wagons filled with coal were pulled along the tracks by horses. In 1804, Richard Trevithick, an engineer in a Welsh tin mine, used a steam engine to pull the wagons. A steam engine uses water heated to steam to produce its power. Trevithick used a steam engine to turn the wheels of a locomotive that pulled the wagons. His locomotive ran on iron rails, but was so heavy that it broke the rails in several places.

The first passenger railway was built by an Englishman called George Stephenson. He was also a mine engineer and he built steam engines to use in his coal mine. In 1829, Stephenson built a locomotive called the *Rocket* to carry passengers. It ran from Liverpool to Manchester and reached a speed of 46 km/hr (29 mph), faster than a horse could run. Some people were worried that passengers might not be able to breathe at these high speeds. However, the railways were successful and soon many more were built. In England, lines ran from London to all the main cities by 1850. In America, the railways helped the pioneers to develop the country. By 1886 a railway ran between east and west coasts.

Steam locomotives were used for over 100 years. Since the 1950s, diesel and electric engines have been used instead of steam engines. A diesel engine is like the engine that drives a car. The main difference is that a diesel engine uses oil as the fuel and not petrol.

The fastest trains are called HSTs, or high-speed trains. HSTs need long, straight tracks with very gentle curves. Usually, the old track is improved so that HSTs can use it. The French railways built special track for their HST, which is called the TGV. It runs from Paris to Lyons. The top speed is 300 km/hr (190 mph). Japan's HST also runs on special track. Most people call it the "Bullet Train", because of its shape. The Bullet Train has a top speed of 250 km/hr (155 mph).

Above **The "Rocket" steam locomotive, built by George Stephenson.**

Below **A steam engine uses steam to push the pistons back and forth, turning the wheels. A valve first lets the steam into the front of the cylinder. This drives the piston back. Then it lets the steam into the back of the cylinder and the piston is pushed forward. Afterwards, the steam escapes through the funnel.**

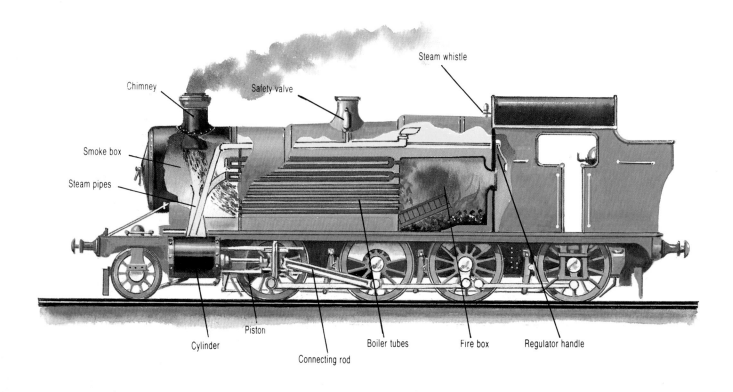

Chimney
Steam whistle
Safety valve
Smoke box
Steam pipes
Piston
Cylinder
Connecting rod
Boiler tubes
Fire box
Regulator handle

Right **A diesel-powered freight locomotive makes its way across Australia.**

Below **Underground trains running in different cities of the world:** (from the left) **New York, Berlin, Montreal and London.**

Bottom **The high-speed "Bullet" train can keep up a speed of 210 km/h (130 mph) for most of its journey from Tokyo to Osaka, in Japan.**

WATER TRANSPORT

The first people to travel by water probably used logs as simple boats. They sat astride the log and used a piece of wood to paddle along. About 5,000 years ago, the Egyptians began to build proper boats. In the early days they simply used bundles of reeds. Later they learnt to make stronger and bigger boats from short planks of wood. They invented the sail and used the wind to push their boats along. They fixed a paddle near the back of the boat to steer it. In these boats, the Ancient Egyptians made long journeys.

Another sea-faring people were the Vikings. They lived in northern Europe about 1,000 years ago. The Viking ships were long and narrow. Each ship had a large, square sail and as many as 80 oars. The Vikings travelled to Iceland and Greenland in their ships.

After the Vikings, even better boats were built. Many explorers used these new ships to make great voyages of exploration. Christopher Columbus sailed to the West Indies in 1492. Vasco da Gama sailed round Africa to India in 1498. Ferdinand Magellan, setting out from Portugal in 1519, sailed right around the world.

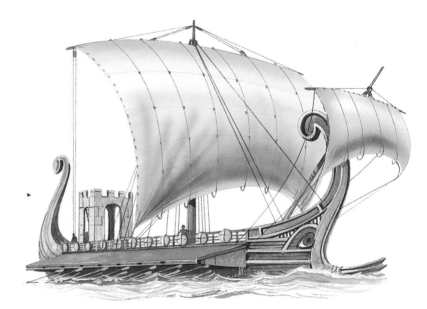

A new type of sailing ship appeared in the 19th century. It was called the clipper. It was long and narrow and had three tall masts, with up to six sails on each mast. The clipper was the fastest ship the world had seen. The *Cutty Sark*, a famous clipper, sailed from Australia to England in 69 days.

The steamship was a great step forward in ship design. An American, John Fitch, first used a steam engine to drive a ship in 1790. His ship, the *Experiment*, had oars that were driven by steam. Soon afterwards paddlesteamers were built with a paddle

Above **Galleys like this Roman one were used as warships.**

Below left **The galleons used in the Spanish Armada of 1588 stood high in the water. They carried many guns on three or more decks.**

Below **A clipper ship. It carried more than 10 miles of rope in its riggings.**

wheel, like the wheel of a water mill, at the side or back of the ship.

In 1894, a British engineer built a new kind of steamship engine. It was called the steam turbine (see page 148). Steam turbines use less fuel and go faster than paddlewheelers. The first steam turbine ship crossed the Atlantic in 1904 and soon all large ships were using turbines as engines. They are still used in ships today, especially large oil tankers. But another type of engine is also used. This is the diesel engine. Most other ships are powered by diesel engines (see page 148).

There was nothing like a hovercraft or a hydrofoil 100 years ago. The hovercraft floats on a cushion of air, which lifts it above the water. It is driven forward by large propellers that spin in the air above the craft. Hovercraft can travel on both land and sea. The hydrofoil has small wings on its underside. These lift the craft out of the water when it is moving, so that it can move more swiftly than an ordinary boat. However, neither hydrofoils nor hovercraft can be used in rough seas. They are used for short journeys in quiet waters.

Navigation

Most ships today use electronic equipment to navigate. Radio stations on land send out radio signals that are picked up by ships. The ships can work out their position from the signals. Ships can also use radar. Radar transmitters on the ship send out radio signals that bounce off the nearby coastline and other ships. This shows exactly where the coast or other ship is.

Above **An ocean liner is like an ocean-going city. It contains everything needed to keep the passengers happy, such as cabins, dining rooms, cinemas and shops. A tug** (right) **tows large vessels into and out of port.**

Below **Oil tankers are slow and clumsy, often being unable to enter port. But they can carry thousands of tons of oil in their huge tanks. They are usually much larger than ocean liners. Rail locomotives and cars are dwarfed by them.**

AIR TRANSPORT

Since the beginning of time, man has dreamed of flying through the air like a bird. The first successful flights were, however, made in balloons. The French brothers, Joseph and Etienne Montgolfier, made the first passenger-carrying hot air balloon. The passengers on its first flight, in 1783, were a sheep, a cockerel and a duck. A few weeks later human passengers went up in a balloon near Paris.

Another pair of brothers, Wilbur and Orville Wright, became the first people to build and fly a powered aeroplane. They made their first successful flight on December 17, 1903, at Kitty Hawk, North Carolina, USA. The aeroplane was made of wood and canvas with a small petrol engine. It flew for 12 seconds and covered a distance of 40 m (130 ft).

A plane gets its lift from its wings. The wings are made in a special shape, called an aerofoil, that lifts the plane as it moves through the air. To help the plane turn, and gain height, there are moving parts on the wings and tail. The pilot can move these from the cockpit, using the control column and footpedals. The flaps on the small tail, or rear, wings are called elevators. These can be moved up and down to make the plane climb or dive. On the main wings there are flaps called ailerons and there is a hinged rudder on the tail fin. Both the rudder and the ailerons are used to make turns. Most small planes have a propeller to move them forward. As the blades turn they push air backwards, driving the plane forward.

Larger aircraft, such as the Boeing 747 or Jumbo jet, are powered by jet engines. Most jet engines are turbofans. They have a fan with many blades on it at the front of the engine. This sucks air into the engine,

Above **The first manned flight in the Montgolfier balloon took place on 21 November 1783.**

The Wright Brothers' machine Flyer 1 (left) **had a wing span of 12.2 m (40 ft) and a length of 6.3 m (21 ft). The Boeing 747** (below) **has a wing span of 59.6 m (195 ft) and a length of 70 m (231 ft). It carries 490 passengers, and is as tall as a six-storey building.**

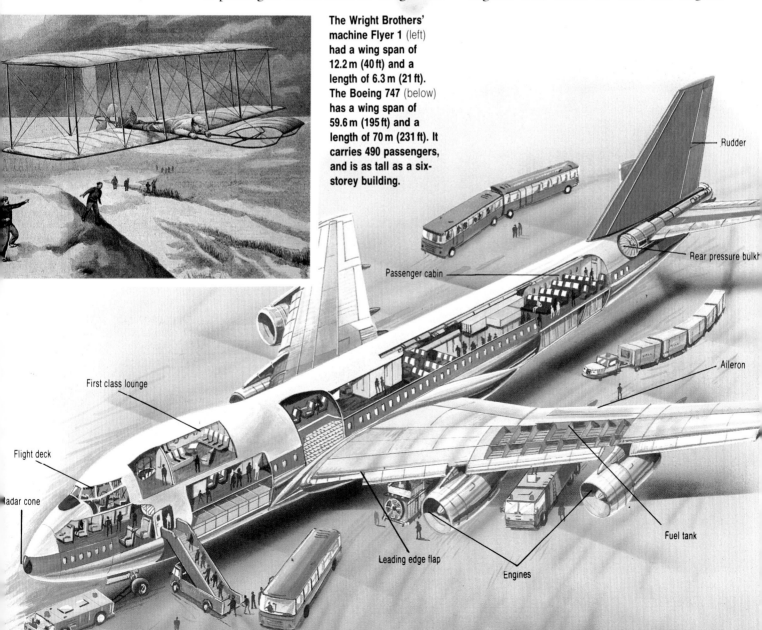

Rudder

Rear pressure bulkh

Passenger cabin

First class lounge

Aileron

Flight deck

Radar cone

Fuel tank

Leading edge flap

Engines

where the air is mixed with burning fuel. The very hot gases produced rush out the back of the jet and the plane is thrust forward.

Modern planes, such as the Concorde, fly faster than the speed of sound (about 1,200 km/hr or 760 mph) and so they are called supersonic aircraft. Concorde is the only supersonic passenger plane and it can cruise at twice the speed of sound. Military planes fly even faster, sometimes over three times the speed of sound.

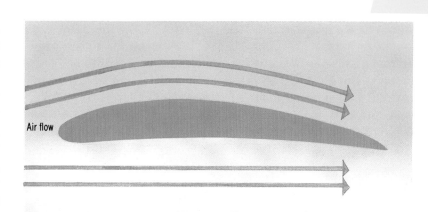

Air flow

Above **The top surface of an aeroplane wing is curved. The bottom surface is almost flat. As the plane moves forward the air pressure on the top of the wing is lower than that below. This gives the wing lift.**

Left **The modern A320 airliner.**

Below **Helicopters use large rotating blades for lift. A small rear propeller stops the craft from spinning. Hand controls and pedals adjust the angle of the blades, giving the pilot control.**

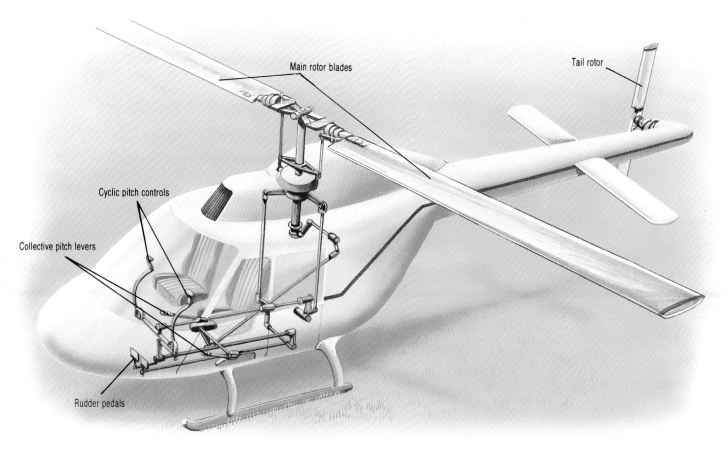

Main rotor blades

Tail rotor

Cyclic pitch controls

Collective pitch levers

Rudder pedals

MAKING A FLIGHT

To make a journey by aeroplane, you must first go to an airport. This is where aircraft take off and land. Millions of passengers pass through a large airport, such as London's Heathrow Airport, each year.

When passengers arrive at the airport, they go first to the check-in desk. Here a computer checks the tickets. The baggage is weighed and sent to the plane to be loaded. Outside on the runway, the plane is being made ready for the flight. Its fuel tanks are being filled up, and the engines, radio, airconditioning and electrics are all carefully checked. When everything is ready the passengers come aboard.

The captain asks Air Traffic Control for permission to take off. Air traffic controllers are in charge of the movement of all planes on the runways and in the sky near the airport. They use radar to watch the movements of planes. Each plane shows up as a spot of light on a screen in front of the controller. No aircraft can take off, or land, until a controller has given permission.

When the plane has reached its cruising height, the flight crew checks the weather reports and navigation. In most busy areas planes navigate by following "pathways" in the sky called airways. The airways are marked by radio beacons, which send out radio signals that the aircraft pick up. The pilot has a map that shows where the beacons are. In remote areas, there are no beacons. Here the plane finds its way by using an inertial navigation system. This is a type of compass that uses gyroscopes to detect changes in the plane's direction. They can work out the position of the plane

Below **A modern airport terminal with loading bays. The circular design of the terminal building enables, the passengers to board aircraft without having to walk far or be exposed to the weather.**

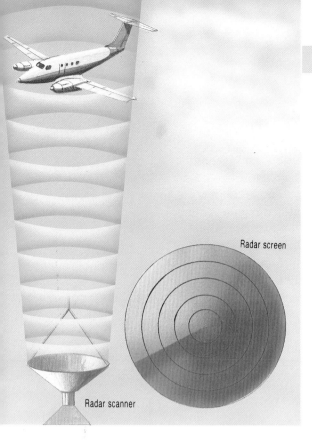

Radar screen

Radar scanner

Left **Air traffic controllers use radar to watch the aircraft. The radar scanner sends out radio signals. When the signals meet a plane, they bounce back. These echoes are shown as a point of light on the radar screen.**

Right **Air traffic controllers follow an aircraft's progress on a radar screen.**

Below **As an aircraft comes in to land it is guided by a radio beam to the runway. A second radio signal tells the pilot if the plane is at the correct height.**

cally controls the height and speed of the aircraft. It can also navigate, using radio beacons and an inertial navigation system.

The final stage of the landing is guided by the instrument landing system. The aircraft picks up a radio beam from the airport, which helps the pilot find the way to the landing strip. It also tells the pilot if the plane is at the correct height. The plane will make a smooth and safe landing if it follows the beam.

by sensing every turn the plane has taken since it left its starting point.

When the plane nears the end of its flight, the flight controllers at the airport give it permission to land. The plane is told to descend to start its approach to the airport. In bad weather this descent will be done using the automatic pilot. This automati-

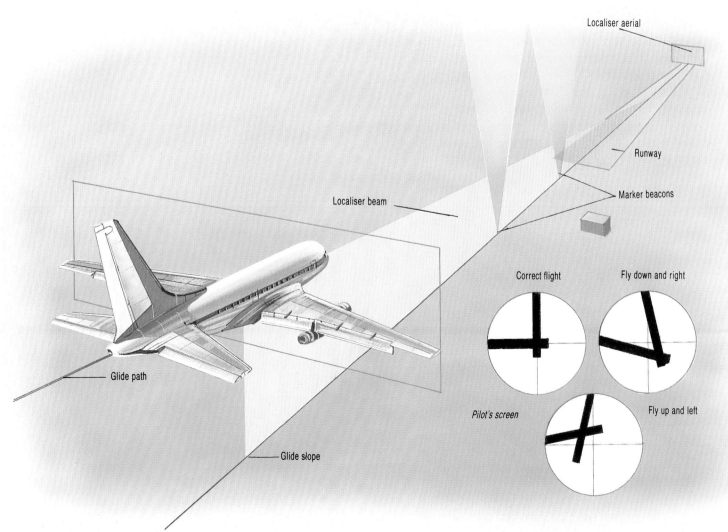

Localiser aerial

Runway

Marker beacons

Localiser beam

Glide path

Glide slope

Correct flight

Fly down and right

Pilot's screen

Fly up and left

SPACE TRANSPORT

To travel in space, we need to escape from the pull of the Earth. This pull is called gravity. Gravity is the force that keeps us on the ground, and makes a ball fall to Earth when you throw it in the air.

A spacecraft has to travel at 38,000 km/hr (24,000 mph) to escape into space. A spacecraft reaches this speed by using rocket engines, the only kind that work in space where there is no air. A Russian teacher called Konstantin Tsiolkovsky first realized in 1895 that rockets were the only way to travel in space. But it was not until 1926 that the American Robert Goddard built the first successful rockets.

Most rockets use liquid fuels carried in separate tanks. When the fuels are mixed in the combustion chamber of the rocket, they burn violently. Hot gases stream out of the rocket, driving it upwards. Because more than one rocket is needed to reach space, one rocket is built on top of another. This is known as a multi-stage rocket. The first rocket (called the first stage) lifts off and when its fuel is used up, it drops away. The second stage then takes over and goes into space. On some rockets three stages are used.

Satellites were the first objects to be launched into space. Satellites circle the Earth in paths called orbits, and they can stay in orbit as long as they are above the atmosphere. The first satellite was launched by the Russians in October 1957. It was called *Sputnik 1*, which means "traveller" in Russian.

Today there are many satellites orbiting the Earth and each has a different task. Some satellites are used to relay telephone messages and television programmes across the world. These are called communications satellites. Other satellites are used to help ships and aircraft navigate. Some satellites contain high-powered cameras and are used to map the Earth. Weather satellites keep watch on clouds and gathering storms, and help meteorologists make weather forecasts.

Another important type of spacecraft is the probe. A probe is an unmanned spacecraft that is sent into space to gather information. Probes were sent to the Moon to help plan the Apollo missions that put a man on the Moon. Probes have been sent to the planets and to Halley's comet. All these spacecraft have sent valuable information about the solar system back to help the scientists on Earth (see page 14).

Above **A probe called Giotto was sent to meet Halley's comet in 1986. The probe went within 1000 km (650 miles) of the centre of the comet.**

Left **Saturn V at the moment of lift-off.**

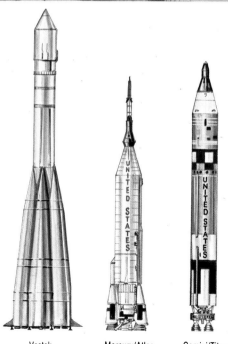

A4/V-2   Sputnik   Vanguard   Juno 1   Vostok   Mercury/Atlas   Gemini/Titan   Soyuz

Right **The solar telescope satellite is designed to observe the Sun.**

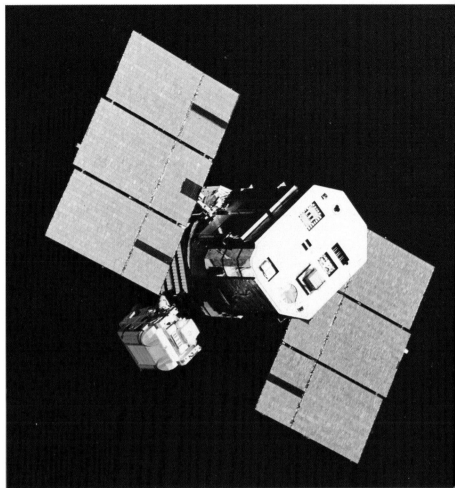

Left **The Saturn V rocket was the biggest rocket ever to fly. It was 111 m (364 ft) high. The scale drawings show how it towers over all the earlier rockets and the Space Shuttle.**

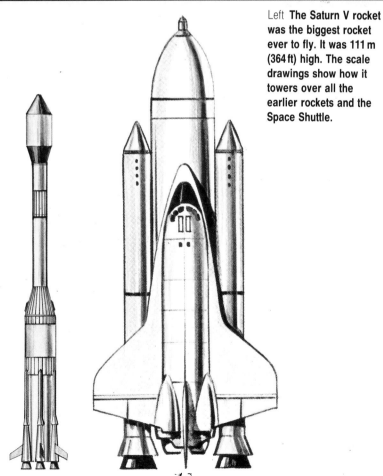

Saturn 1B

Saturn V

Ariane

Space Shuttle

MAN ON THE MOON

Neil Armstrong was the first man to set foot on the Moon. Watched by 500 million television viewers around the world, he climbed down the ladder of the lunar lander and onto the surface of the Moon on July 21, 1969. What he said then will be long remembered: "That's one small step for a man, one giant leap for mankind." Edwin "Buzz" Aldrin joined Armstrong later on the Moon's surface. They spent $2\frac{1}{2}$ hours doing experiments and collecting Moon rocks. Then they returned to the spacecraft and blasted off to rejoin the third astronaut, Michael Collins, who had remained orbiting the Moon while they had visited it.

It was the Apollo 11 mission that carried Armstrong, Aldrin and Collins to the Moon. A giant rocket had been built to power into space the Apollo spacecraft and its astronauts. Called the Saturn V, it was as tall as a

Below and bottom right **Buzz Aldrin at work on the surface of the Moon. He is doing an experiment to study atomic particles from the Sun. The particles are collected by the sheet, called a solar wind sheet. The sheet was brought back to Earth to be studied by scientists.**

30-storey building. It was the most power-ful rocket ever built, with the power of 50 Boeing Jumbo jets.

The spacecraft, carrying Armstrong, Aldrin and Collins, was perched on top of the rocket. It was made up of several main parts. There was the lunar module (or LM) for the descent to the Moon and the return from the surface. This was connected to the command and service module (CSM) that contained the living quarters and com-mand centre. The CSM also held the rocket motor used to correct the course when travelling to and from the Moon.

Earlier Apollo missions had carried out practice runs. Apollo 8 went round the Moon and back to Earth without actually landing. Other missions practised flying the lunar module. There were also other mis-sions to the Moon after Apollo 11. One mission, Apollo 13, went wrong. An oxy-gen tank exploded on the way and the landing on the Moon was cancelled. Luckily the astronauts were able to limp back safely to Earth in the damaged spacecraft.

All the other missions were successful. The astronauts on these missions collected samples of Moon rock which they brought back to Earth. Apollo 15 carried the lunar roving vehicle, or LRV. This was a small four-wheeled car, with a top speed of 17 km/hr (10 mph) and a range of 88 km (55 miles).

The last mission, Apollo 17, was launched in December 1972. Astronauts Eugene Cernan and "Jack" Schmitt were on the Moon for 72 hours. They collected 113 kg (249 lbs) of Moon rock and drove a total

of 34 km (21 miles) in the lunar rover. Before returning to Earth, they remained in orbit around the Moon for a further two days. They spent this time mapping the far side of the Moon. When they splashed down safely in the Pacific Ocean, the three astro-nauts had travelled a total of a little over $2\frac{1}{4}$ million km ($1\frac{1}{2}$ million miles).

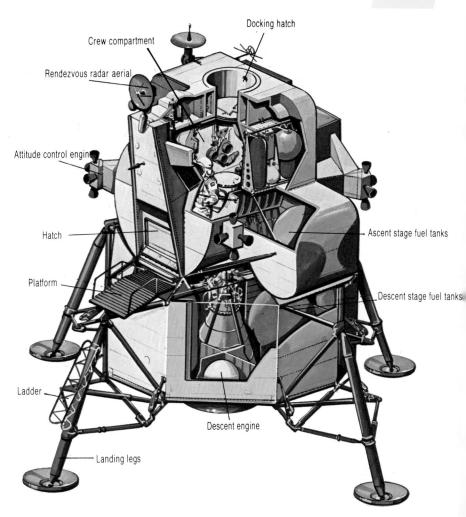

Above **A cutaway diagram of the lunar module which landed on the Moon.**

Below **The CSM has splashed down in the Pacific Ocean, and the astronauts are taken to a waiting ship.**

Left **The first Space Shuttle lifts-off on 12 April 1981**

THE SPACE SHUTTLE

The Space Shuttle is the first space plane. In the future, most space travellers will use the Shuttle, or some craft like it.

The main part of the Shuttle is called the orbiter, which is about the size of a modern passenger plane. It looks like a plane with small wings and rocket engines in the tail. The orbiter carries the crew and cargo into space. It flies in orbit like a spacecraft. When on the launchpad, the orbiter is attached to a large fuel tank. This is called the ET, or external tank. Alongside the ET are two thinner rockets called solid rocket boosters, or SRBs.

Soon after the Shuttle has taken off, the SRBs burn out. They are released and drop into the sea, where they are picked up by ships to be used again. The main engines stop when the Shuttle has reached a height of 112 km (70 miles). The ET is dropped into the sea. The engines at the back of the orbiter are then used to climb into the Earth's orbit. Forty-five minutes after launch, it is in orbit 268 km (168 miles) above the Earth, travelling at a speed of 26,688 km/hr (16,680 mph).

To return to Earth, the orbiter engines are fired while facing forward. This slows the orbiter. It drops out of orbit and enters the Earth's atmosphere. As this happens, the underside of the orbiter becomes very hot. It glides in to land on a very long runway.

Aboard the orbiter, there is a flight deck, like the one on an aircraft. There are two seats for the pilots. In front of the pilots are the instruments that they use to fly the orbiter. Computers are used to control the craft most of the time.

Behind the cabin is the cargo bay. This is about the size of a large railway truck. It is used to carry the cargo of satellites, experiments or materials for building a space station. The cargo bay has two doors that open when the orbiter is in orbit. A long robot arm, called a manipulator arm, is used to move satellites in and out of the cargo bay. This is worked by remote control from inside the orbiter cabin.

Sometimes the astronauts have to work outside the orbiter cabin. For this they wear special suits which protect them in space. On their back packs they wear a life-support system with a vital supply of oxygen. Without these they could not breathe. A manned manoeuvring unit, or MMU, is used to move about in space.

The Space Shuttle has proved its usefulness in space to scientists. However, in 1986, there was a tragedy. The Shuttle *Challenger* exploded just after it was launched, killing all the crew. The United States decided to halt all flights until they could be sure there would be no more accidents.

Above **The Space Shuttle is transported to the launch pad.**

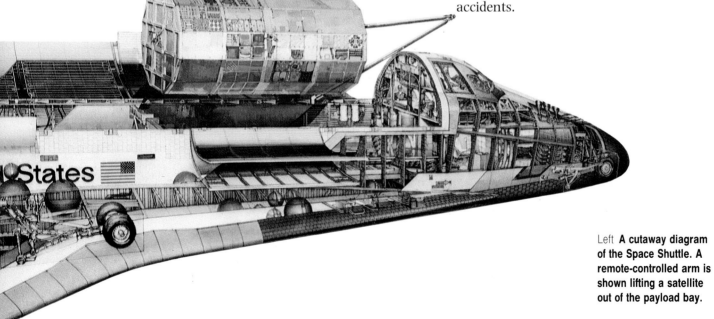

Left **A cutaway diagram of the Space Shuttle. A remote-controlled arm is shown lifting a satellite out of the payload bay.**

HOW WRITING DEVELOPED

If you could not read, you would still be able to tell what this book is about. You would look at the pictures. Pictures are a kind of language.

Long ago, pictures were used by the first writers. The Sumerians, who lived in the Middle East about 5,000 years ago, used picture language. They drew small pictures, called pictographs, on clay tablets. These were pressed into soft clay with a stick (called a stylus) which made wedge-shaped marks. The picture writing came to be called cuneiform, which means "wedge-shaped".

The Egyptians invented a set of pictographs about 3000 BC. These were called hieroglyphs, or "holy carvings", as they were often carved on Egyptian tombs and temples. There were hieroglyphs for spoken sounds, and parts of words, as well as complete words.

It was the Egyptians who invented something very important – paper. They made paper from a plant called papyrus, which was found growing near the River Nile. The Egyptians beat the stems of the plant into thin strips. These were laid side by side, and more strips were laid across them. The strips

Below left **Egyptian hieroglyphics. They tell us about the life of a rich and important person.**

Bottom left **This table shows how alphabets have changed over the years. The Greek alphabet developed into the one used in Western languages.**

Bottom right **Five modern ways of writing: (from the top) Russian, Hindu, Hebrew, Greek and Chinese.**

Ugarit		Phoenician	Greek	Modern	
		K	A	A	O
			B	B	P
			Γ		Q
			Δ	C	R
			E	D	S
				E	T
			Ρ	F	U
			Σ	G	V
			Τ		W
			Υ	H	X
			Z		Y
			Η		Z
			Θ	I	
			I	J	
			K	K	
			Λ	L	
			M	M	
			N	N	

Top left **Deaf people can use sign language to communicate. This uses the fingers and hands to show the letters of the alphabet** (below).

were then soaked in water and beaten flat to make a sheet of paper.

Another great invention was the alphabet. The first true alphabet was used at Ugarit in Syria about 1300 BC. Each letter of the alphabet stood for a single sound and these could be joined together to make words. In time the Ugarit alphabet spread to other people. It had made writing much easier. The Phoenicians, who lived in the country now called Lebanon, taught it to the Greeks. The Greeks added several new letters to the alphabet to make it more useful. The alphabet we use today is adapted from the Greek one.

Left **People who cannot see use the Braille system of writing. It uses patterns of raised dots to stand for each letter which are felt with the tips of the fingers.**

Below **Pens through the ages. Shown in the picture are the quill pen, the fountain pen, the typewriter, the ballpoint pen and the word processor.**

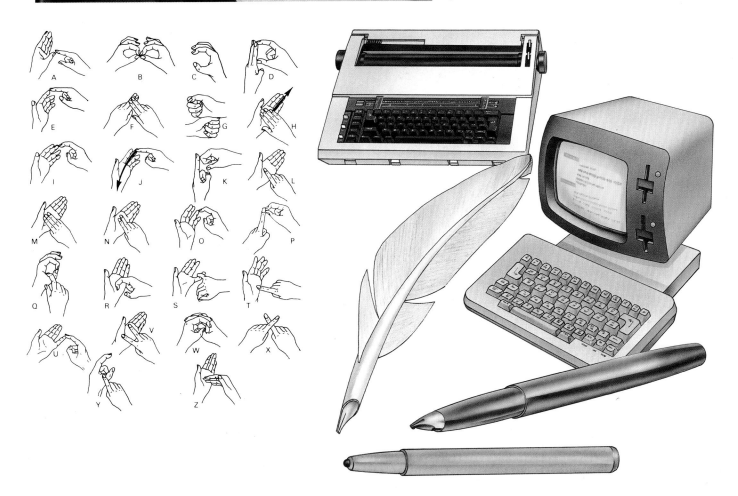

PRINTING AND PAPER

Printing began in China over 2,000 years ago. Parts of a flat wooden plate were cut away to form letters. The raised surface was covered with ink and a sheet of paper pressed down on it.

In the 15th century a German printer, Johann Gutenberg, discovered how to print books more easily. Instead of carving an entire page from one piece of wood, Gutenberg carved each letter separately on a small block. These pieces, called type, could then be placed in any order to make words and sentences. The small wooden pieces could be used more than once. A mechanical device was used to press the paper against the type. These improvements made printing quicker, but it was still slow.

Since then, the speed and quality of printing presses have improved greatly. Type is no longer put together by hand. Modern computers with keyboards like typewriters, are used to assemble pages of type. Typesetting machines produce photographic film of the type. From these, printing plates are made. The plates are used on giant printing presses. These machines can print thousands of books or newspapers every hour.

There are three main ways of printing: letterpress, photolithography and gravure. Letterpress uses plates with raised surfaces. Photolithography uses photographically produced plates with a flat surface. Gravure uses plates with an engraved surface, produced by chemical etching.

There are two main types of printing machine. These are the sheet-fed and the web-fed machines. In sheet-fed machines, single sheets of paper are fed into the machine and printed one at a time. In a web-fed machine, a continuous roll of paper is fed through the printing machine. Both types of machine can print in colour. The paper is printed by a different set of plates for each colour. Some machines can also cut the sheets and fold them into pages. Bookbinding machines are used to sew the folded pages together, and glue a cover on to produce the finished book.

Paper is made from trees in a paper mill. When the trees arrive at the mill, their bark is first removed. Then they are cut into small chips. These chips are treated with chemicals to make a soft mash of white fibres. The mash goes to the papermaking machine. Here it is spread into a long thin layer. It is then dried in steam and wound onto large reels.

Right **The three main printing processes.**

Bottom **Modern printing machines, like this web-offset press, can print, fold, and trim sheets of paper automatically. The type surface is inked by huge rollers, and large rolls of paper are fed into the press. The fastest presses, rotary presses, can print on both sides of the paper at the same time.**

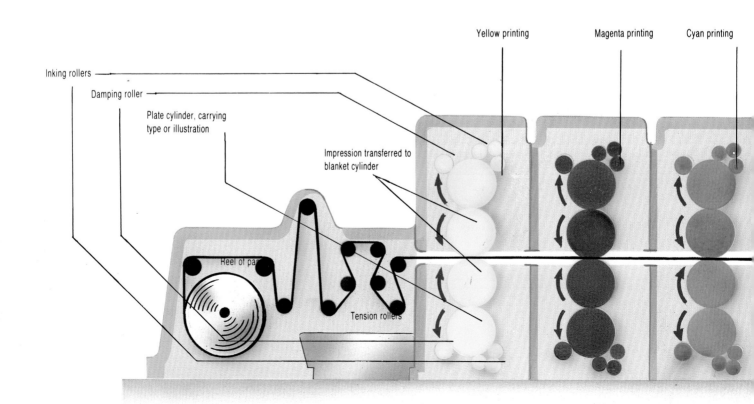

Yellow printing   Magenta printing   Cyan printing

Inking rollers

Damping roller

Plate cylinder, carrying type or illustration

Impression transferred to blanket cylinder

Reel of paper

Tension rollers

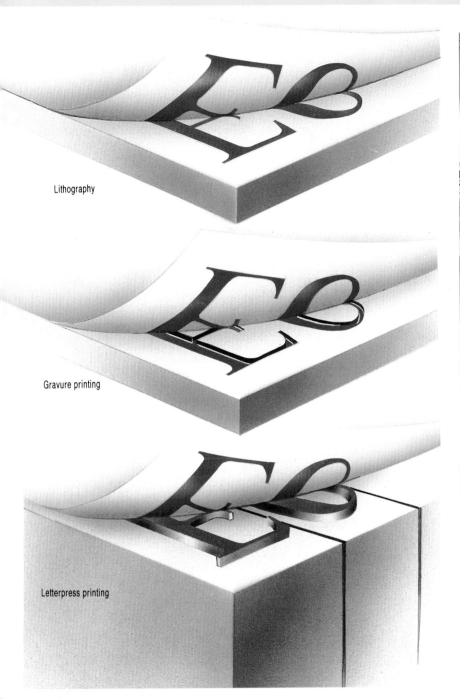

Lithography

Gravure printing

Letterpress printing

Above **In a modern newspaper office, journalists write their stories directly into a computer typesetting machine.**

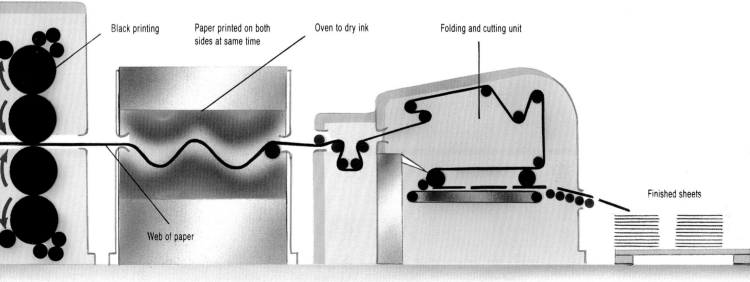

Black printing

Paper printed on both sides at same time

Oven to dry ink

Folding and cutting unit

Finished sheets

Web of paper

TELECOMMUNICATIONS

Telecommunications is the sending of messages over distance by wire or radio signals. The first practical system for electrical signalling was the simple telegraph invented by the Russian Baron Schilling in 1823. A wire carrying an electric current made a compass needle move when a message was sent. An American called Samuel Morse improved on this type of telegraph. He sent messages by using short and long electric pulses. Morse code proved to be fast and reliable and is still used today.

In 1875, the telephone was invented by Alexander Graham Bell. This carried speech along a wire (see page 134). Just three years later, the first telephone exchange was opened in Connecticut, USA. The first long-distance telephone line was set up between Boston and New York in 1884. Since then great changes have taken place in telecommunications.

It is now possible to talk to someone anywhere in the world cheaply and quickly. Cables under the oceans connect all countries together, but a phone does not have to be at the end of a cable. Cordless telephones use radio waves. In fact, many telephone calls travel as radio waves now. Communications satellites, high in space, are linked to the telephone system by microwaves.

Radio phones, such as in-car phones, do not need a connection to the telephone system at all. They work through a network of radio transmitters. Each transmitter covers a small area, called a cell. Calls travel from one cell to another until they reach the transmitter nearest the receiving phone.

The telephone can also be connected to large computers. These computers can be used to shop, bank, work at home or search electronic libraries. The information from the computer is displayed on a television screen in the home or office.

Left **The semaphore telegraph invented by Claude Chappe in 1793.**

Below **Different kinds of telephones through the years.**

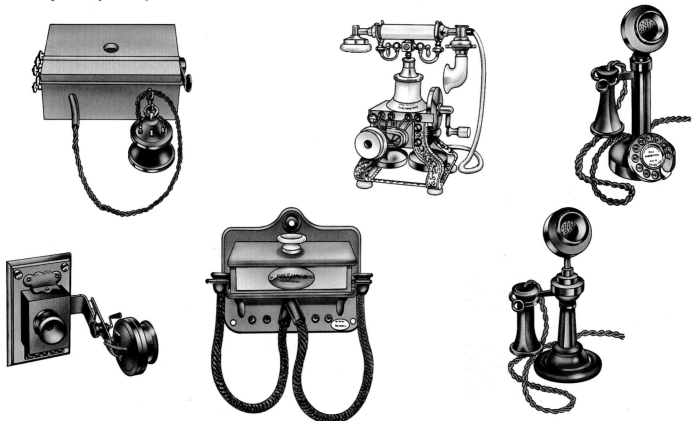

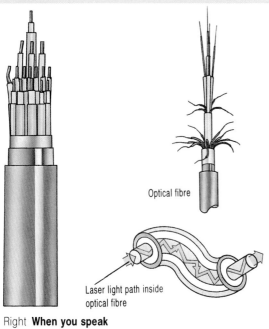

Optical fibre

Laser light path inside optical fibre

Left **Fibre optic cable is now used in telephone links between cities. The cables are made from glass fibres, no thicker than a hair. Messages are sent using pulses of very bright light from a laser. They can carry many more messages than copper wire** (far left).

Right **When you speak into a telephone, your voice makes a microphone vibrate. This produces electrical signals that travel down the telephone wires to the earpiece of the person listening. There, a diaphragm is made to vibrate by the electrical signals. The vibrations of the diaphragm reproduce the sounds spoken.**

Receiver

Metal diaphragm

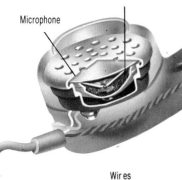

Metal diaphragm

Microphone

Wires

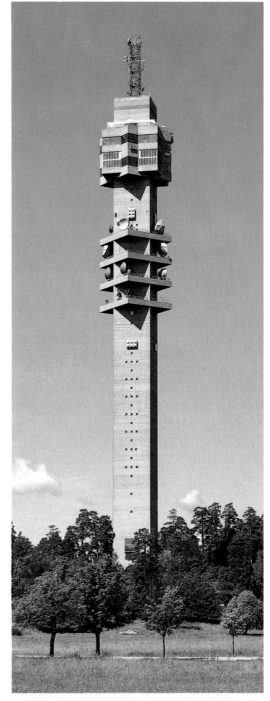

Right **A microwave radio transmitter.**

Below **Satellites are used to send telephone calls around the world.**

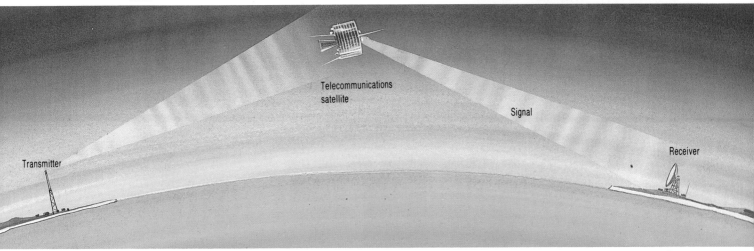

Telecommunications satellite

Signal

Transmitter

Receiver

RADIO AND TELEVISION

Radio and television do not use wires to carry messages. They use a kind of wave. These waves spread out from the radio or television station in much the same way as ripples spread out across the water when a stone is dropped into a pond. We cannot hear or see radio waves. They are electromagnetic waves, ripples of magnetism in space, not sound or water waves.

There are different kinds of electromagnetic waves, all with different wavelengths and frequencies. The wavelength is the distance between two peaks or troughs of the wave. The frequency is the number of waves each second. The shorter the wavelength, the higher the frequency of the wave. There is a wide range of radio waves used for broadcasting. Long and medium wavelength waves are used for local radio. Short wavelengths are used for long-distance broadcasting. These waves can reach right round the world. Television uses even shorter wavelengths.

At a radio station, the announcer speaks into a microphone. The sound of the voice is turned into electric signals (see page 134). These are broadcast as radio waves by the transmitter and your receiver picks them up. It picks out the station you want to hear, as you turn the tuner. Then it makes the

signal stronger. This is called amplification. The signal is turned back into sound and this is played out through a loudspeaker.

At a television station, the main piece of equipment is the studio camera. Light from the scene being broadcast enters the camera through the front lens, or eye, and is changed into electrical signals. The signals from the camera are sent to the transmitter. From there they are broadcast to viewers.

The main part of the television receiver is the cathode ray tube. The big end is the screen you see. At the other end is an

Above **The German scientist, Heinrich Hertz, discovered how to produce radio waves in 1884. In Hertz's apparatus, an electric spark jumped across a small gap on the transmitter.**

Left **The basic radio wave broadcast is called a carrier wave. It is varied or modulated to add the signal. In amplitude modulation, or AM, the strength of the carrier wave is varied. In frequency modulation, or FM, the frequency of the carrier wave is varied. Inside the receiving radio, the signals are separated from the carrier wave and turned back into sound.**

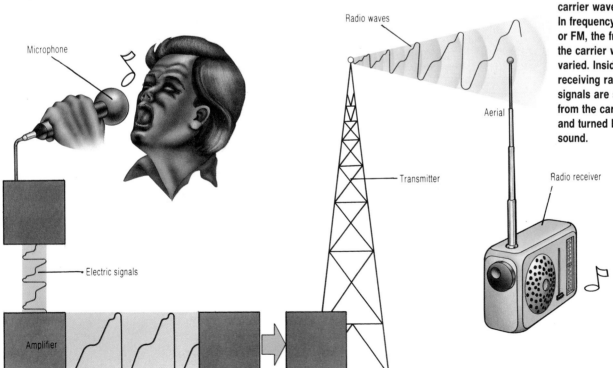

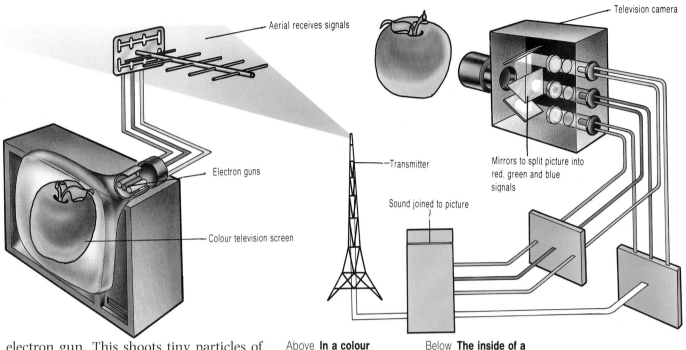

Aerial receives signals

Electron guns

Colour television screen

Television camera

Mirrors to split picture into red, green and blue signals

Sound joined to picture

Transmitter

electron gun. This shoots tiny particles of electricity, called electrons, onto the screen. Where the electrons hit the screen, the screen glows. The beam of electrons produced by an electron gun zigzags across the screen in horizontal lines. As the beam moves across the screen the glow produced forms the picture.

A colour television set has three electron guns: one that produces a red colour, one that produces blue and one that produces green. All the colours you see on the screen are made by mixing these three colours.

Above **In a colour television camera, there are three electronic tubes. One of these picks up the red colour in the scene being broadcast. The second picks up green, and the other blue. The three colour signals are broadcast. The receiver uses three electron guns to fire the colours at the screen.**

Left **Editing a television programme in a studio.**

Below **The inside of a colour television screen is coated with thousands of tiny dots of chemicals called phosphors. Holes in the shadowmask direct the electron beams to the correct colour phosphors, which glow on impact. The electron beams zigzag across the screen in horizontal lines, completing the picture.**

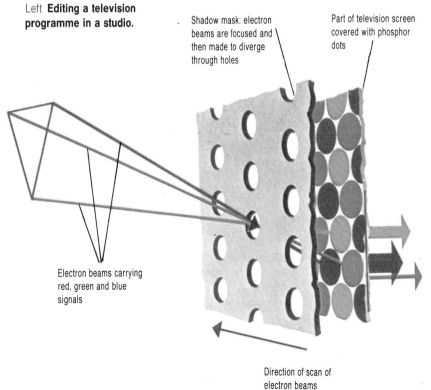

Shadow mask: electron beams are focused and then made to diverge through holes

Part of television screen covered with phosphor dots

Electron beams carrying red, green and blue signals

Direction of scan of electron beams

Technology Factfinder

Alloy A mixture of two or more metals. For example, brass is an alloy of copper and zinc.

Altimeter An instrument for measuring height above the ground, used in aircraft. One type is a kind of barometer, measuring atmospheric pressure, which falls as height increases.

Amplifier An electronic device which magnifies the strength of a signal, such as radio waves.

Automation The use of machines, usually in factories, to do work automatically.

Battery A source of electrical power which produces electricity from chemicals. It often contains many electrical cells, linked together.

Bell, Alexander Graham (1847–1922) US inventor, born in Scotland. He invented the telephone in 1876.

Cathode-ray tube The main unit in a television receiver. It consists of a cone-shaped glass vessel with a long neck. An electron gun in the neck fires electrons at the fluorescent screen, producing spots of light.

Computer An electronic device for storing and manipulating a large amount of information. Their great advantage is the speed with which they do calculations and retrieve information.

Diesel A type of oil used by engines of locomotives, lorries, buses, etc. In a diesel engine, the fuel is ignited (set alight) by hot, compressed air. Unlike a petrol engine, it has no spark plugs.

Drag The resistance of the air or water to the movement of anything moving through it, for example, an aircraft, ship or car.

Dynamo *see* Generator.

Edison, Thomas (1847–1931) US inventor. Among his many inventions, the most famous are the phonograph (the first record player) and the electric light bulb.

Fibre A long, thread-like structure, such as protein fibre in animals (for example, silk) or cellulose structures in plants (for example, cotton). Many artificial fibres, such as nylon, have been developed.

Ford, Henry (1863–1947) US engineer. The famous Model T Ford was the first motor car produced cheaply on a factory production line.

Fulcrum The point from which a lever moves, or pivots. For example, in a seesaw (which is a kind of lever), the fulcrum is at the centre.

Galvanometer An instrument which detects and measures very small electric currents.

Geiger counter An instrument which detects and measures radioactivity.

Generator A machine that converts mechanical energy into electrical energy. A dynamo produces direct current (DC) electricity. An alternator produces alternating current (AC) electricity.

Gyroscope An instrument used in navigation. It is a wheel which spins inside a framework. The wheel

can turn freely in all three dimensions and remains in the same position whatever the movements of the aircraft or ship.

Holograph A photograph in three dimensions, which is made possible by laser light.

Hovercraft A propeller-driven vehicle which moves on a cushion of air. The "cushion" is held in place by a "skirt" and supplied by fans. Hovercraft can travel over sea or land or swamp.

Hydroelectric power Electricity which is generated from the power of falling water ("hydro" means "water").

Hydrofoil A type of boat mounted on underwater "foils" or wings. When it has reached a certain speed, the hull rises out of the water. This reduces drag and allows the boat to go faster.

Information technology A name given to the methods of sending, obtaining and storing information by electronic methods.

Internal combustion engine A petrol or diesel fuel-burning engine, as used in most motor vehicles. In the petrol engine, a mixture of petrol vapour and air is exploded by a spark inside cylinders. The gases produced expand, driving pistons down the cylinders, producing power.

Jet engine A type of gas-turbine engine used in most large aircraft. A stream of hot gases is expelled from the rear of the engine, driving the aircraft forwards.

Laser A device which projects a narrow, intense beam of light. Among other uses, lasers make precise cutting tools, used by surgeons. They are also important in fibre-optic communications, as a laser beam can carry a huge amount of information.

Lever A machine for lifting a heavy weight. In principle, a lever consists of a bar which turns on a fulcrum. A wheelbarrow and nutcrackers represent other types of levers.

Marconi, Guglielmo (1874–1937) Italian physicist. He invented the first workable system of wireless telegraphy (radio), transmitting signals across the Atlantic Ocean in 1901.

Metals Elements that are normally solids (mercury is one exception). They are good conductors of heat and electricity, and they can be "worked" by beating, hammering, heating, etc. into sheet, wire or other forms.

Microphone An instrument for changing sound waves into electric signals. The variations of the current can be recorded or amplified and then changed back to sounds by a loudspeaker.

Microscope An instrument for magnifying the appearance of a small object. The simplest example is a magnifying glass. Laboratory instruments are more complicated and make use of two lenses. An electron microscope can produce a magnified image of many thousands of times using a focussed beam of electrons rather than light.

Microwave A form of electromagnetic radiation of very short wavelength. Microwaves are used in communication (e.g. radio) and in cookery. In a microwave oven, the molecules of water in the food are made to vibrate very fast, causing heat.

Top **A ruby laser in action in a laboratory.**

Above **A sea-water distillation plant.**

Montgolfier, Joseph (1740–1810) and Etienne (1745–99) French balloonists. Their hot-air balloon flight of 1783 was the first manned flight. They travelled nearly 2 km in about ten minutes.

Morse, Samuel (1791–1872) US inventor. He invented the telegraph, and also the system of dots and dashes called the Morse Code, used for sending messages by telegraph.

Nuclear power Energy obtained from the nucleus of certain atoms, by nuclear fission. In a nuclear power plant, the energy is released in a nuclear reactor and changed into electricity.

Nylon A man-made plastic and synthetic fibre. The raw materials come from oil or coal. Many different types of nylon are made, including nylon thread.

Optical fibre A very thin, bendable glass thread which can transmit light by internal reflections. They are used in making surgical examinations as well as in communications.

Pendulum A weight (called a bob) swinging at the end of a rod. The regularity of a pendulum's swing was used in building the first really accurate clocks in the 17th century.

Petroleum A liquid mineral fuel containing hydrocarbons, which is found trapped in between rocks below the Earth's surface.

Plastics Man-made materials in which the molecules are joined together in a long chain (polymer). They can be shaped by pressure and heat. Many types of plastic are made, with different properties for different purposes.

Pulley A tool for lifting weights. It consists of a wheel with a groove around the rim in which a rope runs.

Radar A method of detecting and locating the position of objects. Microwaves, electromagnetic waves of very short wavelength, are reflected by the object and recorded on the screen of a cathode-ray tube.

Radio The transmission and reception of messages through the air by means of electromagnetic (radio) waves.

Robot A machine which can do a job that is usually done by a human being. Robots are used on factory assembly lines to do one particular job which is continually repeated.

Rocket An engine driven by burning gases, like a jet engine. It is the only kind of engine that works in space because it carries its own oxygen.

Sextant An instrument used in navigation. It measures the angle of the Sun or other stars above the horizon at a certain time. From this it is possible to work out a ship's position.

Shuttle The first reusable space vehicle. An American craft, it is launched into space by rockets, but lands like an aeroplane.

Skylab The first American space laboratory. It was launched in 1973 and was visited by three teams of astronauts for periods of 28, 95 and 94 days.

Smelting The method used to extract a metal from its ore by heating.

Software The program (instructions) and data (information) which are fed into a computer. The computer itself and all machinery connected with it are called hardware.

Sonar A system that uses sound waves to find the position of an object underwater. It was first designed to detect enemy submarines. Sound waves are sent out and their echo is registered by microphones.

Sputnik A Soviet space satellite. Launched 4 October 1957, Sputnik I was the first man-made satellite to orbit the Earth.

Steam engine An engine in which the energy of hot steam is converted into work by moving a piston inside a cylinder.

Stephenson, George (1781–1848) British railway pioneer. His *Rocket* was the first successful steam-driven locomotive built for a public railway.

Telegraph A system for sending messages over a long distance by an electric signal along a wire. Messages were sent in Morse code by breaking up the signal into "dots" and "dashes".

Telephone A device for transmitting speech along wires or by radio waves. The mouthpiece converts sound waves into an electric signal. In the receiver the incoming signal vibrates a diaphragm which recreates the sound waves.

Television A broadcasting system which sends pictures by radio waves to a television receiver containing a cathode-ray tube. The picture is built up from hundreds of horizontal lines.

Thermometer An instrument for measuring temperature. A home thermometer consists of a thin glass tube containing (usually) mercury. Heat causes the mercury to expand in the tube, and the temperature is shown on a scale alongside the tube.

Thrust The force produced by an aircraft engine, which drives the aircraft forwards.

Transistor A semiconductor electronic device which controls the flow of an electric current. It is used as an amplifier in radios and television sets and has made possible advances in computers.

Turbine An engine in which a shaft is turned by a flow of gas or water directed through the blades of a kind of fan which are attached to the shaft. Water turbines are used in hydroelectric power stations, gas turbines in jet engines.

Ultrasound Sound waves of very high frequency which are beyond human hearing.

Video recorder An electronic device for recording and replaying television pictures.

Volta, Alessandro (1745–1827) Italian physicist. Among other discoveries in electricity, he found that a wire connecting two different metals placed in a salt solution carries an electric current. This is the principle of the battery.

Watt, James (1736–1819) British inventor. His improved version of the steam engine, using a separate condenser, was the main source of power for factories and machines in the 19th century.

Wright, Orville (1871–1948) and Wilbur (1867–1912) US engineers. They made the first successful powered flight in a heavier-than-air machine, an aeroplane which they built themselves, in 1903.

The Human Body

The skeleton

The skeleton is the framework of bones which supports the body. It gives the body its shape, and surrounds and protects all the soft parts of the body. For example, the heart and lungs are protected by the ribs, and the brain is protected by the skull (made up of 29 bones). Another important reason why we have a skeleton is that, together with the muscles, it enables us to move.

There are more than 200 bones in the human body. They are all shapes and sizes from the tiny bones in your fingers to the much larger bones of your hips. Bones are hard on the outside, but inside they are hollow. The space is filled with criss-crossing fibres, which make the bone strong but light. In the centre is the marrow, which is a soft, fatty tissue. It makes new cells for the blood system.

The places where bones meet and are held together are called joints. Shoulders and hips have ball-and-socket joints, which allow movement in any direction. Elbows, knees, toes and fingers have hinged joints, which only allow them to move in one or two directions.

At joints, the ends of the bones are covered with cartilage, which is a tough, gristly material. It prevents the bones rubbing together and damaging each other. Joints also have a special liquid, called synovial fluid, which acts like oil and keeps them moving easily. A special layer of tissue prevents the fluid leaking away and helps hold joints together.

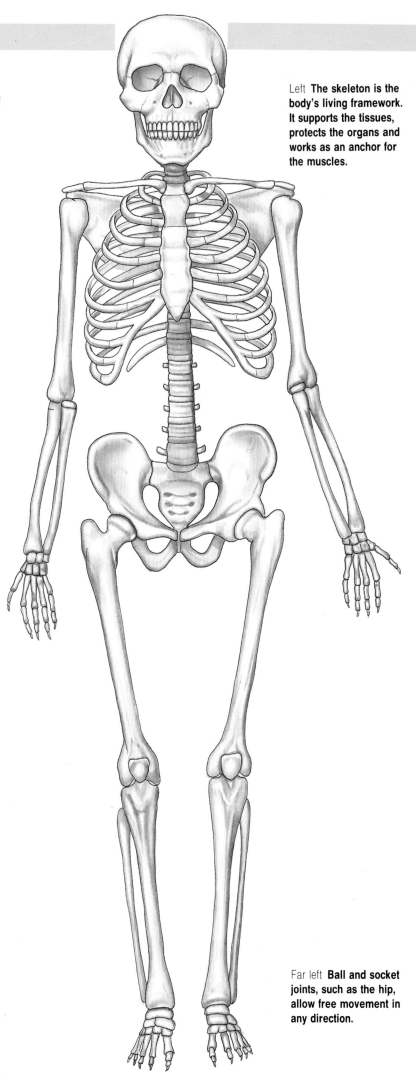

Left **The skeleton is the body's living framework. It supports the tissues, protects the organs and works as an anchor for the muscles.**

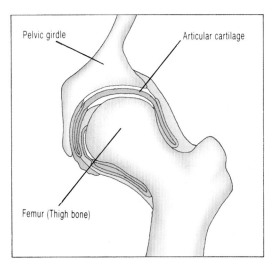

Pelvic girdle

Articular cartilage

Femur (Thigh bone)

Far left **Ball and socket joints, such as the hip, allow free movement in any direction.**

The muscles

The muscles allow the parts of the body to move. Muscles come in many shapes and sizes. Some are large and flat like a sheet. Others, like the biceps in the upper arm, are more fleshy.

Muscles are joined to bones by strong cords called tendons. They reach from one side of a joint to the other. When a muscle is tightened, it grows shorter, pulling the bone after it. This is what happens when you bend your elbow. When you relax the muscle again, your arm straightens.

Muscles cannot push, they can only pull. So most of them work in pairs. When you move your arm to the right, one muscle tightens. When you move it back, another muscle tightens to move it in the opposite direction.

There are over 600 muscles in the body. Many are used to move legs, arms, head and so on. But other muscles have different jobs. Some make the lungs expand and draw in air. Some move food from the mouth down into the stomach. The heart itself is one big muscle.

The brain

The brain is the control centre of the body. It is made up of millions of tiny cells, which are connected to the rest of the body by cables called nerves.

The body sends messages along the nerves to the brain. Besides feelings of pain, or warmth or wetness and so on, the messages may be sounds (from the ears) or sights (from the eyes). The brain receives the message and decides what action to take. It may store the message in its memory. It may order part of the body to move.

The brain has three main parts. The brain stem connects the nerves with the upper brain and controls breathing and heart beat. The cerebellum controls movement by giving orders to the muscles. The cerebrum, the largest part of the brain, does the work of thinking and remembering.

The brain is just as important to an athlete as it is to a learned professor, because it is the brain which makes legs and arms move and keeps the body balanced.

Above **The gymnast's brain co-ordinates messages, controlling** her muscle and limb position, balance and sight.

Below **The human brain is made up of three parts: the greatly folded cerebrum, the cerebellum situated beneath it, and the brain stem.**

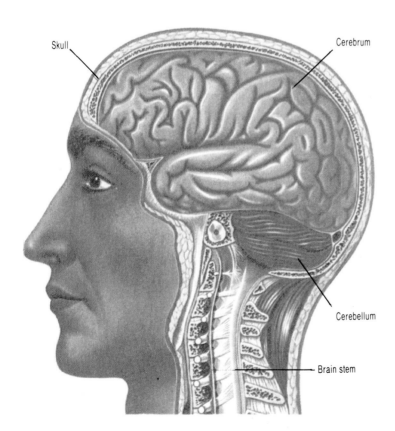

Skull

Cerebrum

Cerebellum

Brain stem

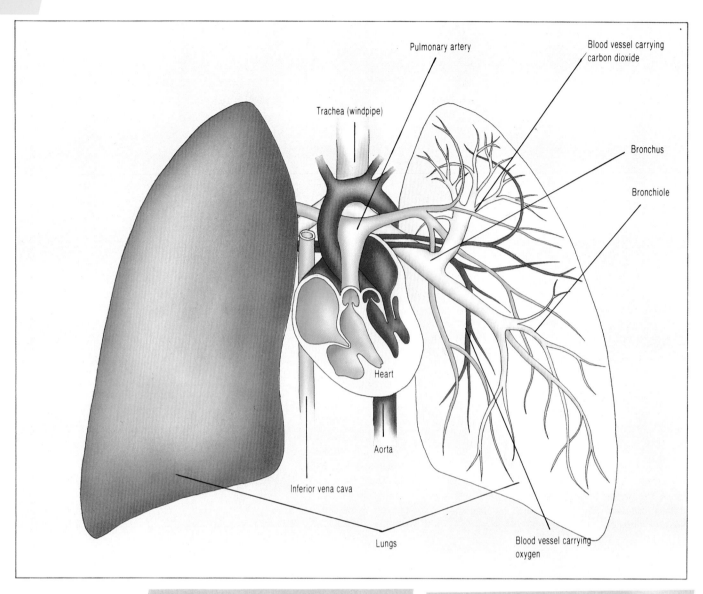

Pulmonary artery

Blood vessel carrying carbon dioxide

Trachea (windpipe)

Bronchus

Bronchiole

Heart

Aorta

Inferior vena cava

Lungs

Blood vessel carrying oxygen

Above **The lungs contain thousands of airways ending in air sacs called alveoli. There are over 300 million altogether. The blue blood vessels carry carbon dioxide towards the alveoli ready for breathing out, while the red vessels carry fresh oxygen to cells all over the body.**

The lungs

Like all living things, the human body needs oxygen, which it gets from the air. When we breathe in, air passes into the lungs, which are two spongy sacs in the chest. The air is drawn in through the nose and mouth. On the way to the lungs it is warmed, and dust and germs are caught by tiny hairs in the nose and windpipe.

The lungs are full of tiny pipes ending in air sacs called alveoli. Oxygen from the air is absorbed into the blood stream. Waste gas in the form of carbon dioxide is breathed out again.

The lungs are worked by a big muscle called the diaphragm, helped by smaller muscles attached to the ribs. As air is breathed in, these muscles make the chest expand, pushing the ribs out. The ribs are pulled in again as air is breathed out.

The blood

The job of the blood is to carry oxygen, and other materials needed by the body, to every part, and to carry waste materials away. It travels in hollow tubes called blood vessels.

The main blood vessels are the arteries, which carry fresh blood from the heart, and the veins, which carry the blood back again. Smaller branch vessels called capillaries form a huge mesh throughout the body.

Blood can only travel in one direction through the system. Every blood vessel has a series of flaps, or valves, which prevent it from flowing backwards.

Blood is mostly made up of plasma, which is a clear, watery fluid. Floating in the plasma are the blood cells. Red blood cells carry the oxygen, and give the blood its colour. White cells help defend the body against germs. The blood also contains small cells called platelets. When a blood vessel is injured, the platelets cluster together and make the blood clot, preventing more blood flowing from the injury.

There are about 4.5–6 litres (8–10 pints) of blood in a human body. When blood is lost, the body can make more quickly. If too much blood is lost, a blood transfusion is necessary.

The heart

The heart is a powerful muscle, whose job is to pump the blood through the body. It beats about seventy times a minute, each beat pumping blood around the system.

Fresh blood, loaded with oxygen from the lungs, enters the heart and is pumped through the arteries. When the oxygen has been absorbed by the body through the walls of the capillaries, the blood returns to the heart through the veins.

The heart is divided into four chambers, two auricles and two ventricles. Blood from the veins enters the right auricle, passes to the right ventricle and from there to the lungs, through the pulmonary artery. Fresh blood enters the left auricle and passes to the left ventricle. From there it is squeezed into the aorta, the main artery, and carries oxygen to all parts of the body.

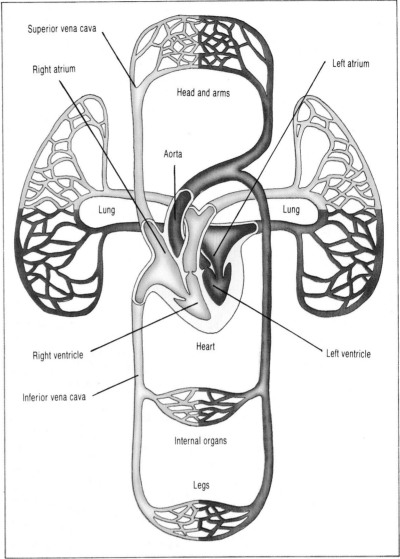

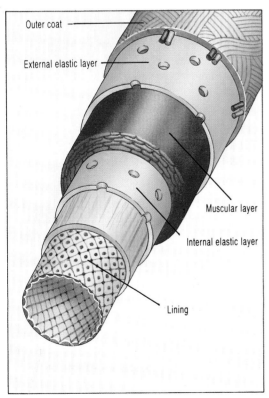

Left **The body's network of arteries helps to make sure that blood is delivered swiftly wherever it is needed.**

Above **Blood is pumped by the heart throughout the body in a complicated network of blood vessels.**

Below **Blood transfusions (removing blood and injecting new blood) occur regularly in modern hospitals.**

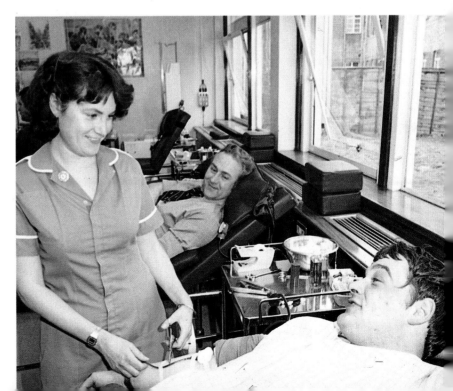

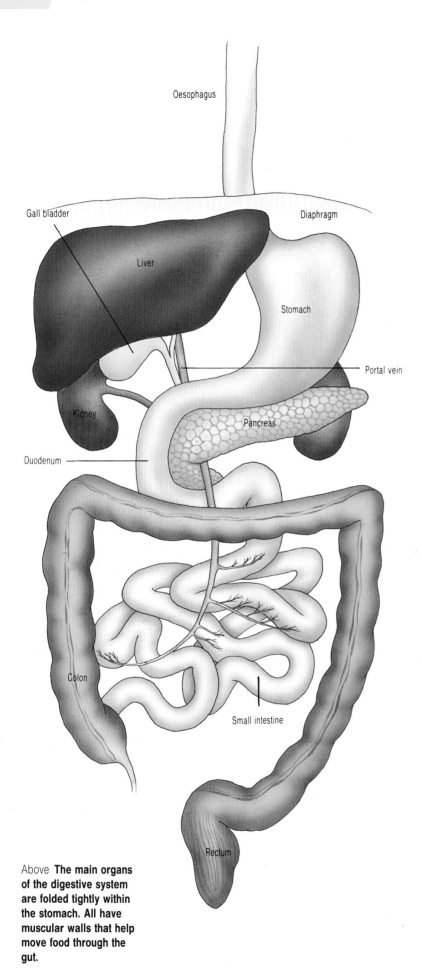

Oesophagus

Gall bladder

Diaphragm

Liver

Stomach

Portal vein

Kidney

Pancreas

Duodenum

Colon

Small intestine

Rectum

Above **The main organs of the digestive system are folded tightly within the stomach. All have muscular walls that help move food through the gut.**

The stomach and intestines

Like an engine, the body needs fuel to keep it working. It gets it from food. But the food we eat has to be processed by the body before it can be used to build cells or give energy. This is the job of the digestive system.

The body needs different kinds of food. These are the main types: proteins, which help the body grow and repair itself; starches and fats, which provide energy and warmth; vitamins and mineral salts, which keep the body healthy. As about two-thirds of the human body is water, it also needs a good supply of this.

The job of processing the food, or digestion, begins in the mouth, where it is chewed up and mixed with saliva. That makes it easier to swallow. It passes through the throat and down the gullet to the stomach, where strong muscles churn it up and digestive juices begin to break it down into a form which the body can use.

It spends more than two hours in the stomach, and then passes into the small intestine. This is an amazingly long tube – about 6 m (20 ft) – but it is tightly coiled into a small space. Here the process of digestion is completed, helped by the ridged lining of the small intestine and the millions of tiny hairs, called villi, which cover it.

Almost all the food the body can use is digested in the small intestine and passes through the walls of the tube into the blood stream. Undigested waste material moves into the large intestine and, after further processing, leaves the body through the rectum.

The whole process, from putting something into your mouth to getting rid of what's left in the lavatory, takes roughly 24 hours.

The kidneys

Human bodies contain two kidneys. They are filters, which keep the blood clean and healthy. Every hour, about 70 litres (120 pints) of blood are pumped through them. They take out waste material and unwanted water, which together become urine. The urine is stored in the bladder, which has to be emptied every few hours.

The kidneys have another important job. They control the amount of salt and water in the blood. Too much salt is damaging, and too much water weakens the blood.

The liver

The liver is a remarkable organ, because it carries out so many tasks. Blood reaches the liver from the intestines, where it has absorbed the useful materials from food. The liver controls the flow of these useful substances – fats, carbohydrates and proteins – in the blood. It acts as a storehouse for fats and carbohydrates, and as a factory, converting protein to make energy. It is also a cleaner, destroying old red blood cells and poisons in the blood.

The liver also produces bile. This is a bitter green liquid which is used to break down the food in the intestines and release its goodness.

The liver is the busiest organ in the body, with as many as 500 different jobs. Not surprisingly, it is also the biggest organ.

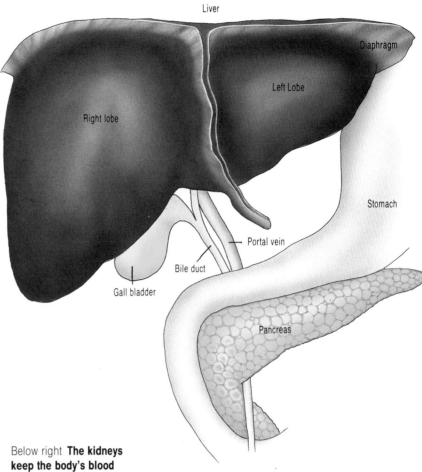

Below **The body has developed all sorts of ways of breaking down the food we eat – whatever shape it comes in!**

Above right **The liver has many jobs. One is to control the flow of useful substances in the blood.**

Below right **The kidneys keep the body's blood clean and healthy. They hold back water or let it run out as urine.**

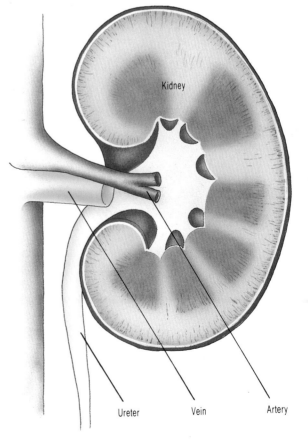

THE SPREAD OF HUMAN BEINGS

The first human beings probably lived in east central Africa about two million years ago. At that time, much of the Earth was covered by ice and was not a fit place for human beings to live.

As the Ice Age came to an end, the Earth grew warmer and the ice sheets retreated. Much more of the Earth became suited to human life. Over many thousands of years, human beings spread to every continent except Antarctica.

The last continents to be populated were the Americas and Australia. The Americas were settled by people who came from eastern Asia, crossing from Siberia to Alaska when there was still a land link between them. In the same way, people entered Australia from south-east Asia, though they may have used boats for part of the distance.

All human beings belong to the same species, *Homo sapiens*. They are really all very much alike. But there are a great many small differences between groups of people living in different parts of the world. One of

Below **All skin types contain a range of nerve endings sensing touch, pressure, heat, cold and pain.**

the most obvious differences is skin colour. There are also differences in size, type of hair, size of teeth (Australian Aborigines have the largest teeth, Lapps from Scandinavia have the smallest) and other minor features. Blood types differ too. For example, blood type B is hardly ever found among North American Indians. It is rare among Europeans – less than 15 per cent of Europeans have blood type B. But in many parts of Asia and Africa it is quite common, with nearly half the population having blood of this type. Diseases also affect different groups. Sickle-cell anaemia is a hereditary blood disease which is common in parts of Africa, but unknown in other countries.

No one knows for certain why different groups or races of people developed differences in their appearance or other features, but the main reason is probably connected with the kind of place in which they lived. Over thousands of years, races of people changed to suit the climate of their homeland.

Australian aborigine

Dark-skinned people

All people can be roughly divided into three groups, called Caucasoid, Mongoloid and Negroid, or "white", "yellow" and "black". This is not a scientific division and it is not really very accurate (most "blacks" are brown, most "whites" are pink), but at least it is simple!

Negroid people are believed to have developed in central Africa. They later spread

Opposite **A map showing the distribution of the Caucasoid peoples.**

Below **A map showing the distribution of the Negroid peoples.**

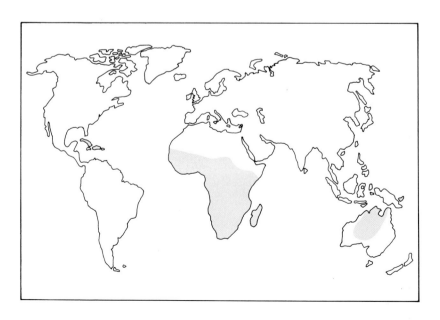

Below **Negroid people are believed to have originated in central Africa. They include the shortest people in the world, the pygmies of Zaire, and the tallest, the Masai of Kenya.**

African pygmy

Pacific islander

Bantu

throughout southern Africa, mixing with different peoples. As they came from one of the hottest parts of the world, they developed ways of protecting their bodies from the heat of the sun. The dark colour of their skin prevented the sun's rays penetrating. Broad lips and noses also helped to keep the body cool.

However, there are today many different peoples or races in Africa. They include, for example, the shortest people in the world, the pygmies of the Zaire River valley who average less than 1.5 m (5 ft) tall, and one of the tallest people in the world, the lanky Masai of Kenya.

The bushmen of southern Africa, many of whom used to live in the harsh Kalahari Desert, are another unique African people. Yet they share many of the features of other Africans, including a dark skin, since they too come from a hot region.

In the last few centuries, black Africans have spread throughout the world. Many were taken to the Americas as slaves, and millions of their descendants now live in North America, the West Indies and Brazil.

Besides the bushmen, whose ancestors were much more widely spread in Africa and probably occupied all the open land, and the Negroid peoples, who came from the tropical forest but spread throughout the continent, there were other groups not related to either of them. In the north-east were people who are sometimes called Hamitic. Although they were fairly dark-skinned, they belonged to the Caucasoid group.

Below **The Caucasoids include the Nordic, Mediterranean, Indic and Alpine peoples.**

Arab

Indian

Nordic

Celtic

The Caucasoid peoples

The Caucasoid peoples include the white-skinned people of Europe, whose descendants today also make up most of the populations of North America, Australia, New Zealand, and some other non-European countries. However, not all Caucasoids are white-skinned. In fact they vary from very pale, fair-haired people in north-west Europe to people of the Indian sub-continent, some of whom are darker than most Africans.

They are called Caucasoid because a fair-skinned people, who may have been the ancestors of most Europeans, appeared at a very early time in the region of the Caucasus Mountains, between the Black Sea and the Caspian Sea.

In cooler climates, like that of north-west Europe, it was not necessary for human bodies to protect themselves against the heat of the sun. Europeans therefore have pale skins and narrow noses and lips.

However, many other causes have been at work in creating racial differences, besides climate. Today, for example, Americans of Chinese parents are in general taller than their fathers and mothers. This must be due to a different way of life, including a different diet.

Caucasoid peoples can be divided into a number of different groups. The main ones are Nordic (fair-skinned, mainly northern European), Mediterranean (southern Europe, the Middle East and North Africa – including the Arabs), Indic (mainly northern India) and Alpine (from south-west Europe to western Asia). Variations exist between these main groups, besides skin colour. For example, the Alpine type is shorter and stockier, with round head and wide cheekbones.

The Mongoloid peoples

This is the largest group of peoples, which contains more than two-thirds of the world population today. Mongoloid peoples are sometimes described as yellow-skinned. Really, they are no more yellow than Caucasoids are white, although some Mongoloid people have a faint yellowish tint.

One group, the North American Indians, used to be called "redskins", which is equally inaccurate!

The name Mongoloid comes from Mongolia, in east-central Asia. Mongoloids are supposed to look like the Mongols, and perhaps to be related to them. Certainly, the native peoples of eastern Asia do have some similar features, such as dark eyes, dark straight hair and smooth faces. Most of them have an extra fold of skin on the inner edge of the eyelid, which gives them a slant-eyed look. These features may be explained as the result of climate, because they are all features which give protection against cold, and these groups, which are sometimes called Late Mongoloid, were originally trapped to the north of mountain glaciers, in a very cold climate.

However, the American Indians do not have these features. They are classed as Early Mongoloid, and they have other features which they do share with peoples of eastern Asia, such as the shape of their incisor teeth and the way their hair grows from the crown of the head.

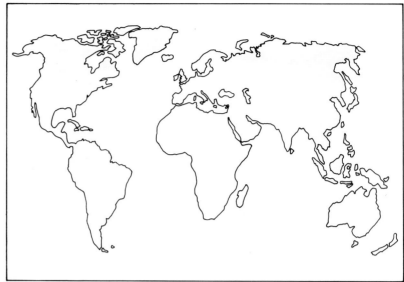

Above **A map showing the distribution of the Mongoloid peoples.**

Below **The Mongoloids contain more than two-thirds of the world population today.**

Japanese

Chinese

Eskimo

Mongolian

Mexican indian

Human Body Factfinder

Acupuncture A method of stopping pain and curing disease by sticking needles into certain parts of the body. Acupuncture was originally practised in China, but is now used in Western countries too.

AIDS An infectious disease caused by a virus which leads to a breakdown in the body's normal defences against infection. It cannot be cured and usually ends in death.

Allergy A condition in which pain or illness is caused by touching, breathing or eating some substance which is harmless to most people. Hay fever is caused by an allergy to pollen.

Anaemia A disease in which the number of red blood cells circulating in the body, or their ability to carry oxygen, is reduced. Anaemic people lack energy and are short of breath.

Anaesthetic A substance used in medicine to take away feeling. A local anaesthetic makes an area numb; a general anaesthetic makes the patient unconscious.

Anatomy The study of the parts of the body and how they work.

Antibiotic A type of medicine which stops infections caused by bacteria. Antibiotics are made from living things such as fungi.

Antibody A substance produced by the body which fights against antigens, poisonous substances produced by bacteria.

Antiseptic A chemical substance, such as iodine, which kills bacteria. Antiseptic is put on wounds to prevent them becoming infected.

Artery A blood vessel like a tube with a tough muscular "wall" which carries oxygen-rich blood from the heart to all parts of the body.

Barnard, Christiaan (born 1922) South African surgeon. He carried out the first human heart transplant operation, in 1967.

Blood pressure The pressure of the blood on the walls of the blood vessels. Abnormal blood pressure is a sign of ill health.

Bone The hard parts of the body which make up the skeleton and support and protect the softer parts. There are 206 bones in an adult human body.

Brain An organ consisting mainly of a large spongy mass of cells inside the skull. The brain controls the nervous system of the body as well as thought and memory.

Bronchial tubes The tubes of the lungs. In human beings, each lung has one main bronchus, which divides again and again into small tubes called bronchioles.

Cancer A diseased growth of abnormal cells in the body, called a tumour. There are many kinds of cancer, and they can affect almost any part. Cancers keep growing, and although most can be easily cured, they are a common cause of death.

Chromosome A thread-like structure in the nucleus of a cell. They are always in pairs, and every human cell contains 23 pairs of chromosomes.

They contain the genes, which control the inherited characteristics of a person, such as height, hair colour, etc.

Circulatory system The arrangement of arteries, veins and other organs through which blood flows, carrying food and oxygen to all parts of the body.

Deficiency disease A condition caused when the body does not receive enough of one or more of the substances such as vitamins or proteins it needs to stay healthy.

DNA (deoxyribonucleic acid) A substance found in the nucleus of a cell, where it combines with protein to form chromosomes. Its molecular structure contains instructions, called genes, which pass on hereditary characteristics from parent to child.

Diagnosis The explanation of the cause and nature of an illness. Until a disease is diagnosed, it cannot be properly treated.

Diaphragm A large band of muscle between chest and stomach. The main task of the diaphragm is to control breathing by expanding and contracting the lungs.

Digestive system All the organs of the body which turn food into the substances which the body can absorb. The system includes the stomach and the intestines.

Drug A medicine, or a chemical used in medicines. Some drugs are substances taken because they give a pleasant physical sensation. Drugs of this kind are dangerous and often addictive.

Epidemic An outbreak of an infectious disease in which many people within the same area are affected at the same time.

Enzymes Substances produced by cells which help in many kinds of chemical reaction in the body. For example, certain enzymes help the digestive process.

Fleming, Alexander (1881–1951) British bacteriologist. In 1928 he discovered, by chance, a mould which proved to be a powerful antibiotic – penicillin.

Freud, Sigmund (1856–1939) Austrian psychiatrist. He was the founder of psychoanalysis, a method of treating nervous illness by searching the patient's unconscious mind, revealed through memories and dreams, for a hidden cause.

Galen (died about 200 BC) Greek physician. He studied the anatomy of animals and discovered that blood flowed through the arteries. He was the chief authority on the body up to the time of Vesalius.

Gene *see* DNA.

Gland An organ which takes substances from the blood and converts them into the chemicals which the body needs, for example, saliva.

Harvey, William (1578–1657) English physician. He discovered that blood is pumped around the body by the heart – an enormous step forward in understanding how the body works.

Heart A muscular organ in the body which acts as a pump to circulate the blood.

Hippocrates (lived around 400 BC) Greek physician. He was the most famous doctor of ancient

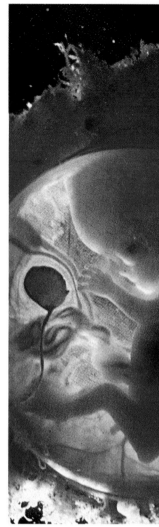

Top **A human embryo in the womb.**

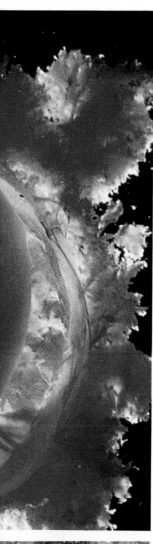

Above **Aborigines, natives of Australia.**

times. The Hippocratic Oath is his statement of how a doctor should behave towards his patients.

Hypochondria The belief of a person that he is suffering from a disease he has not got, or is more ill than he really is.

Immune system The natural defences which protect the body against disease. A person can be immunized against a particular disease by vaccination.

Insulin A substance produced by a certain gland, which controls the amount of glucose in the blood. Lack of insulin causes a disease called diabetes.

Intestine The long tube between the stomach and the anus. The upper part is known as the small intestine, the lower part as the large intestine. It absorbs food and carries waste away.

Jenner, Edward (1749–1823) British physician. He discovered vaccination as a means of preventing the deadly disease of smallpox.

Kidneys A pair of glands which control the amount of water and salt in the body, and take waste products and water out of the blood and turn them into urine.

Lister, Joseph (1827–1912) British surgeon. He realized that infections were easily spread during operations and was the first to use antiseptics during surgery.

Liver A large gland in the body below the diaphragm. The liver does a great many jobs, mainly concerned with processing and storing food products.

Lungs A pair of organs in the chest. They take in air from which oxygen is absorbed by the blood. Carbon dioxide is removed from the blood and breathed out.

Muscle A bundle of tissue in the body made up of cells which can contract or relax to produce movement in joints or organs.

Nerve A thread-like tissue in the body, which carries messages to and from the brain.

Pathology The study of diseases. The person (usually a doctor) who examines a dead body to discover the cause of death is called a pathologist.

Pediatrics The branch of medicine concerned with children.

Penicillin An antibiotic which is obtained from a fungus mould called *penicillium*.

Pharmacology The study of drugs. A pharmacist, or chemist, makes and supplies drugs.

Physiology The study of how living things work.

Physiotherapy The improvement or strengthening of bodily movements by exercise or massage.

Pneumonia An infection of the lungs which causes inflammation and difficulty in breathing.

Polio (short for poliomyelitis) An infectious disease which affects the nerves of the backbone, leading to paralysis and sometimes, especially in small children, death.

Protein A chemical compound made up of amino-acids, which the body needs to grow and repair itself. Protein is obtained from meat, eggs, fish, cheese, etc. Much of the body itself is made up of proteins.

Psychiatry A branch of medicine dealing with the treatment of diseases of the mind.

Psychology The study of the mind and the way it works, and especially the way it affects human and animal behaviour.

Pulse The expansion and contraction of an artery at each beat of the heart. An irregular or abnormal pulse rate is a sign of ill health. The pulse can be measured at the wrist.

Respiration Another word for breathing, the process of taking in oxygen from the air and giving out carbon dioxide.

Stethoscope The instrument used by doctors to listen to sounds inside the body, such as the heartbeat.

Stomach A sack-like organ at the end of the oesophagus, a tube that leads from the throat. The stomach receives food which it turns into a semi-liquid mass, partly by muscular movements and partly by adding a digesting liquid called gastric juice.

Stroke A sudden illness in part of the brain which can cause permanent damage or death. A stroke is caused by loss of blood in the brain following a blockage or a burst blood vessel.

Surgery The branch of medicine which treats disease by direct operation, usually by cutting open the body.

Tendon A band of strong tissue, made up of fibres running the same way, by which a muscle is attached to a bone.

Tissue A collection of similar cells which make up a particular organ. For example, the lungs are made of lung tissue, muscles of muscle tissue.

Transplant In surgery, the replacement of a diseased or damaged organ with a healthy one from another person.

Tumour A growth caused by abnormal growth of tissue. A benign tumour is usually not dangerous; a malignant tumour, or cancer, may spread and cause damage.

Vaccination Protecting against a particular disease by inoculation with vaccine, a substance containing a virus in a weakened form. It causes production of the right antibodies.

Vein A blood vessel which carries deoxygenated blood towards the right upper chamber of the heart (*see* Artery). Veins have valves so the blood cannot travel the wrong way.

Vesalius, Andreas (1514–64) Flemish anatomist. From his work on dissecting the human body, he accurately described how the parts worked. One of his many conclusions was that the brain, not the heart, controlled personality.

Virus The cause of many diseases. A virus can only reproduce itself inside a living cell.

Vitamin One of several substances needed by the body and obtained from food. For example, Vitamin C is obtained from fresh fruit and vegetables. Deficiency of Vitamin C causes scurvy.

Religions and Governments

WORLDS OF MYTHS AND LEGENDS

A myth is a story, usually a very old story, which has some special meaning. It explains something mysterious, and it is usually religious.

Myths began almost as soon as human beings learned to think about the world. Everything they saw and heard and felt was mysterious. They had no idea what the Sun was, or why it shone, or how it moved. But human beings cannot live comfortably without finding things out. So they invented myths which explained such things. They wondered what the world was. How did it begin? Who made it? The myths that explained these questions developed over many hundreds of years. Some of them became the basis of great religions.

Every people or nation, so far as we know, has had myths about the creation of the world. An old Chinese myth tells how the universe began inside an egg. All things on Heaven and Earth were mixed inside the egg. Then the first being, called Pangu, was formed. He broke open the egg. Heavy parts sank down and became land. Lighter parts rose and became the sky.

The Maya, people of Mexico and Central America, believed that the universe began as nothing but sea and sky. Hidden beneath the water were the Creators, who planned the world. They made mountains and valleys rise above the sea, and they made the animals to live there. But the animals could not speak, so the Creators made human beings out of wood and corn.

In the mythology of northern Europe, the first living being was a cruel giant named Ymir. He was attacked and killed by three gods. His huge body formed the Earth, and his blood ran out to form the sea. His skull became the sky above. Then the gods took two pieces of driftwood – or, in another version of the myth, trees – and made them into the first man and the first woman.

There are also myths and legends about real people. Rama, an important figure today for many Hindus, is a god but also a hero. Baldur, the god of light in Scandinavian and Germanic mythology, is another hero-god.

Gods and goddesses

According to the myths of nearly all ancient peoples, the world was ruled by many gods and goddesses. The mythological world we know best is that of the ancient Greeks. The Greek gods were powerful creatures, full of magic, but they were also very like ordinary human beings in their behaviour. Zeus, the chief god, sometimes lost his temper, and would hurl thunderbolts. (This was, in origin, an explanation of the thunderstorm.) Zeus's wife, Hera, was jealous, as Zeus often took up with other goddesses – or human women. Other important gods were Apollo, who probably began as a kind of sun god; Aphrodite, goddess of love; Athena, who was not only the daughter of Zeus but also the special goddess of the city of Athens; and Hermes, the young messenger-god. There were many others, and they were all supposed to live on Mount Olympus in Greece, though they often visited ordinary people.

The ancient Egyptians also had many gods. The most important was Ra, the sun god. In statues of him, he was often given the body of a man and the head of a falcon.

Egyptian gods were often associated with animals. Anubis, the judge of the dead, had the head of a jackal. Other important gods were Osiris, god of farming and fertility, and Isis, his wife, whose tears were said to cause the annual flooding of the Nile. The worship of Isis was an early rival of Christianity.

Among the early civilizations of the Middle East, there were few religions which had only one supreme god. The Persian religion known as Zoroastrianism was one, and the religion of the ancient Hebrews was another. From that, the Jewish and Christian religions developed.

Above **The demon king appears in the *Ramayana*, one of India's great epic stories. A religious teaching to Hindus, the characters Rama and Sita represent the ideal man and woman.**

Below **According to the famous Scandinavian myth, Balder was the god of the Sun and of light, the noblest and happiest of gods.**

Left **Magnificent statues that we can still see today remind us of the powerful, mythological world of the ancient Greeks.**

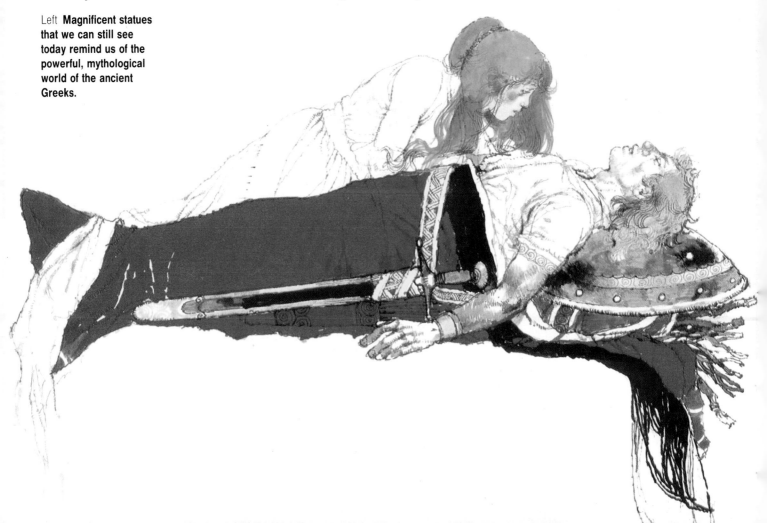

RELIGION

Most people believe in the existence of supernatural beings who are in some way superior to human beings. Religion is the relationship that people have with the supernatural beings in which they believe.

There are many hundreds of different religions. But besides a belief in supernatural beings, most of the major religions have some things in common. They contain a set of beliefs about the world which people share. Most religions tell people how they should behave – towards God and towards each other. In some, this code of behaviour is more important than worship of God.

Christianity

Christianity began as a reform movement in Judaism. It was founded by Jesus, called Christ ("Saviour") by his followers, in the 1st century AD. (The Western calendar is dated from the birth of Jesus, although in fact a mistake was made and Jesus was probably born about 4 BC (BC means "Before Christ"). Christians believe that Jesus was divine, the Son of God, the all-powerful creator of the universe. The Christian god is made up of God the Father, God the Son, and God the Holy Spirit.

Jesus taught that people should love God and also love each other. He said he had come to prepare for the Kingdom of God, by which he meant the perfect state of a person's soul. But it was thought that he meant a political kingdom, and he was treated as a dangerous revolutionary. He was crucified in Jerusalem, but his teaching spread beyond the Jewish kingdom, carried by his apostles, especially St Paul. Christianity eventually became the official religion of the Roman Empire (see page 63).

Below **The Church of England is one of the many Protestant churches of the Christian world.**

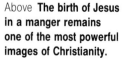

Above **The birth of Jesus in a manger remains one of the most powerful images of Christianity.**

Above **The Orthodox Church spread through the Eastern Empire of the Roman Empire and later to south-east Europe and Russia.**

Left **Many Roman Catholic churches have highly decorated interiors, as in this Mexican church.**

Above **At the age of thirteen, Jewish boys can have a Bar Mitzvah. The ceremony celebrates the fact that a boy has become a man. The menorah** (right) **holds nine candles and is lit at the Jewish festival of Hanukkah.**

Above **The Kaaba is an important Muslim shrine in Mecca. All Muslims try to visit Mecca once in a lifetime.**

When the Roman Empire became divided into a Western Empire (with Rome the capital) and an Eastern Empire (with Constantinople the capital), Christianity was also divided. The Greek Orthodox Church developed separately in the east, and later spread to south-east Europe and Russia. In the west, Christianity remained a single Church under the rule of the Pope in Rome until the 16th century, when another split took place as a result of differences of belief. The Pope remains head of the Roman Catholic Church, but there are many other Churches, including the Church of England, which together are known as Protestant.

Judaism

Judaism, the religion of the Jews, may be the oldest religion in the world. It can be traced back to the figure in the Bible called Abraham, who probably lived about 4,000 years ago. At the least, it goes back to Moses, who received the basic law of God known as the Ten Commandments in about the 13th century BC. The religion of the Jews was based on the idea that God had a special covenant, or agreement, with them. They were his Chosen People. At that time they were a very small nation in the Middle East, often under foreign rule. Later, they spread all over the world, but not until this century did they again have their own state in the Middle East (Israel).

Because of the special relationship between God and the whole Jewish people, Judaism has no single great figure, like Jesus or Muhammad, but a succession of prophets, speakers of God's will, of whom Moses is the greatest. The Torah (Law), the Talmud (Learning) and other sacred writings are the basis of Judaism.

Islam

The civilization of Islam includes all those who follow the Muslim religion. Muslims believe in a supreme god, Allah. They recognize many religious prophets who founded other faiths. They include Abraham, the supposed founder of Judaism, and Jesus, the founder of Christianity. But the greatest prophet of Islam, and the founder of the Muslim religion, was Muhammad (AD 570–632), who came from Mecca in Arabia. Mecca is still the chief religious centre of Islam. Devout Muslims make the great pilgrimage to Mecca at least once in their lifetime.

Inspired by the new religion taught by Muhammad, the Arabs set out on a great period of conquest, which spread Islam over a huge area – from Spain to India. At first Islam was more or less an Arab empire, but as time went by it became international, and at different periods other peoples –

Persians, Turks, etc. – played the leading part.

The sacred book of Islam is the Koran, which consists of revelations (statements directly from God) to Muhammad, which were written down as Muhammad repeated them.

Hinduism

It is impossible to say when Hinduism began because it developed over many centuries out of earlier customs and beliefs. Its most distant origins may be even older than Judaism.

Hinduism is the chief religion of India. Like other Eastern religions, it is as much a social system, or code of behaviour, as a religion. It has no firm principles or creeds, although it has a rich store of sacred literature which goes back over 3,000 years. In spite of the caste system, which divided people into rigid classes by birth and

Above left **Hinduism is India's main religion. Hindus believe that they are born again many times. Washing in the Ganges, their sacred river, is an important ritual.**

Above centre **Shinto is the main religion of Japan. It is a mixture of nature-worship and ancestor-worship. Ceremonies like this are part of Shinto's colourful tradition.**

Above **Siddhartha Gautama, the founder of Buddhism, is called the Buddha or the "enlightened" one. Buddhists believe that people can reach happiness by living the right way.**

Far left **The choir of the Mormon Tabernacle, Salt Lake City, Utah, is famous all over the world. Their church was founded in 1830.**

Left **Gurus, or teachers, help Hindus to live a series of better and better lives until they reach a state of *Moksha*. At this point they are freed from the need to be born again.**

occupation, Hinduism has always been a flexible religion, able to take in foreign influences and also to influence other religions. It contains a great many different sects or divisions, which are especially attached to a particular Hindu god. There are many gods, but the most important are Vishnu, the preserver of the universe, and Shiva, the "Lord of the Dance", who often appears in statues dancing in a ring of fire. The most popular god is Krishna, said to be an incarnation, or another form of, Vishnu, of whom many exciting and humorous stories are told. The supreme god Brahma, sometimes shown with four heads as a sign of great wisdom, has become less important as Hinduism has developed.

Buddhism

Buddhism is really a way of life rather than a religion like Christianity or Judaism. There is no all-powerful god in Buddhism. It is based on the teachings of an Indian prince Siddhartha Gautama, renamed Buddha ("the Enlightened One") after his death, who lived about 500 BC. He taught that people can reach peace and happiness by living in the right way. He was more interested in the urgent problems of everyday life than in ideas about the creation of the world. Buddhists hope to reach the state called *Nirvana*, perfect peace of mind, by living an unselfish life. Perhaps the most important belief in Buddhism is in *Karma*, the law of cause and effect. A good cause will have a good result, a bad cause a bad result. There are no prayers in Buddhism because there is no god to whom people can pray.

Buddhism began in India and spread to Tibet, China, Korea, south-east Asia and Japan. There are two main forms of Buddhism and many different sects. Zen, a Japanese sect, which teaches self-discipline, has been the most influential form of Buddhism outside Asia.

Above **The distinctive orange robes of the Hare Krishna, followers of the Buddha.**

GOVERNMENTS

When people live together in a society, they must have a government. This is true of a small tribe of just a few families and it is true of a large, modern nation containing millions of people. A government exists to make rules and to see that they are carried out.

In Europe 200 years ago, most governments were headed by a king. The king had very great powers. Although he had advisers, and perhaps groups of representatives of the people (parliaments), he did not have to do what they said. Of course, if he completely ignored them, he would have risked losing his throne, but to a great extent he was an absolute ruler or a dictator.

Today, many governments are said to be democratic. They exist for the good of the people they govern. They are usually elected by the people, and the laws they make are agreed to by a majority of the people – or by their representatives in parliament.

Unfortunately, although governments may profess to believe in democracy – the

Democracy in practice all over the world: votes being cast in Algeria (above) **and Britain** (right).

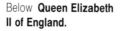

Below **Queen Elizabeth II of England.**

Below **Emperor Bokassa I of the Central African Republic was overthrown in 1979 and the empire was abolished.**

right of the people to choose the government – they do not all behave in that way. In some countries, the government depends not on the votes of the people, but on military force.

In democratic countries, such as those of western Europe, an election is held every few years. The way a government is elected differs from one country to another. In Britain, the country is divided into 650 constituencies. In each constituency, people vote for the candidate of their choice, who belongs to a particular party. The party which wins most constituencies or "seats" in the election forms the government. The leader of that party becomes the head of the government, and he or she chooses ministers to form the cabinet.

In the United States, France and many other countries, people vote for a president as well as for a national assembly (parliament). The president chooses the cabinet and has great individual powers.

The cabinet is the heart of government – the part that gets things done. But if the cabinet wishes to make a new law, it must get the approval of the elected assembly, or parliament, which contains all the successful candidates at the election, of all parties.

The government has to make decisions about everything from – for example – building a new motorway to declaring war. It controls industry and agriculture, defence and safety, health and education, foreign trade and social welfare. In fact, anything that happens in the country is the responsibility of some government department.

However, the government is concerned with national affairs – its decisions affect the whole country. It may decide to change the way schools are organized, for example, but it does not appoint a new teacher to a particular school. That is the job of local government.

Most of the actual work of government, both national and local, cannot be done by the people who are elected to parliament or to the local council. It is done by civil servants. They are full-time officials, who are paid to carry out what the elected government decides. They include a vast number of people doing thousands of different jobs, from sweeping roads to planning the country's future.

Above **As the world's supply of nuclear weapons has multiplied, so have intense anti-nuclear demonstrations. Governments all over the world have had to face vast, and angry crowds.**

Left **During the Russian revolution of 1917 Lenin became the country's leader. Posters throughout Russia were meant to remind the people of the revolutionary way forward.**

THE LAW

The rules which control the way people behave in a society are called the law. Law is a part of government, but it is usually independent of the rest of the government. The law is enforced by judges in law courts. They are called courts because, centuries ago, the chief judge in the country was the king and a person looking for justice came to the king's court.

The first written laws that we know of are the Code of Hammurabi, king of Babylon nearly 4,000 years ago. All ancient societies had laws, however, even if they were not written down. The laws of the ancient Hebrews, for example, are recorded in the Bible.

Law as we think of it, with courts and judges and professional lawyers, dates from the time of the Romans. Roman law was very advanced. It was one of the main reasons for the success of the Roman Empire, and it has had great influence on the development of law in Europe ever since.

Common Law

In England, however, the Roman law was less important than what is called the Common Law. It was built up over the centuries by the judgements and orders given by courts, and was called the Common Law because it was "common" to the whole kingdom.

In time, the English Common Law became the basis of the law in other countries, especially the United States and many countries of the Commonwealth. It also had some influence in other countries with different traditions.

The Common Law has several principles which have become very widely accepted.

Below **Most policemen and policewomen wear uniforms, although detectives usually wear "plain" clothes. The picture shows policemen from** (left to right) **Nigeria, France, Canada and Britain.**

Above **The Courts of Justice, Washington DC.**

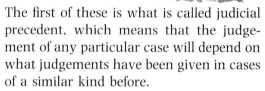

Above **Inside the courts of the Old Bailey, London.**

The first of these is what is called judicial precedent, which means that the judgement of any particular case will depend on what judgements have been given in cases of a similar kind before.

Another important feature of the Common Law is trial by jury. When a person is accused of a serious crime, he or she is entitled to a trial in which a decision about his or her guilt or innocence is given by a jury of 12 ordinary people.

Juries of a kind were used in the Middle Ages, when it was still the custom for a person's guilt to be established by "ordeal". (This meant, for example, that the accused person was tied up and thrown into a river. If he survived, he was innocent!) Gradually, trial by jury came to be the accepted system, and today it exists in most countries.

A third important feature of the Common Law is the supremacy of law. Everyone, including the government, must obey the law. There is no higher authority.

Of course, the law can be changed, but only by act of parliament. Law made by acts of parliament is called Statute Law.

Codes of law

A code in law is a complete, systematic statement of (usually) a branch of the law. The most famous legal code of modern times is the Code Napoléon, introduced in France after the French Revolution. Its official name is the *Code Civil*, and it applies only to civil law. Civil law deals with property, contracts, and relations between people, not with criminal matters.

The Police

Every country has a police force. The job of the police is to preserve public law and order. This means preventing crime and catching criminals, but it also means protecting lives and property, controlling traffic and many other services.

The earliest civilizations had to have some kind of force for law and order, but the job was often done by soldiers or part-time amateurs. Professional police forces were not created until the early 19th century, when crime and disorder had resulted from the sudden growth of cities. The first full-time, uniformed, professional police force was the London Metropolitan Police, founded in 1829.

The police patrol the streets and are called to the scene when a crime takes place. Although they have many other jobs, crime control and detection is the main one. In most countries of the world, crime has been increasing in recent years, bringing extra pressure on police forces. Often, other forces are needed to help the police. In some countries, there is little difference between the army and the police.

In the fight against crime, the police today have many advantages resulting from scientific and technological developments. The identity of a criminal can be proved by a fingerprint or even a hair. Police laboratories make use of very complicated technical processes to help solve crimes and convict criminals. Computers are widely used in most police forces, and the police have a wide range of tools and weapons. Most police forces are armed.

Above and below **The police may use dogs or may rely on clues left by criminals. Different photos fitted together may help to reveal the criminal's face.**

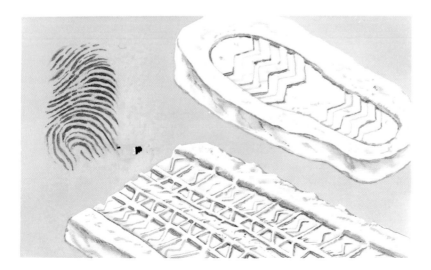

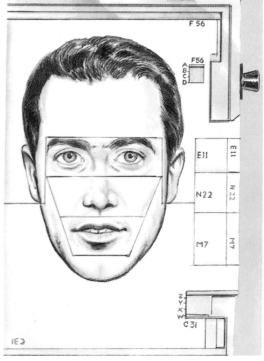

Left **"Open" prisons are a recent idea. They are designed for less serious offenders, and there are far fewer restrictions. Prisoners may receive training in a new craft.**

Right **Many prisons built in the 19th century are still in use today. Although conditions have improved since then, overcrowding remains a serious problem.**

But the police also still employ traditional methods. In searching for illegal drugs or a lost child, dogs are more efficient than any other method.

Courts

In every country there are many different kinds of law court, but a person who is charged with a serious crime will usually find himself in a criminal court. What happens there is controlled by professional officials, and the case is conducted by lawyers. Usually, a lawyer for the prosecution tries to prove the prisoner guilty, using evidence and witnesses found by the police, while another lawyer tries to prove the prisoner is not guilty. Usually, the final decision is up to a jury, though in some places and for some crimes it may be a judge or group of judges. The sentence is given by the judge, who is in overall charge of the trial, making sure the correct legal principles are obeyed.

Prison

In many countries, if a person is convicted of a serious crime, such as murder, he or she may be sentenced to death. More often, the sentence is a term in prison, the length depending on the seriousness of the crime.

The earliest prisons were brutal and filthy places. The only idea behind them was punishment. Today, in Western countries especially, prisons, though still overcrowded, are supposed to make some effort to turn criminals back into good citizens.

INTERNATIONAL ORGANIZATIONS

In the past, when countries acted together, it was usually because they were members of some military alliance. Military alliances are still very important. The main ones in the world today are NATO (North Atlantic Treaty Organization) and the Warsaw Pact. NATO consists of the United States and its allies in western Europe; the Warsaw Pact is made up of the Soviet Union and its allies.

But today there are many other types of international organization, besides military alliances. In the 20th century the world seems to have grown smaller as the result of technological advances, especially in communications and transport. It is now very much easier for different peoples to work together and exchange views. We now think of ourselves as members of one community—the world. On the other hand, military weapons have also advanced, so that full-scale war would probably cause the death of most people on Earth.

The United Nations

The United Nations was created mainly in the hope of preventing future wars. It was founded in 1945 by the nations fighting against Nazi Germany and Japan, including the Soviet Union and the United States. Today, almost every country in the world is a member of the United Nations.

There has been no world war since 1945, and perhaps the UN has been partly responsible. However, there have been a great many smaller wars, such as the Korean War, the Vietnam War and various wars in the Middle East, Africa and Central America. The UN has sometimes played a part in limiting the fighting, but its success in stopping war has on the whole been limited.

However, the UN includes a number of world bodies which have achieved marvellous results. They include the World Health Organization (WHO) and the Children's Fund (UNICEF).

Above **The headquarters of the European Economic Community are in this impressive building in Brussels, Belgium. The EEC began as an economic treaty signed by France, West Germany, Italy and the Benelux countries in 1958. By 1988, the UK, Ireland, Denmark, Greece, Spain and Portugal had made the numbers up to 12.**

Below **The Red Cross has had a big part to play in famine-struck Ethiopia.**

Bottom right **Meetings between the Soviet leader Mr Gorbachev** (left) **and US President Reagan** (right) **gave the world new hope for peace in the late 1980s.**

Economic Organizations

Countries have also joined together in larger groups in order to gain a larger market for the goods they produce and more co-operation. They hope this will lead to greater wealth for them all. The most successful of these groups has been the European Economic Community, which consists of most of the nations of western Europe.

Some groups have been formed by countries which specialize in producing one product. The best-known of these is OPEC (Oil Producing and Exporting Countries).

In some other international groups, economic matters are less important than culture and tradition. The Commonwealth of Nations is an association of countries which once were members of the British Empire and share a common language and certain customs.

International Charities

There are a great many international organizations whose aim is to help people or preserve the environment. One of the first was the Red Cross, founded by a Swiss businessman in 1864. Its purpose was to help those hurt in wars, but it now helps those hurt in other disasters such as earthquakes or famine.

Amnesty International tries to help political prisoners – in all countries. The World Wildlife Fund is concerned with preserving species of animals that are likely to become extinct. Greenpeace tries to protect the natural environment against those who threaten to pollute or destroy it for whatever reason. Survival International is devoted to those dwindling people with an ancient lifestyle who live in remote regions like the South American jungle and are being steadily ruined by the advance of 20th-century progress.

World Leaders

Akbar the Great (1542–1605) Greatest of the Mughal emperors of India. He conquered all northern India and brought peace and justice to Hindus and Muslims.

Alexander the Great (356–323 BC) King of Macedon from 336. He led the Greeks against the Persians and conquered the largest empire of ancient times, spreading Greek ideas as far as India.

Alfred the Great (849–899) King of Wessex from 871. He defeated the invading Danes when other English kingdoms had fallen, and his descendants ruled over a united England.

Attila (406–453) Leader of the Huns, warlike nomads from Asia. Attila's conquests created an empire which stretched from Germany to China.

Augustine (354–430) Greatest of the early "fathers" of the Christian Church. His character and writings were a powerful influence on Christianity.

Augustus (63 BC–AD 14) First Roman emperor. As Octavian, he was the adopted son and heir of Julius Caesar. As emperor, Augustus (a name which means "sacred") strengthened the empire and rebuilt Rome.

Bismarck, Prince Otto von (1815–98) German statesman. A Prussian, he created a united Germany under Prussian leadership and made it the greatest power in Europe.

Buddha (about 560–480 BC) The name given to Prince Siddhartha, the founder of Buddhism. Son of an Indian rajah, he gave up riches to become a teacher. What he taught became one of the world's great religions.

Caesar, Julius (100–44 BC) Roman general and statesman. He conquered Gaul (France), invaded Britain, and became ruler of the Roman republic before he was murdered by jealous politicians.

Castro, Fidel (born 1927) Cuban statesman. He became prime minister in 1958 after leading a revolution. He made Cuba a Communist state.

Catherine II, the Great (1729–96) Russian empress from 1762. A German princess, she became a patriotic Russian, and under her rule the lands of Russia were greatly increased.

Charlemagne (742–814) King of the Franks from 768. He ruled wisely over the great empire he created in western Europe. Both Germans and French think of him as their national hero.

Charles V (1500–58) Holy Roman Emperor from 1519 and king of Spain. He inherited a huge personal empire, including Spanish colonies in the Americas, and defended the Church against Protestant reformers.

Chiang Kai-shek (1887–1975) Chinese general and statesman. He was president of the Chinese republic but, defeated in civil war by the Communists, set up a separate Chinese state in Taiwan.

Churchill, Winston (1874–1965) British statesman. He was prime minister during the Second World War (1940–45), and again in 1951–55. An inspiring speaker, he was Britain's greatest leader in war.

Confucius (551–479 BC) Chinese philosopher. His teachings, known as Confucianism, were a strong influence on the Chinese up to this century.

Constantine the Great (274–337) Roman emperor. He founded Constantinople (Istanbul), and made Christianity the official religion of the Roman Empire.

Cromwell, Oliver (1599–1658) English statesman. He was Parliament's best general in the English Civil War and became head of state as "Lord Protector" (1653–58).

Cyrus the Great (died 529 BC) Founder of the Persian Empire. He united the Medes and Persians and conquered the biggest empire the world had ever seen.

David (died about 1000 BC) King of Israel. He was a great Hebrew hero, who killed Goliath and, as king, made Israel strong.

De Gaulle, Charles (1890–1970) French statesman. General de Gaulle was leader of the Free French in exile during the Second World War and later became president of the French Republic.

De Valera, Eamon (1882–1975) Irish nationalist leader. Ireland's most famous statesman, he was prime minister or president for most of the period from 1932 to 1973.

Eisenhower, Dwight D. (1890–1969) US general and statesman. He was Allied commander-in-chief during the Second World War (from 1944–45) and US president (1953–61).

Franco, Francisco (1892–1975) Spanish dictator. General Franco defeated the republican government in the Spanish Civil War (1936–39) and ruled as dictator until his death.

Frederick I "Barbarossa" (1123–90) Perhaps the greatest Holy Roman Emperor (reigned from 1152). He ruled half Europe, crushed many rebellions and died leading the Third Crusade against Saladin.

Frederick II, the Great (1712–86) King of Prussia from 1740. A great general, he fought against a large European alliance and prepared the way for Prussia's greatness.

Gandhi, Mohandas (1869–1948) Indian nationalist hero, known as Mahatma ("great soul"). He opposed British rule in India by peaceful methods, as he hated violence as well as injustice.

Garibaldi, Giuseppe (1807–82) Italian hero. A great guerilla leader, his band of 1,000 "Red Shirts" helped win Italy's independence.

Genghis Khan (1162–1227) Mongol leader. A skilful governor as well as a great conqueror, he ruled an empire which stretched from south-east Europe to the Pacific.

Gustavus Adolphus (1594–1632) King of Sweden. The victories of this warrior-king made Sweden the greatest power in northern Europe.

Hannibal (247–182 BC) Carthaginian general. Crossing the Alps, with elephants, he invaded Italy and defeated the mighty Romans, but could not capture Rome.

Hitler, Adolf (1889–45) German dictator from 1933. The Nazi leader believed in force, not justice, and headed the cruellest, most vicious government Europe has ever known. Hitler's armies conquered most of Europe before Germany's defeat in 1945, when Hitler killed himself.

Top **Mao Tse-tung, Chinese leader from 1949 to 1976.**

Ho Chi-Minh (1892–1969) Vietnamese statesman. He won Vietnam's independence from France (1954) and directed North Vietnam's victory over the South (with its American allies) in the 1960s.

Ivan IV, the Terrible (1530–84) Russian tsar. Though a brutal man, he was a powerful ruler who greatly enlarged the lands of "Muscovy" (Russia).

Jesus Christ (?5BC–AD 29) Founder of Christianity. To Christians he is the Son of God, who came to Earth to save humanity from sin (Christ means "saviour") and was crucified in Jerusalem.

Joan of Arc (1412–31) French heroine. A peasant girl, Joan became leader of the French armies against the English.

Justinian I (482–565) Byzantine emperor. His reign was the most brilliant of the Byzantine (eastern Roman) empire, but he is remembered especially for his system of laws.

Kenyatta, Jomo (1889–1978) Kenyan statesman. He led the Mau Mau guerillas against British rule and became first prime minister of independent Kenya in 1963.

Lenin, Vladimir (1870–1924) Russian revolutionary leader. He led the Bolshevik revolution in 1917 which established the Communist system in the Soviet Union.

Lincoln, Abraham (1809–65) US president. Because he opposed slavery, the Southern states broke away from the North when he was elected. That caused the Civil War. Soon after the victory of the Union, Lincoln was assassinated.

Louis XIV (1638–1715) King of France from 1643. He was the grandest and most powerful monarch in Europe, but his mighty armies were defeated in the War of the Spanish Succession (1700–13).

Luther, Martin (1483–1546) German religious reformer. He was the leader of those who were later called Protestants during the Reformation, when the Christian Church became permanently divided.

Mao Tse-tung (1893–1976) Chinese statesman. A teacher, Mao became leader of the Chinese Communist revolution and, from 1949, leader of the Chinese People's Republic.

Maria Theresa (1717–80) Austrian empress from 1740. She had to fight against Prussia and others for her right to reign, but became one of the greatest rulers of the Holy Roman Empire.

Moses (?15th century BC) Hebrew leader. He led the ancient Hebrews from slavery in Egypt to independence in the "Promised Land" of Israel, and was the founder of the Jewish law.

Muhammad (570–632) Founder of the Muslim religion. As the Prophet of Allah (God), he inspired the Arab people, and their conquests created the religious empire of Islam.

Mussolini, Benito (1883–1945) Italian dictator. Leader of the Fascists, he gained power in 1922. His brutal policies made him an ideal ally for Hitler and he led Italy to defeat in the Second World War.

Napoleon Bonaparte (1769–1821) French emperor. A brilliant general, he gained supreme power after the French Revolution and conquered most of Europe. His invasion of Russia (1812) was a

Above **Pope John Paul II, formerly Cardinal Karol Wojtyla.**

disaster, and he was finally defeated at Waterloo (1815).

Nasser, Gamal Abdel (1918–70) Egyptian leader. He was behind the plot that overthrew the Egyptian monarchy (1952). President from 1954, he was the greatest Arab leader of recent times.

Nehru, Jawaharlal (1889–1964) Indian statesman. Leader of the Indian nationalist movement, he became prime minister of India from its independence (1947).

Nkrumah, Kwame (1909–72) Ghanaian statesman. A leader of African nationalism, he led Ghana to independence from Britain (1957). His government was overthrown in 1966.

Paul (died about AD 64) Christian apostle. The greatest of the apostles, he travelled widely spreading Christianity among the Gentiles.

Pericles (490–429 BC) Greek statesman. He led the democratic government of Athens in its greatest days, but could not avoid a fatal war with Sparta.

Peter I, the Great (1672–1725) Russian tsar. His energy and intelligence made backward Russia a great power in Europe for the first time.

Robespierre, Maximilien de (1758–94) French Revolutionary leader. Leader of the Jacobin party, he held supreme power during the Terror, when hundreds were beheaded at the guillotine.

Roosevelt, Franklin D. (1882–1945) US president 1933–45. His "New Deal" programme restored the country after the Great Depression, and he led his country during the Second World War.

Saladin (1137–93) Sultan of Egypt. The greatest of Muslim generals during the Christian Crusades, he was a wise ruler of the empire he conquered.

Shaka Zulu (1787–1838) Zulu king. He raised his people from a small tribe to a powerful warrior nation.

Stalin, Joseph (1879–1953) Soviet statesman. He gained supreme power after Lenin's death (1924), and held it by murder and oppression until his own death.

Sun Yat-sen (1866–1925) Chinese revolutionary leader. He led the successful revolution of 1911. Civil war followed, but Sun laid the plans for Chiang Kai-shek's unification of China.

Tamerlane (1336–1405) Tatar conqueror. He was the last of the great leaders from Mongolia, and defeated even the powerful Ottoman Turks.

Washington, George (1732–99) US president. He commanded the Americans in their successful War of Independence against the British, and was elected first president of the new republic (1789–97). The capital city was named after him.

Wellington, Duke of (1769–1852) British general and statesman. After fighting against the French in Spain, he was in command at Waterloo, where Napoleon was finally defeated. He entered politics and was prime minister, 1828–30.

William I, the Conqueror (1027–87) King of England. As duke of Normandy, he invaded England in 1066, and won the Battle of Hastings and the English Crown.

Arts and Entertainment

Above **A Stone Age cave painter at work.**

Left **An Egyptian tomb painting, from Thebes.**

Below left **A Chinese artist painting on silk.**

Below **A Michelangelo pencil sketch and painting.**

PAINTERS AND PAINTINGS

The first painters were at work over 20,000 years ago. They were Stone Age cave painters and they painted pictures of animals on the rock walls of caves. They had no written language, and so they had no books. Instead they painted pictures. Possibly they thought that painting a deer or wild ox would give a hunter power to kill those animals for food.

Much primitive art has a magical or religious meaning. Australian aboriginal people still decorate their secret magical places with paintings that tell a hidden story. As well as painting (using coloured earth, clays and vegetable oils for paint), ancient peoples also carved figures in wood, ivory and bone and made figures from wet clay. The civilizations of ancient Egypt, China, India, Greece and Rome were rich in art. Wealthy rulers wished to live in luxury and they paid painters to decorate their palaces. The Egyptian pharaohs (kings) were buried in tombs decorated with beautiful wall paintings.

The Greeks were marvellous artists and the Romans copied many Greek styles. We can tell from the ruins of the Roman town of Pompeii (buried by the volcano Vesuvius in AD 79) what fine artists were at work in those times.

Many of these early paintings were made on walls. Wall paintings are called frescoes. During the Middle Ages frescoes were painted inside churches and monasteries. Monks copied books by hand and painted

Left ***The Battle between Carnival and Lent*** by Pieter Brueghel (detail).

Above ***The Straw Hat,*** painted by the Flemish artist Rubens.

brightly coloured "illuminations" as illustrations on the pages. Painting on canvas began in Europe at this time, while in the East, Chinese and Japanese artists drew delicate landscapes (paintings of trees, mountains and rivers) with brush and ink on silk.

European painters often used religion as their subject since much of their work was done for churches. During the Renaissance (see page 69) painters such as Leonardo da Vinci, Raphael, Michelangelo and Titian brought a new genius to painting. They studied the human body, so as to paint it more accurately. Artists also took more interest in perspective (the way things look from different distances and angles). They set up workrooms or studios where young painters could learn the secrets of the older "masters". Italy became the great centre of European painting.

During the 1600s and 1700s painters began painting landscapes, and also still-life and portraits. Fashionable people liked to have their portraits painted in family groups. In the 1800s and 1900s painters often tried to make their picture tell a story. They also tried new ways of using paint.

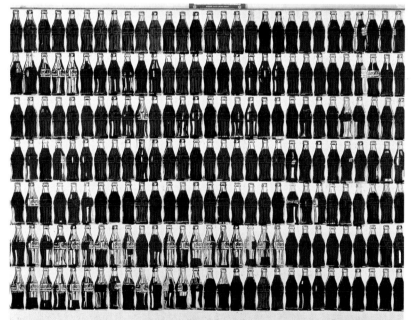

The Impressionists were a group of painters who wanted to show how light and colour affect the way we see things. Abstract painters tried to express feelings and ideas through shapes and colours. The most famous painter of the 20th century was Pablo Picasso and many of his pictures are abstract.

Above **Modern painters, such as the Pop artist Andy Warhol, often surprise us by choosing everyday objects for their subjects. Warhol painted these *Green Coca Cola Bottles* in 1962.**

ARCHITECTURE AND SCULPTURE

Architecture is the art of planning buildings. As new tools and building materials have been discovered, so building styles have changed. Early builders used wood, but by the time of the ancient Egyptians, temples and pyramids were cut from huge blocks of stone. So accurate was the planning of Egyptian architects that their buildings have lasted for thousands of years. The peoples of the Middle East used bricks made from clay hardened in the sun. Brick-built mounds, or ziggurats, were built by the Babylonians for their temples.

Many of these buildings were decorated by artists called sculptors, who make solid forms from materials such as clay, wood, stone or metal. Egyptian rulers set up huge statues as monuments to their power, but craftsmen also modelled small images of their gods to use in religious ceremonies or to place in the tombs of the dead.

Sculptors decorated buildings with rounded figures, and with pictures carved from flat stone. These carvings are called reliefs. The ancient Persians and Assyrians carved scenes of battles and hunting on their palaces. The Mayan people of Central America also carved pictures on their buildings, which included pyramids like those in Egypt.

Ancient Greek architects preferred a simple, graceful style, building tall columns to hold up heavy marble beams. These columns had various names, according to their decoration. The three most important are Doric, Ionic and Corinthian. The Greek "Classical" style has been copied ever since, especially by the Romans. Perhaps the most famous Greek building is the Parthenon in Athens, which was built under the direction of the sculptor Pheidias.

Roman architects invented the arch, using it to span wide distances as they built forts, bridges and aqueducts all over their empire. They used small stones and concrete instead of heavy marble. Roman sculptors decorated triumphal arches and columns with pictures of famous generals and emperors.

As practical as the Romans were the builders of ancient China. The Great Wall of China, set up to keep out warring invaders, was probably the biggest building project of all time. Chinese sculptures include life-like figures, such as the army of clay soldiers found in the tomb of the first emperor.

The architecture of many peoples is seen at its best in their religious buildings. The Muslims of the Middle East made domed mosques, decorated inside and out with geometric patterns. In Europe during the Middle Ages, cathedrals and churches were made of stone, as were forts and castles. Architects first followed the Roman style, but by the 1200s built tall "Gothic" buildings with pointed arches and windows. Craftsmen and stone masons adorned them with wood carvings and statues.

During the 1400s and 1500s, architects and sculptors went back to the "Classical" style. The great painter and sculptor, Michelangelo, carved life-like statues from huge lumps of marble. In the 1600s sculptors like Bernini worked in the ornate "baroque" style, very different from the simple "abstract" shapes created by modern sculptors and architects.

New materials such as steel, reinforced concrete, glass and plastics have helped architects to build higher and higher. The "skyscrapers" (see page 145) which dominate most modern cities first appeared in the United States.

Above **A Mayan stone carving of a figure, probably representing one of the Mayan gods.**

Above left **The Chinese were the first to master the art of casting in bronze.**

Left **A Greek bronze figure of the god Zeus.**

Below **An abstract sculpture by the 20th-century artist Henry Moore.**

Right **A classical Greek temple with graceful columns in the Ionic style. Greek architecture influenced the Renaissance period.**

Below **The *duomo* (cathedral) in Florence, Italy, is one of the glories of European Renaissance art. Begun in 1296 but not finished until 1434, it contains work by such great artists as Michelangelo and Donatello.**

Right **The shell-like "sails" of Sydney's opera house, opened in 1973, are one of Australia's most famous landmarks. Inside are concert halls, theatres, cinemas and recording studios. The building stands on the shore of Sydney Harbour.**

Far right **New York, and particularly the Manhattan district, is the home of the skyscraper. Towering buildings crowd the city skyline.**

MUSIC AND DANCE

Music and dance are arts which grew up together. Dance is perhaps the older of the two, as from the earliest times people have expressed in movement their feelings of joy, anger, or hatred of an enemy. Dance was often led by a magic-maker as part of a religious ceremony. He would lead war and hunt dances, dances to bring rain and celebrate the return of spring.

The oldest dances known today are probably the religious temple dances of the East. In the West, folk dances among country people grew from earlier dances such as the Morris. From folk dancing developed the ballroom and disco dancing of today.

From folk dances also grew a new form of dancing performed for an audience. Such dancing began in the courts of Italy and France in the 1500s and 1600s and from it came the art of ballet. Many of the great ballet dancers have been Russian, including the famous Nijinsky, and much ballet music was written by the composer Tchaikovsky. Although dancers need only rhythm, or a steady beat, to accompany them, they often perform to music.

Music is a set of sounds arranged in a way to please the listener. It must have rhythm and often has a melody, or tune, as well. Early people copied natural rhythms by beating sticks on stones, and then made drums to play. In time, many musical instruments were invented.

Wind instruments, such as a flute, are played by blowing down a pipe or tube. Stringed instruments have strings stretched across a hollow box. The strings can be plucked or played with a bow. Percussion instruments are those like drums, cymbals and bells which are struck with a hammer or stick. Keyboard instruments like the piano and harpsichord have strings which are tapped by a key or little hammer.

Music is made up of notes or sounds of a different pitch. They may be high or low, long or short. Notes follow each other in order in what is called a scale. But there are great differences between scales in Eastern and Western music. This makes the music of one sound strange to people used to hearing the other.

Hardly any early music is known because it was not written down. During the 1100s and 1200s music grew more complicated. Two or three melodies were sung or played

Above left **A minstrel of the Middle Ages playing a stringed instrument called a lute.**

Left **Drums are important in the music and dance of Africa.**

Below **Jazz players from the Deep South USA.**

Right **A concert pianist during a performance.**

Below **Young ballet school students practise at the barre.**

Right **A concert pianist during a performance.**

Below **Young ballet school students practise at the barre.**

together at the same time in music called counterpoint. In the Middle Ages, monks chanted music in churches and minstrels wandered from court to court, singing and playing the music they had written.

Soon composers began to group notes together in harmony, making chords which sounded well together. Singers sang a melody and instruments played with them in harmony. In this way operas, or musical dramas, began.

Some of the greatest music was written in the 1700s by the composers Bach, Handel, Mozart and Haydn. These are called "classical" composers. They wrote for voices and the group of instruments called an orchestra. One of the greatest writers for the orchestra was Beethoven, who composed some of the finest symphonies. After Beethoven, composers began to experiment with new forms and music became more complicated. Today, music is composed for electronic instruments as well as those of the symphony orchestra, and recording has made possible all kinds of new sounds.

"Classical" music is heard in the concert hall and on records. But all the time it was developing, people continued making popular music of their own, such as folk songs. From the folk songs of black slaves in the United States grew the jazz and pop music of today.

Above **Young people enjoy a disco.**

Far left **An Indian performs a ritual dance to bring rain.**

Below **The Hollywood film stars Fred Astaire and Ginger Rogers. Their 1930s musicals included many dazzling dance routines.**

LITERATURE AND DRAMA

Long before people learned to write, they told stories. These stories were passed down from generation to generation, carefully retold word for word. They are known as oral, or spoken, literature. Literature is the most important way in which human beings record thoughts and ideas. Drama, the acting out of stories, often in poetry and music, is one of the most enjoyable forms of literature.

The Greeks loved drama and the plays written by their greatest dramatists, such as Sophocles and Aeschylus, are still performed today. The Greek poet Homer told the story of the Trojan War in a long epic story-poem, the *Iliad*, and of the wanderings of the hero Odysseus in the *Odyssey*. Later, the epic form was used by the Roman poet Virgil, writing in Latin. In ancient Persia, China and India, poets wrote about the creation of the world, and the mysteries of life and death.

English poetry was first written down in Anglo-Saxon in about AD 700. Early literature had to be written by hand, since printed books were unknown in Europe before the 1400s. Few people could read. The first great English writer was Geoffrey Chaucer (1340–1400), who is famous for his *Canterbury Tales*, a collection of stories told by travellers.

DRAMA AND THE THEATRE

In a Greek and Roman theatre, the audience sat in the open air. The actors, all men, wore masks and there were two kinds of play: tragedy (with a sad ending) and comedy

Above **Storytellers have enthralled children throughout the ages.**

Left **A page from the 8th-century Book of Kells, a gospel written and illuminated by hand.**

Bottom left **Over 2,000 years ago audiences watched plays in this open-air Greek theatre.**

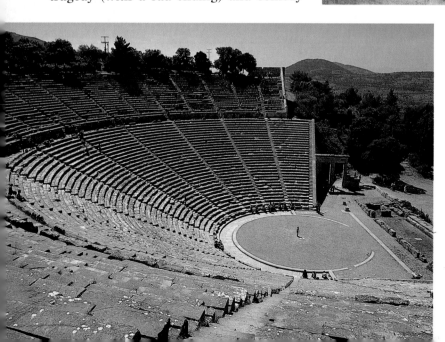

Right **A Japanese Kabuki actor.**

(with a happy ending). During the Middle Ages in Europe, the Church used drama as a way of teaching people about good and evil, using stories from the Bible. These plays are called mystery or miracle plays. Proper theatres were not built in England, France and Germany until the late 1500s. The greatest of all dramatists of this period was William Shakespeare (1564–1616). Most people agree that he is the greatest writer of all time.

Drama declined during the 1600s, but later going to the theatre became part of fashionable town life. Some plays were witty comedies, others exciting spectacles with fights, thunderstorms and other "special effects". In the late 1900s plays became more concerned with everyday life. Musical theatre, including opera (developed in Italy), became popular. Today, dramatists write not only for the theatre but also for films and television.

POETRY AND PROSE

Poetry is the art of putting together words in an interesting way. Some poetry sounds "musical" it is written in verse that has rhythm (a beat) and has lines that end in words that rhyme.

Literature that is not poetry is prose. Prose writing may be fiction (stories) or non-fiction (including history, biography – the story of a person's life – and so on). A novel is a long story in prose. Novels became popular in the 1700s, when books were printed more cheaply and more people could read. Some of the novels of Charles Dickens (1812–70) came out in weekly parts in magazines, as a serial.

All over the world there are writers at work, for people still enjoy reading a story or a poem. Literature remains the way in which people attempt to understand the world and themselves.

Below **The Globe theatre in Elizabethan London was open to the sky. Shakespeare's plays were performed here.**

Bottom **400 years later, audiences still enjoy Shakespeare. This is a scene from *A Midsummer Night's Dream*, performed by the Royal Shakespeare Company.**

218

ENTERTAINMENT FOR ALL

The first entertainers performed at religious festivals, the courts of kings, and at markets and fairs. One of the most famous fairs in old London was Bartholomew Fair, which was founded by a monk called Rahere in the 12th century. People came to buy and sell goods, and to enjoy themselves watching the sideshows. There were conjurers, tumblers, actors, musicians, dancing bears, performing dogs, puppets and fire-eaters! When the River Thames froze in bitterly cold winters, fairs were held on the ice. So popular were these English fairs that they went on even when the Puritans closed the theatres in the 1600s.

Dressing up is an important part of carnival. In Christian countries, carnivals have traditionally been held to celebrate the

Above **Clowns and jugglers have always been popular.**

last day before the fasting period of Lent. Another name for carnival is Mardi Gras, which is French for "fat Tuesday" (Shrove Tuesday being the day on which people ate up the last of their meat before fasting began). There are famous Mardi Gras parades in Nice (France) and New Orleans (USA). Caribbean and Brazilian carnivals are famous for music and dancing.

FAIRGROUNDS AND CIRCUSES

Fairground entertainers travelled the country to give their shows. From these shows grew the circus. One of the first European circuses was staged by Philip Astley in England in the late 1700s. At first horses were the only performing animals but later lions, elephants, bears, sealions and other animals became part of the

Left **Home of fantasy and fun: Disneyland in California, USA.**

Below **Mardi Gras is carnival time.**

Right **A television outside broadcast. Pictures from the cameras pass through the control unit in the van and reach our TV sets at home.**

circus. The circus took place inside a huge tent called the Big Top. The sawdust-strewn arena inside was the ring, and the man who introduced the circus acts was the ring master. As well as animals, there were clowns, jugglers, horseback riders, strong men, trapeze artists and tightrope walkers. The world's largest circus was Barnum and Bailey's, in the United States. It was proudly called "The Greatest Show on Earth". Today, the Moscow State Circus of the USSR is one of the best circuses. There are even world championships for circus performers. Animal acts are not so popular now, for many people do not enjoy seeing wild animals being made to perform tricks.

It is exciting to go to a fairground, with its whirling rides, dodgem cars, big wheels, rollercoasters and roundabouts. Lights flash, machinery roars, and music plays as the crowds enjoy all the fun of the fair. Some of the largest amusement, or theme parks are to be found in the United States. Walt Disney, the famous film-maker, built the first Disneyland park, to recreate the scenes and cartoon characters of his films. Today, millions of people visit Disneyland and other similar parks.

PUPPETS AND MUSIC HALL

People all over the world have always enjoyed puppet shows. In Southeast Asia there are shadow puppets, worked from behind a brightly lit screen. Mr Punch, the star of the seaside Punch and Judy show, has been performing his antics for hundreds of years.

Going to the seaside for a holiday only became possible for most people after the

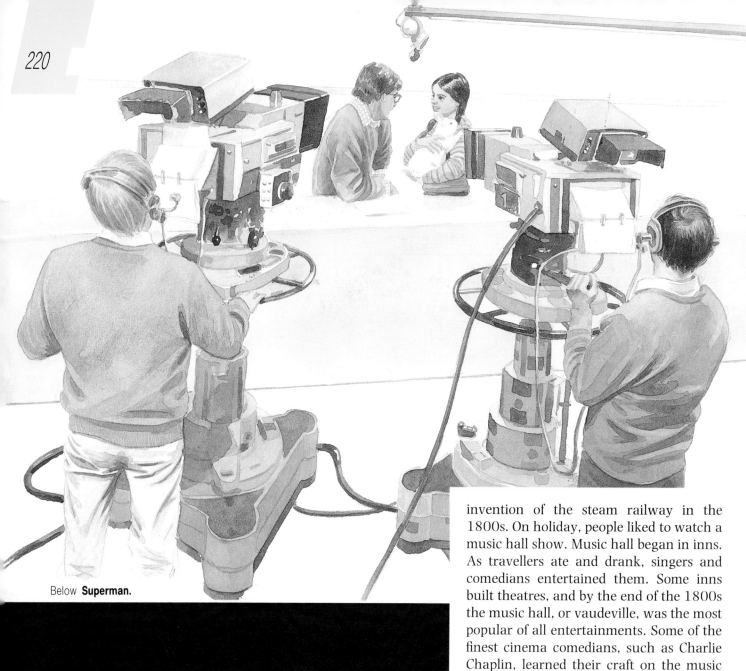

Below **Superman.**

invention of the steam railway in the 1800s. On holiday, people liked to watch a music hall show. Music hall began in inns. As travellers ate and drank, singers and comedians entertained them. Some inns built theatres, and by the end of the 1800s the music hall, or vaudeville, was the most popular of all entertainments. Some of the finest cinema comedians, such as Charlie Chaplin, learned their craft on the music hall stage.

RADIO AND CINEMA

Some people still entertain themselves by singing, or playing musical instruments. Once, almost all entertainment was "live". But this changed with the invention of radio by Guglielmo Marconi in the 1890s (see page 178) and the arrival of the cinema. Soon after the First World War (1914–18) radio stations began to broadcast programmes of talks, plays and music. People bought "wireless sets" to listen and enjoy a new experience: home entertainment over the radio waves.

Millions of people visited the cinema every week during the 1930s and 1940s. Films were invented at about the same time as radio. At first there was no sound and the films were in black and white only. Talking pictures arrived in 1927, soon followed by colour. In the 1930s, Hollywood became the "movie capital of the world", and audiences in every country watched westerns, gangster films and musicals.

RECORDING SOUND AND PICTURES

Sound recording was invented in the 1870s. The first gramophones were boxlike machines, with loudspeakers shaped like trumpets. They were worked by a spring and had to be wound up each time a record was played.

Radio broadcasting helped to sell records. In the 1940s long-playing records first appeared, followed by cassette tapes in the 1970s and more recently compact discs. The modern home sound system has a record player, tape deck and compact disc player. It has stereo speakers that make it sound as if the musicians on the record or tape are actually in the room.

With the radio and the gramophone, people could enjoy sound entertainment at home. On television, they could see pictures too. Television was invented in the 1920s and the first regular TV broadcasts were begun in Britain in 1936 (see page 178). It rapidly took over from radio as the most popular form of home entertainment, and as a result fewer people went to the cinema.

In some countries, all broadcasting is controlled by the government. In others, there are many small independent radio and TV stations, which transmit programmes paid for by advertising. Satellites in orbit around the Earth can now relay TV signals around the world, so a viewer in the United States can watch a live programme from Europe, India, or Australia. With a dish aerial, a viewer can pick up hundreds of programmes in different languages from different countries: a wonder undreamed of 100 years ago.

In the 1950s engineers developed video tape; a way of recording TV pictures electronically as signals on tape. This allowed "instant playback" (of a goal in a soccer match, for instance) and also made possible the home video system. So we can now not only tape programmes from the television, but also hire or buy videos to enjoy at home. The home is now, once again, most people's entertainment centre.

Opposite **Cameras in a TV studio.**

Above **Meryl Streep, movie star.**

Above right **Pop superstar Madonna.**

Right **Rock n' Roll legend, Elvis Presley.**

Below **Making an animated cartoon.**

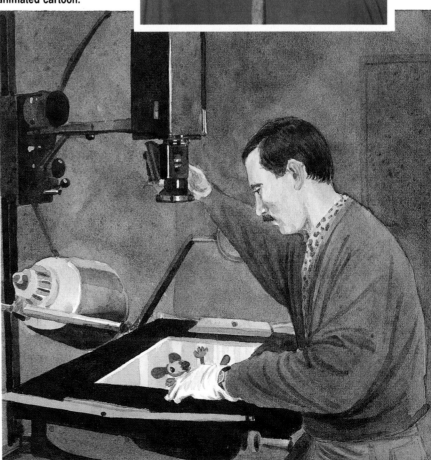

Famous figures in the Arts

Austen, Jane (1775–1817) English novelist. Her novels, like *Pride and Prejudice* and *Emma*, wittily describe middle-class customs and behaviour.

Bach, J.S. (1685–1750) German composer. The greatest composer of religious music, he made important advances in the art of polyphony – combining different sounds and voices.

Beethoven, Ludwig van (1770–1827) German composer. Beethoven is thought to be one of the greatest composers ever. Beethoven's most popular works are his nine symphonies and one opera, *Fidelio*.

Berlioz, Hector (1803–69) French composer. Berlioz was one of the first to write music for the large, modern orchestra. His works include the *Symphonie Fantastique* and the opera, *The Trojans*.

Botticelli, Sandro (1444–1510) Italian painter. He was one of the greatest painters of the Renaissance in Florence. His *The Birth of Venus* and *Spring* (*Primavera*) are two of his finest works.

Brahms, Johannes (1833–97) German composer. He wrote romantic music in the Classical tradition. His symphonies and concertos are played by every orchestra today.

Brontë, Charlotte (1816–55) Emily (1818–48) and **Anne (1820–49)** English novelists. The most famous of the sisters' books are Charlotte's *Jane Eyre* and Emily's *Wuthering Heights*.

Breughel, Pieter (1520–69) Dutch painter. He painted chiefly scenes from the life of Dutch peasants.

Burns, Robert (1759–96) Scots poet. Scotland's national poet, he wrote songs and ballads, often humorous, about ordinary people.

Cervantes, Miguel de (1547–1616) Spanish novelist. He wrote one of the world's finest novels, *Don Quixote*, with its crazy but gallant hero.

Cézanne, Paul (1839–1906) French painter. He was interested especially in the shape of things, and had great influence on later painters.

Chaucer, Geoffrey (1340–1400) English poet. The "father of English literature", he wrote *The Canterbury Tales*, amusing stories in verse.

Chekhov Anton (1860–1904) Russian writer. A doctor, he wrote short stories but is more famous for his plays, such as *The Cherry Orchard*.

Chopin, Frédéric (1810–49) Polish composer. Himself a pianist, he was one of the greatest composers of piano music.

Constable, John (1778–1837) English painter. He lived in a pretty part of Suffolk and became England's leading landscape painter.

Dante Alighieri (1265–1321) Italian poet. His *Divine Comedy* is the greatest work of medieval literature. It made Italian a "respectable" written language.

Diaghilev, Sergei (1872–1929) Russian ballet producer. His productions of Russian ballet in Paris laid the foundations for modern ballet.

Dickens, Charles (1812–70) English novelist. He had an amazing talent for creating characters, like Sam Weller in *Pickwick Papers*, Fagin in *Oliver Twist* and hundreds more.

Dostoyevsky, Fyodor (1821–81) Russian novelist. He wrote powerful, realistic novels, such as *Crime and Punishment* and *The Brothers Karamazov*.

Dürer, Albrecht (1471–1528) German artist. He was one of the finest artists of the Renaissance in northern Europe, and was an especially brilliant engraver.

El Greco (1548–1614) Spanish painter, born in Greece (El Greco means "the Greek"). He was a passionate painter with a unique style. His long and willowy human figures are easy to recognise.

Eliot, T.S. (1888–1965) American-British poet. His poetry, such as *Four Quartets* and *The Waste Land*, is sometimes hard to understand but had deep influence on other poets.

Gauguin, Paul (1848–1903) French painter. He gave up money and luxury in Europe to live in Tahiti, painting its people and customs.

Goethe, J.W. von (1749–1832) German writer. The author of *Faust* and other plays, he became a giant influence on German literature and culture.

Goya, Francisco (1746–1828) Spanish artist. He painted people – and life – as he saw them, however frightening or horrible.

Handel, G.F. (1685–1759) German composer. He lived in England from 1713, where he composed the *Messiah*, 46 operas and many other works.

Holbein, Hans (1497–1543) German painter. He painted many portraits in England, where Henry VIII made him court painter.

Homer (9th century BC) Greek poet. Homer's *Iliad* and *Odyssey*, about the Trojan wars and wanderings of Odysseus are the first great works of European literature.

Ibsen, Henrik (1828–1906) Norwegian playwright. His powerful plays, like *Ghosts*, *The Wild Duck* and *Hedda Gabler*, brought new ideas and new subjects to the theatre.

Johnson, Samuel (1709–84) English writer. He wrote *A Dictionary of the English Language*, but he is remembered as a great character as much as a great author.

Joyce, James (1882–1941) Irish writer. Novels such as *Ulysses* and *Finnegan's Wake* broke all the rules of novel-writing and had great influence on later novelists.

Kipling, Rudyard (1865–1936) English writer. He was born in India, where many of his best stories and poems are set. His *Jungle Books* and *Just So Stories* are children's classics.

Lawrence, D.H. (1885–1930) English novelist. He was a Nottinghamshire miner's son and his best books are about the lives of working-class people.

Le Corbusier (1887–1965) Swiss architect. His real name was Charles-Édouard Jeanneret. He had great influence on modern architecture through his use of industrial forms and concrete.

Leonardo da Vinci (1452–1509) Italian artist. Leonardo was one of the greatest geniuses of the

Top **A self-portrait by Rembrandt.**

Above **"Woman Weeping"**, by Picasso.

Renaissance. He was a sculptor, an inventor and much more, but he is best known for paintings, especially the *Mona Lisa*.

Liszt, Franz (1811–86) Hungarian composer. A famous pianist, he also created a new kind of orchestral music in his "symphonic poems".

Michelangelo Buonarroti (1475–1564) Italian artist. He was one of the greatest sculptors who ever lived. Michelangelo was also an architect and a poet, but is best remembered for his paintings, especially the ceiling of the Sistine Chapel, Rome.

Milton, John (1608–74) English poet. His most famous work is the great religious poem, *Paradise Lost*, in blank verse (no rhymes).

Molière (1622–1732) French playwright. His real name was Poquelin. He wrote brilliant comedies, like *Tartuffe* and *The Misanthrope*.

Mozart, Wolfgang Amadeus (1756–91) Austrian composer. He started writing music at a very young age, and made his first tour as a performer when aged six. He wrote over 600 compositions, including many operas and symphonies. Three of his greatest operas are *The Magic Flute*, *Marriage of Figaro* and *Don Giovanni*.

Olivier, Laurence (born 1907) English actor. He has played many parts, but is best remembered for the great Shakespearean roles, on stage and film. He was the first director of the National Theatre.

O'Neill, Eugene (1888–1953) US playwright. The first truly great American playwright, he wrote long, powerful dramas like *The Iceman Cometh* and *Long Day's Journey into Night*.

Picasso, Pablo (1881–1973) Spanish painter. He was the most admired artist of this century, and a leading figure in many of the new developments in modern art.

Raphael (1483–1520) Italian painter. He was one of the greatest painters of the Italian Renaissance. He painted many beautiful pictures of the Madonna (Mary, mother of Jesus).

Rembrandt van Rijn (1606–69) Dutch painter. Many people call him the greatest painter of all. His portraits, including self-portraits, show wonderful understanding of human nature.

Renoir, Auguste (1841–1919) French painter. He was one of the Impressionists but later painted in more Classical style, especially loving portraits of young women.

Rodin, Auguste (1840–1917) French sculptor. The finest sculptor of his time, he was full of new ideas and methods and had a marvellous eye for movement.

Rubens, Peter Paul (1577–1640) Flemish painter. His pictures are full of life and energy, and painted in rich colours.

Shakespeare, William (1564–1616) English playwright. Most people agree that he was the greatest playwright, not only in English, but in any language. His tragedies, *Hamlet*, *Othello*, *Macbeth* and *King Lear*, are perhaps his finest works, but his comedies and history plays are no less famous.

Sibelius, Jean (1865–1957) Finnish composer. His orchestral music, especially *Finlandia*, seems to echo with Finland's forests and rivers.

Stevenson, Robert Louis (1850–94) Scottish writer. He wrote a great deal in his short life, including famous tales like *Treasure Island* and *Kidnapped*.

Stravinsky, Igor (1882–1971) Russian composer. His ballet music for Diaghilev made him famous. Later, his experiments with harmony had a strong influence on modern music.

Swift, Jonathan (1667–1745) English–Irish writer. He was a brilliant master of satire – mocking human behaviour – but his *Gulliver's Travels* is also a splendid adventure story.

Tchaikovsky, Piotr (1840–93) Russian composer. His beautiful melodies made him the most popular Russian composer. His ballet music, *Swan Lake*, *Sleeping Beauty*, *Nutcracker*, is best known.

Tennyson, Alfred (1809–92) English poet. He was the most popular poet of the 19th century. His poems include *The Lady of Shalott* and *Morte d'Arthur*.

Titian (died 1576) Italian painter. He was the greatest painter of the school of Venice, especially famous for his colours. Princes and emperors were eager to employ him.

Tolkien, J.R.R. (1892–1973) English novelist. A professor of Anglo-Saxon, he wrote strange and gripping fairy tales, especially *The Hobbit* and *The Lord of the Rings*.

Tolstoy, Leo (1828–1910) Russian novelist. His finest works were *Anna Karenina* and *War and Peace*, which took six years to write.

Turner, J.M.W. (1775–1851) English painter. He was a master of landscape, and often painted in watercolours. He was interested in effects of light, and some paintings are really paintings of light itself.

Twain, Mark (1835–1910) US writer. Samuel Langhorne Clemens (his real name) grew up on the Mississippi, and his best, most amusing stories (*Tom Sawyer*, *Huckleberry Finn*) were based on that boyhood.

Van Gogh, Vincent (1853–90) Dutch painter. No one put more feeling (or stronger colours) into painting than Van Gogh. He died poor, but today his paintings are sold for millions.

Velazquez (1599–1660) Spanish painter. One of Spain's greatest artists, he was a court painter who did not flatter his subjects.

Verdi, Giuseppe (1813–1901) Italian composer. He heads the list of Italian operatic composers, with operas such as *Rigoletto*, *La Traviata* and *Otello*.

Virgil (70–19 BC) Latin poet. The greatest poet of ancient Rome, he wrote the *Aeneid* at the request of the emperor. It took eleven years.

Wagner, Richard (1813–83) German composer. He wrote spectacular, dramatic operas which were based on German folktales (as in the *Ring* cycle).

Wordsworth, William (1770–1850) English poet. He is the great poet of the English countryside. His *Lyrical Ballads* marked a new age in English poetry.

Wren, Christopher (1632–1723) English architect. His greatest building is St Paul's Cathedral, London.

The Story of Sport

People have played games of various kinds since our early ancestors lived in caves during the Stone Age. The oldest of all sports is probably hunting. Prehistoric people had to hunt animals for food, but they would also have been proud to show off their skill with the spear or bow.

The ancient Egyptians enjoyed hunting and chariot racing 4,000 years ago, while the wall paintings from their temples show people fishing and catching wild birds.

Centuries later, in 776 BC, the Greeks, who much admired physical strength and skill in sporting contests, began a series of competitions known as the Olympic Games. Runners, throwers and wrestlers took part, as did poets and artists. The Romans also appreciated athletic skill, although they preferred sporting spectacles which attracted huge crowds. In Roman times, throughout the empire, people flocked to the arenas to watch races and fights between gladiators, who were trained to fight one another. In Rome itself was the Circus Maximus, a huge arena used for horse races. It was even bigger than the sports stadiums of today, holding 250,000 people.

Many Roman athletes were professionals who were paid to run, wrestle, ride horses or fight. They were all men, as it was unknown for women to take part in organized sport

Below **A thrilling spectacle in ancient Crete was bull-leaping. Athletes vaulted over the horns of wild bulls.**

Below **Roman gladiators fought in the arena. The one with net and trident was called a *retarius*.**

until modern times. Many women from wealthier families, however, enjoyed horse riding and other outdoor sports such as falconry (hunting birds with trained falcons).

A number of traditional sports were warlike, and were helpful in training men for battle. In Europe during the Middle Ages there were tournaments at which armoured knights fought mock battles called jousts. Warriors on horseback loved to show off their skill. The ancient Persians and Indians played polo, a game a little like hockey on horseback that was invented by the skilful horsemen of the Central Asian plains. Archery, or shooting at targets with bows and arrows, was also a favourite sport in many parts of the world, and continues to this day.

However, not all sports were connected with war. People also enjoyed playing ball games and many different forms were invented. The Mayan people of Central America played a game that involved throwing a ball through a ring on the wall of a specially-built court (rather like basketball), but it is not known exactly how it was played. In North America, the Indians

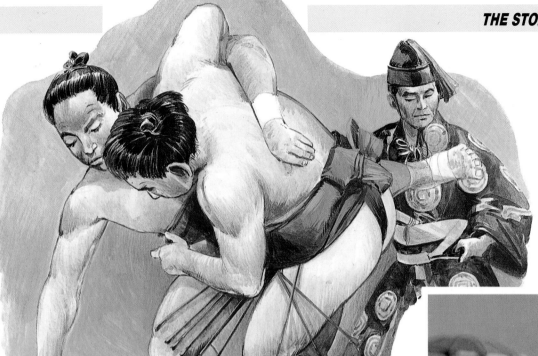

Left **Japan is famous for martial arts. Heavyweights take part in Sumo wrestling, which has a strict code of rules.**

Below **Hurdling is an athletics track event. Competitors race over a series of barriers, taking them in their stride. The longest hurdle race is 400 metres.**

enjoyed a game called baggataway, from which grew the modern game of lacrosse. In Europe, an early form of tennis was played in a walled court. Henry VIII of England, a keen sportsman, built a court at Hampton Court Palace in 1529.

At country fairs and markets, ordinary people liked to watch wrestlers, jugglers, acrobats and archers. They also watched cruel sports such as bear-baiting and cock-fighting. Bowls and skittles were played in the Middle Ages in much the same way as we know them today.

SPORT FOR ALL

The ancient Greeks knew that sport was good exercise for the body. They also believed that it helped to develop the mind and character. They thought of sport as being just as important as science or the arts. During the 19th century people in Europe and America began to think in the same way, and as a result organized sport began.

The 19th century was the time of the Industrial Revolution. More and more people were moving from the countryside to work in factories in towns. Schools and

Below **The Olympic Games begin with the arrival of a torch carried from Greece.**

universities were the first to take sport seriously, but town workers soon followed their example and formed their own sports clubs. Games such as football and cricket had grown up in a haphazard way, with no fixed rules. Now they were "organized", with governing associations, rules and proper clubs playing matches against each other. The modern rules of many games, including football, cricket, hockey, baseball, tennis and many more, were drawn up at this time.

As sport developed, argument arose over the difference between a professional (a paid player) and an amateur (one who plays only for enjoyment). In 1896, the Olympic Games, which had died out in AD 394, were revived by a Frenchman, Baron Pierre de Coubertin. He believed that international sporting competition would encourage goodwill and peace between nations. Since 1896, the Olympic Games have been held every four years (except during the two World Wars, 1914–18 and 1939–45). All Olympic competitors were supposed to be amateurs, but in recent years a number of sports have removed the distinction between amateurs and professionals. Sports-

Above **Soccer demands skilful ball control.**

Left **American footballers wear protective padding and helmets.**

Right **A gymnast performs on the beam.**

men and sportswomen today may be full-time athletes, earning a living from their sport.

At the Olympic Games and world championships, people thrill to the strength and grace of the gymnasts, and the track and field athletes. In athletics, competitors try not only to beat each other, but to improve the performance of their individual events. There are running races at distances ranging from 100 metres to the Marathon (26 miles 385 yds, or 42,195 m), and field events that include the high jump, long jump, javelin and discus throwing and shot-putting. Athletics events may be held indoors as well as outdoors, and the foremost athletes train for hours each day to keep their bodies at the peak of physical fitness.

POPULAR TEAM GAMES

Almost everyone enjoys playing with a ball. The simple act of throwing, hitting or kicking a ball has been developed into many different games. Football is the most popular team ball game in the world. Some people believe that the Romans played a form of football, but it is known that it was played in the Middle Ages as a rough-and-tumble village game with few rules. Later, different forms or "codes" of football were invented.

The most popular type of football is Association football, or soccer, which is played in almost every country. The World Cup finals, for the best national soccer teams, are held every four years and are enjoyed by millions watching televised matches. Soccer is particularly popular in Europe and South America. A soccer ball is round, whereas that of another popular game, rugby, is egg-shaped. Rugby football began in 1823 when a boy at Rugby School in England picked up the ball and ran with it. Britain is therefore the home of rugby, which is also played to a high standard in France, Australia, New Zealand, South Africa, Argentina and Fiji. American "grid-iron" football dates from 1873 when college students agreed a set of rules. It is very popular in the United States and has spread to other countries. Australia and Canada also have their own national football games.

Above **Fielders near the wicket watch as a batsman strikes during a cricket match.**

Right **A swimmer doing the butterfly stroke.**

Below **Tennis player Boris Becker was a world champion at 17.**

Cricket, which dates in its modern form from the 18th century, is the national summer game in England, and is played in other countries, especially the West Indies, Australia, New Zealand, South Africa, India, and Pakistan. A cricket international, or Test match, can last five days, but there are also one-day match competitions.

A bat-and-ball game very different from cricket is baseball, which is something like the old game of rounders, and is very popular in the United States.

A stick, rather than a bat, is used for hockey. Field hockey is played either on grass or on hard pitches, while ice hockey, the fastest of all team games, is played on an indoor ice rink.

Basketball, volleyball and handball are indoor team games. Netball, similar to basketball, is usually played outdoors.

Professional team sports are today big business. Famous players earn lots of money and huge crowds pay to watch the top teams. Yet, even more people have fun playing in local matches where the only prize is the excitement of winning.

SINGLES AND PAIRS

Apart from the well-known team games, there are many sports in which players compete either alone or with a partner. They include indoor court games such as badminton and squash, and table tennis, which developed from a game played on a dining table. The most popular court game is tennis, which originally was played on a

Above left **A skier twists through a "gate" during a slalom event.**

Left **Formula One racing cars at the start of a Grand Prix.**

Above **A boardsailer, or windsurfer, balances to keep the board riding the waves.**

Above right **Rock climbers on steep cliffs fasten themselves to ropes with snap links. Helmets protect them from rock falls.**

grass lawn but is now played mostly on hard surfaces. The most famous tennis championship of all is the Wimbledon tournament, first held in 1877 in London and now the only important championship still played on grass.

Croquet and bowls are two more sports played on well-tended lawns. Golf too has its carpet-like putting greens. Golf began in Scotland some time in the 15th century, but there are now golf courses and golfers in countries all around the world. In golf, as in some other sports, the best players can earn valuable money prizes in competitions. Many more golfers play purely for pleasure and to take exercise. They may play against a rival or on their own, aiming to improve their skill. Yet another solo sport is angling (fishing), which is among the most popular of all sports.

FAST AND DANGEROUS SPORTS

Winter sports were originally enjoyed by people living in cold climates who had to travel over snow and ice on skates, skis or sleds. Today, many more people can travel to enjoy a winter sports holiday at a tourist resort. Here beginners learning to keep their balance on ice skates can admire the speed and grace of expert skaters. Skiers race downhill over the snow slopes of the mountains and ski-jumpers launch themselves into the air from the tops of high ski-ramps. Toboggan and bobsled racers hurtle down twisting courses such as the famous Cresta Run in Switzerland. Every four years the best winter sports athletes meet in the Winter Olympics, first held in 1924.

Speed sports can be dangerous, but they attract many people. Motor car racing started soon after the invention of the motor car in the 1880s. Today, there are Grand Prix races for high-speed motor cars, rallies across country roads, drag races and stockcar races for specially adapted vehicles. Motor cycles too are raced, on road circuits and over muddy "scramble" courses. Speedway races for motorcycles are held on special dirt tracks. Cycle racing demands only the pedal power of the rider, who must be a highly trained athlete. Huge crowds follow the progress of the cyclists in important road races such as the Tour de France.

Adventure sports may take people underground, or high in the air. Cavers explore deep under the earth in sunless caverns. Climbers scale steep rock faces and high snow-capped mountains. In the air soar sailplane gliders and hang gliders, while hot-air balloons rise silently on the wind. Flying is an enjoyable, though expensive, pastime. Some people prefer the thrill of skydiving, in which they freefall through the air before opening a parachute to float gently down to earth.

Water sport is fun all year round and swimming is one of the best forms of exercise. So too is rowing. Rowing, yacht racing, boardsailing, surfing, powerboat racing, water-skiing and scuba diving are all popular water sports. The Eskimos of the Arctic invented the kayak canoe, which today is paddled by many for fun.

INDOOR GAMES, PASTIMES AND HOBBIES

Board and table games are among the oldest games known. Chess, for example, was first played some 1,500 years ago, probably in India or China. A similar but simpler board game is draughts or checkers. It is fascinating to think that people have been playing board games like "snakes and ladders" for thousands of years. In prehistoric times, the players probably used animal bones or stones as dice and counters.

Playing cards were first used in the ancient Far East and arrived in Europe during the 14th century, possibly introduced by returning Crusaders. Some games, such as bridge, require considerable skill;

Below left **A snooker player pots a ball into one of the six pockets around the table.**

Below **Some young chess players are world class. The very best may one day become Grand Masters.**

Left **Looking after pets properly takes time and effort. Each animal needs its own special care to stay healthy and contented.**

others, such as snap or poker, depend largely on the luck of the player and his ability to bluff opponents. Another table game that has been known since the Middle Ages is billiards, which is played with coloured balls and long sticks called cues. From billiards developed the games of snooker and pool.

A pastime is something which can be enjoyed alone or with friends. Today, as in the past, most people begin following a hobby or pastime in childhood, often with toys, including traditional dolls or mechanical toys, as well as the latest electronic versions. Collecting one kind of toy can be an interesting hobby. In fact, people collect all kinds of things, like antiques, coins, postcards, stamps, matchbox labels, or fossils.

Making things also gives many people satisfaction. Painting, modelling, wood carving, needlework and knitting are just a few of the many creative craft hobbies. Model-making demands patience and skill. By building a model theatre, for example, plays can be staged using model puppets. Many modellers build scale models of famous aircraft and ships, starting with a simple kit bought from a model shop. To see a working model in action may give even more satisfaction: a home-made glider, for example, or a model steam engine. Railway enthusiasts can build their own model railway layout, with hand-made scenery and stations. Those who prefer electronics can build their own circuits or invent a new computer game.

Right **You can use a personal computer to help with all kinds of hobbies, as well as for playing computer games. You can even make up your own computer programs.**

Left **One of the most enjoyable outdoor pursuits is walking, or rambling. Exploring the countryside on foot keeps you fit as you enjoy watching the scenery and wildlife.**

Champions of Sport

Ali, Muhammad (born 1942) US Boxer. As Cassius Clay he became World Heavyweight boxing champion in 1964. Famous for his catchphrase "I'm the greatest", Ali lost and regained his title several times before retiring in 1980.

Ballesteros, Severiano (born 1957) Spanish golfer. He won the Open Golf Championship in 1979 at 22, the youngest for a century to hold the title.

Banks, Gordon (born 1937) English footballer. One of the best-ever goalkeepers in the world, he won a winner's medal in the 1966 World Cup Final.

Bannister, Roger (born 1929) English athlete. He earned his fame in 1954 when he became the first to run a mile in under four minutes.

Beckenbauer, Franz (born 1945) West German footballer. Known for his elegant style of play in his role as attacking centre-back, Beckenbauer played in three World Cup finals for his country. He later became manager of the national side.

Best, George (born 1946) Northern Irish footballer. Best was a colourful "pop-star" personality in his day, and was frequently in trouble with his club, Manchester United. He was also hailed as one of the geniuses of modern football.

Blankers-Koen, Fanny (born 1918) Dutch athlete. She was one of the greatest athletes of this century. Excelling at the sprint distances, hurdles, high and long jumps, she was nicknamed "The Flying Dutchwoman".

Borg, Bjorn (born 1956) Swedish tennis player. He won the Wimbledon Men's Singles Championships five times in a row (1976–1980). Borg is regarded as one of the finest players the game has ever known.

Botham, Ian (born 1955) English cricketer. He made his debut for England against Australia in 1977 and quickly established himself as one of cricket's greatest-ever all-rounders. He has scored more than 4000 runs and taken more than 300 wickets in Test matches.

Bradman, Donald (born 1908) Australian cricketer. Most people are agreed that he was the greatest batsman of all time. His Test average at the end of his career was 99.94.

Charlton, Bobby (born 1937) English footballer. He was an attacking midfield player, famous for his thundering shot. Charlton played more than 100 matches for England, scoring a record 49 goals.

Coe, Sebastian (born 1956) English athlete. One of the greatest ever middle-distance runners, in 1975 he became the first to hold all three world records for 800m, 1500m and the mile at the same time.

Comaneci, Nadia (born 1961) Romanian gymnast. At the age of 14, she became the first to score 10 out of 10 in a gymnastics event, winning gold in the beam and asymmetric bars at the 1976 Montreal Olympics.

Connolly, Maureen (1934–69) US tennis player. She won Wimbledon three times in a row, 1952–54, the first when she was only 17. A horse-riding accident in 1954 ended "Little Mo's" career.

Court, Margaret (born 1942) Australian tennis player. Between 1960 and 1976, she won 90 championships, including 24 singles titles in Grand Slam tournaments.

Cruyff, Johan (born 1947) Dutch footballer. Famed for his speed and superb ball control, he captained the great Dutch national team of the 1970s.

Dalglish, Kenny (born 1951) Scottish footballer. He is one of the greatest British players in recent years. A gifted goalscorer for Celtic, Liverpool and Scotland, he became manager of Liverpool in 1985 and won the League and Cup double in his first season.

Davies, Mervyn (born 1946) Welsh rugby footballer. Possibly the best British forward of the modern game, he played 38 consecutive internationals in the great Welsh national side of the 1970s.

Davis, Steve (born 1957) English snooker player. Since 1981, when he won the World Championship, he has been generally regarded as the World's number one.

Edwards, Gareth (born 1947) Welsh rugby footballer. A gifted scrum-half, he played in all 53 international matches from his debut in 1967 to his retirement in 1978.

Ender, Kornelia (born 1958) East German swimmer. An extremely powerful freestyle swimmer, she won four gold medals in the 1976 Olympics. During her career she broke 23 world records.

Evert, Chris (born 1954) US tennis player. Since her first Wimbledon Championships in 1974, she has, with Martina Navratilova, dominated world tennis.

Fangio, Juan (born 1911) Argentinian racing driver. He was the greatest driver in the world in the 1950s, perhaps of all time. He won the World Championship five times, winning 24 of his 51 races.

Gavaskar, Sunil (born 1949) Indian cricketer. An opening batsman, he was ever-present in the national team since his debut in 1970. He holds the record for the greatest number of runs scored in a Test career.

Grace, W.G. (1848–1915) English cricketer. He was the first great figure in the history of cricket. His career lasted more than 40 years (1865–1908) during which he scored nearly 55,000 runs and took 2,876 wickets.

Hobbs, Jack (1882–1963) English cricketer. He was one of the greatest-ever batsmen, holding a record for the most first class runs (61,237) and the most centuries (197), in a career lasting from 1905 to 1934.

King, Billie Jean (born 1943) US tennis player. She was one of the toughest competitors the game has seen. She first the Wimbledon Singles Championship in 1961 and triumphed for the sixth and last time in 1975.

Koch, Marita (born 1957) East German athlete. Responsible for lowering the world 400m record 7 times between 1978 and 1985, she dominated 200m and 400m running until her retirement in 1987.

Korbut, Olga (born 1955) Soviet gymnast. Her

Top **Racehorses in full flight at a steeplechase meeting**

performance at the 1972 Munich Olympics brought huge popularity to women's gymnastics.

Lauda, Niki (born 1949) Austrian racing driver. Twice World champion in the 1970s, Lauda narrowly escaped death in a crash during the 1976 German Grand Prix. He won the Championship again in 1984.

Laver, Rod (born 1938) Australian tennis player. Nicknamed the "Rocket", he was one of the greatest players of recent years. He won Wimbledon four times in the 1960s.

Lenglen, Suzanne (1899–1938) French tennis player. She was the first superstar of women's tennis. She lost only three sets during the seven years of her reign as Wimbledon champion in the 1920s.

Lillee, Dennis (born 1949) Australian cricketer. He was one of the most formidable fast bowlers of recent years. By the time he retired from Test cricket in 1984, he had taken 355 Test wickets, then a record.

Louis, Joe (1914–81) US Boxer. Known as "The Brown Bomber", he held the World Heavyweight Championship for the longest-ever period, nearly 12 years (1937–49).

McEnroe, John (born 1959) US tennis player. A highly-gifted, but controversial player, he won Wimbledon three times in the early 1980s.

McKay, Heather (born 1942) Australian squash player. Her career record shows she was the world's greatest-ever squash player. She was unbeaten in 16 years.

Maradona, Diego (born 1960) Argentinian footballer. He is widely regarded as the finest player in the world in the 1980s. He captained Argentina to their World Cup victory in 1986.

Marciano, Rocky (1923–69) US Boxer. A tough, aggressive heavyweight, he retired as world champion in 1955 unbeaten in 49 professional bouts.

Matthews, Stanley (born 1915) English footballer. Famous for his skilful dribbling on the right wing, the highlight of his long career was his brilliant performance for Blackpool in the 1953 FA Cup Final.

Moody, Helen Wills (born 1905) US tennis player. She dominated women's tennis from 1922 to 1938, winning 19 major singles' championships.

Moses, Ed (born 1955) US athlete. From 1977 he utterly dominated his event, the 400m hurdles, remaining unbeaten for more than 10 years.

Navratilova, Martina (born 1956) US tennis player born in Czechoslovakia. She was the most successful player in tennis from the late 1970s, winning Wimbledon six times in a row.

Nicklaus, Jack (born 1940) US golfer. Perhaps the world's greatest-ever player, he has won the most major championships in the history of golf.

Nurmi, Paavo (1879–1973) Finnish athlete. Between 1923 and 1931, he broke 29 world records at distances from 1,500m to 20,000m.

Ovett, Steve (born 1955) English athlete. In the late 1970s and early 1980s he swapped world records in the middle distance events with Sebastian Coe.

Owens, Jesse (1913–80) US athlete. A world record holder in the sprint, hurdles and long jump. He will always be remembered for his four gold medals in the 1936 Berlin Olympics.

Pelé (born 1940) Brazilian footballer. His real name was Edson Arantes do Nascimento, and he was probably the most famous footballer of all. A brilliant attacking player, Pelé played in four World Cup tournaments and scored 97 goals in 110 matches for Brazil.

Piggott, Lester (born 1935) English racing jockey. He achieved a record-breaking nine victories in the Epsom Derby between 1954 and 1983.

Platini, Michel (born 1955) French footballer. A gifted midfield player, he captained the exciting French national side of the 1980s.

Player, Gary (born 1935) South African golfer. He was one of the finest golfers of the 1960s and 70s. Player was the first non-American to win each of the four Grand Slam tournaments.

Puskas, Ferenc (born 1927) Hungarian footballer. Famed for his long-range shooting, he was one of the stars in the great Hungarian team of the 1950s. He later captained Real Madrid, and helped them to win the European Cup five times in a row 1956–60.

Richards, Viv (born 1952) West Indian cricketer. He is probably the greatest batsman of the 1980s. He played his first Test match in 1974 and since then has maintained an average of well over 50.

Rudolph, Wilma (born 1940) US athlete. Until the age of 11, her leg was paralysed after a childhood illness. But in the 1960 Olympic Games she won gold medals in three sprint events.

Ruth, George Herman ("Babe") (1895–1948) US baseball player. One of the greatest baseball players of all time, he set many hitting records in his career with the New York Yankees (1920–34).

Sobers, Gary (born 1936) West Indian cricketer. He is one of the finest all-rounders the game has ever seen. In his career he scored over 28,000 runs and took over 1,000 wickets. He was the first professional player to hit six sixes in an over.

Spitz, Mark (born 1950) US swimmer. He burst to fame in 1972 when he won seven gold medals in freestyle and butterfly events. He broke or equalled 32 world records in his career.

Thompson, Daley (born 1958) English athlete. A magnificent all-round athlete, he dominated the decathlon event in the 1980s, winning Olympic golds at the 1980 and 1984 Games.

Tyson, Mike (born 1966) US boxer. He won the WBC World Heavyweight title in November 1986 by defeating Trevor Berbick. At 20 he was the youngest title claimant in heavyweight history.

Williams, J.P.R. (born 1949) Welsh rugby footballer. Playing at full back, he was first choice for his country and the British Lions in the 1970s. He is regarded as one of the greatest rugby full-backs of all time.

Zatopek, Emil (born 1922) Czech athlete. In the 1950s, he broke world records in both 5,000 and 10,000 metres. He won Olympic golds in all three long-distance events in 1952.

Above **Success! An American athletic team wins the relay.**

Index

Ink 211
Insect 89, 90, 93, 94–5, 103–4, 116
Insect pest 152
Insectivore 109
Instrument Landing System 165
Insulin 193
Internal combustion engine **149, 157,** 180
International Organization 206
Interstellar space 18
Intestine 186, 187, 193
Invertebrates 90, **90,** 92, 93, 121
Ion 137
Ionic column 212
Iowa 47
Iran 38, 87
Iraq 38
Irawaddy, River 41
Ireland 35
Iron **138,** 138–9
Iron Curtain 83
Isfahan 71
Isis 195
Islam **65,** 65, 71, 198
Israel 38, 85, 87, 197
Israelite exodus 86
Italy 32, 35, 68, 211
Ivan IV (the Terrible) 86, 209
Izalco 50

Jamaica 50, 51
Janissaries 71, **71**
Japan 38, 41, 72, 82, 83, 84
Jazz 215
Jenner, Edward 193
Jersey cattle 155
Jerusalem 196
Jesus Christ 86, 196, **196,** 198, 209
Jet engines 148, **148,** 162, 180
Jewish religion *see* Judaism
Jews 197
Joan of Arc 209
Johnson, Samuel 222
Joint 182
Jousting 224
Joyce, James 87, 222
Judaism 195, 196, 197, **197,** 198
Judge 202, 205
Judicial precedent 203
Julius Caesar **63**
Jupiter 12, 14, 15, **18,** 132
Jury 203, 205
Justinian I 209
Jutland 34

Kaaba **197**
Kabuki **216**
Kalahari Desert 42, 45, 189
Kampuchea 41
Kangaroo 106
K'ang-hsi 72
Kansas 47
Karma 199
Kells, Book of **216**
Kennedy, John F. 87
Kenya 42, 45
Kenyatta, Jomo 209
Kepler, Johannes 18
Kerosene, 147
Keyboard Instrument 214
Khomeini, Ayatollah **84**
Kidneys 186–7, **187,** 193
King, Billie Jean 232
Kingdom 66, 70, 200
Kikuyu people 42
Kipling, Rudyard 222
Koala 106
Koran 198
Korbut, Olga 233
Korea 38, 41
Korean War 85, 87, 206

Krishna 199
Kublai Khan 86
Kuwait 38
Kyushu 41

Labrador 49
Lacrosse 225
Lagos 44
Lamprey 96, **96**
Landholder 66
Landlord 66–7
Laos 41
Lauda, Niki 233
Landscape 211
Language 32, 172
Lapps 34, 188
Larva 94, 129
Laser 180, **180**
Lava 23, 31
Laver, Rod 233
Lavoisier, Antoine 87, 137
Law 200, 202–5
Lawrence D.H. 222
Lawyer 205
League of Nations 82
Leeward Islands 51
Lenglen, Suzanne 233
Lenin, Vladimir 81, **201,** 209
Lens 178
Lent 218
Leonardo da Vinci **68,** 69, 86, 211, 223
Lesser Antilles 51
Letterpress 174, **175**
Lever 180
Liberalism 75
Libya 44
Lichen **120**
Light 137
Light-year 18
Lightning 31, **133**
Lillee, Dennis 233
Lincoln, Abraham 78, 209
Lion **108, 118**
Lion fish **96**
Liquid 131
Liquid gas 131
Lister, Joseph 193
Liszt, Franz 223
Literature 69, 216–7
Litmus 137
Little brain *see* Cerebellum
Liver 187, **187,** 193
Liverwort 110
Livestock farming 154–5
Livingstone, David 87
Lizard 100, **101**
Local Government 201
Locomotive 158
London Metropolitan Police 204
Lord of the manor 66
Louis XIV 70, **70,** 209
Louisiana Purchase 78
Louis, Joe 233
Lubrication system 148
Lugworm **92**
Luminosity 18
Lunar module 169, **169**
Lunar roving vehicle 169
Lungs 184, **184,** 193
Lute **214**
Luther, Martin 68, 86, 209
Luxembourg 34, 35

Machiavelli 69, 86
Machine 142
Machine tools 142
Madonna **221**
Magellan, Ferdinand 86, 160
Magnet 21, 137
Magnetism 133, **133**
Maidenhair tree 113
Malaria 121

Malawi 45
Malaysia 41
Mammals 89, 90, 106–9, **106–9,** 116, 129
Manchu, 72, 86
Manitoba 49
Manor 66, **66**
Mantle (Earth) **20,** 21, 31
Manufacturing 142
Mao Tse-tung 87, **208,** 209
Maradona, Diego 233
Marathon 227
Marciano, Rocky 233
Marco Polo 86
Marconi, Guglielmo 87m 180, 220
Mardi Gras 218, **218**
Maria Theresa 209
Mars 12, 14–15, **15**
Marsupials 106, 129
Martinique 51
Martians 14
Martinique 51
Marx, Karl 79
Maryland 77
Masai 42, 189
Mass 137
Matter 130–1
Matthews, Stanley 233
Mayan mythology 194, **212**
Mayan people 212, 224
"Mayflower", The 86
McKinley, Mt 47
Mecca **65, 197,** 198
Mediterranean Sea 32, 35, 190
Mediterranean countries 35
Mekong, River 41
Melanesia 54, 55
Melbourne 54
Memory 183
Mercury (metal) 139
Mercury (planet) 12, 14
Meridian 18
Mesopotamia 38, 61
Mesozoic era 88, 89
Metals 138–9, 180
Metamorphic rock 25, 31
Metamorphosis 129
Meteor 13, 18, 19
Meteorite 13, 19
Meteorologist 28, 166
Meteorology 31
Mexico 50
Mexico City 50, **50,** 76
Michelangelo 69, 86, **210,** 211, 212, 223
Micronesia 54, 55
Microphone 134, 178, 180
Microscope **136,** 180
Microwave 176, **177,** 180
Middle Ages 67, 203, 210, 212, 215, 217, 224, 225, 227, 231
Middle East 38, 65, 85, 212
Migration 123
Mildew 111
Military alliances 206
Military planes 163
Military weapons 206
Milk 155, **155**
Milking machine 155, **155**
Milky way 19
Millipede 93
Milton, John 223
Mineral 25, **25,** 31, 139
Mineral salts 186
Ministers 201
Minoan age 62
Minoan palace 86
Minstrel **214,** 215
Missionary 72
Mississippi, River 46, 47, 48
Missouri, River 46
Mite **93, 120**
Model-making 231

Mole **106**
Molecule 137, 140
Molière 223
Molluscs 92, 93, 129
"Mona Lisa" 86
Money 70
Mongolia 41
Mongoloid people 188, 190–1, **191**
Monkey 109, **109**
Monkey Puzzle tree 113
Monocotyledons 114–15, 129
Monsoon climate 38
Monotremes 106, 129
Montgolfier, Joseph and Etienne 162, **162,** 181
Moody, Helen Wills 233
Moon, The 12–13, **14,** 19, 132, 166, 168, 169
Moons 12
Moore, Henry **212**
More, Sir Thomas 69
Mormon Tabernacle choir **199**
Morocco 44
Morris dancing 214
Morse, Samuel 176, 181
Morse code 176
Moscow 36, **36,** 37
Moscow State Circus 219
Moses 197, 209
Moses, Ed 233
Mosque **65,** 212
Moss 110
Motor-cycle racing 229
Motor racing **228,** 229
Mountain **22,** 23, 30, 124
Mozart, Wolfgang Amadeus 87, 215, 223
Mughal court **71**
Mughal Empire 71, **80,** 86
Muhammad 65, 86, 198, 209
Multi-stage rocket 166
Muscle 183, **183,** 185, 193
Music 135, 214
Music Hall 220
Musical instruments 214
Mushroom 111
Muslims 65, 71, **197,** 212
Mussolini, Benito 82, 209
Mycenaeans 62
Mystery play **67,** 217
Myth 194

Nairobi 44
Nansen, Fridtjof 56
Nantes, Edict of 86
Napoleon Bonaparte 75, **75,** 87, 209
NASA (National Aeronautics and Space Administration) 19
Nasser, Gamal Abdel 209
National Assembly 75, 201
Nationalism 75, 79
NATO (North Atlantic Treaty Organization), **83,** 206
Natural fibres 141
Natural gas **146,** 150
Naval conflict, 74, **74**
Navigation 161
Navratilova, Martina 233
Nazis 82
Neanderthal Man 60
Nebula **9,** 10, 19
Nectar 95, 129
Negroid people 188–9, **188–9**
Nehru, Jawaharlal 209
Nepal **39,** 40, 41
Neptune 12, 14
Nerve 183, **188,** 193
Nerve cells **183**
Nest 105
Netball 228
Netherlands 34, 35

["